DIGITAL TRANSFORMATION

DIGITAL TRANSFORMATION

BUILDING INTELLIGENT ENTERPRISES

Anup Maheshwari

WILEY

For general information on our other products and services or for technical support, please
contact our Customer Care Department within the United States at (800) 762-2974, outside
the United States at (317) 572-3993, or fax (317) 572-4002.

Wiley publishes in a variety of print and electronic formats and by print-on-demand. Some
material included with standard print versions of this book may not be included in e-books or in
print-on-demand. If this book refers to media such as a CD or DVD that is not included in the
version you purchased, you may download this material at http://booksupport.wiley.com. For
more information about Wiley products, visit www.wiley.com.

Library of Congress Cataloging-in-Publication Data is Available

ISBN 978-1-119-54083-0 (Hardcover)
ISBN 978-1-119-54086-1 (ePDF)
ISBN 978-1-119-54085-4 (ePub)

Cover Design: Wiley
Cover Images: © Erikona/Getty Images, © Nikada/Getty Images

Printed in the United States of America

V10012661_073119

CONTENTS

CHAPTER 8 Machine Learning   179

CHAPTER 9 Blockchain   191

CHAPTER 10 Drones   221

PREFACE

We are living in the era of digital revolution where new products and technologies are disrupting the existing businesses while at the same time creating opportunities and paving the way for new businesses to flourish and make a mark of their own.

I am extremely thrilled and excited to present in this book the enterprise path to digital transformation and the adoption of new IT methods and tools and emerging technologies to build intelligent enterprises. Every enterprise is looking for nirvana in digital transformation but it takes a complete restructuring within the enterprise to make that change and be successful.

Through this book, I have made an attempt to discuss all the methodologies, tools, technologies, and platforms that an enterprise needs to consider and evaluate to reach the end goal. Every enterprise is unique and is at various levels of technological adoption maturity. Though the book provides a holistic view of all the emerging technologies, the enterprise needs to choose the right fit that would bring the maximum value to their business, make them stand above the competition, and help them succeed as the enterprise of tomorrow.

I hope you enjoy reading this book, as every attempt has been made to discuss all the technologies from a business perspective with industry-specific use cases so that a business case can be established towards implementing a specific tool or technology. I have discussed the methodology and tools that the enterprise can utilize to implement emerging technologies on the correct platform with correct data sets and then integrate for exposure to the outside world.

SAP Leonardo is an innovative solution helping clients achieve digital transformation. I have reviewed the end-to-end offering of this product to provide an overview of the functionality and capabilities to my treasured readers.

I hope you will find reading this book a worthwhile investment of your time.

Anup Maheshwari
Dallas, TX
2019

ABOUT THIS BOOK

Who Should Read This Book

The book provides a solid theoretical and practical application for various emerging technologies that help in building intelligent enterprises. Though there are individual books available for each of the subjects covered in this book, this book provides all the topics "under one roof" so that the readers can gain substantial knowledge on any subject of their interest. No prior understanding of any technical coding or language is necessary to understand the content of this book.

The book is very well suited for C-suite executives comprising CEOs, CFOs, CIOs, CDOs, and CMOs, IT leaders and executives, IT managers, project/program managers, solution architects, business leaders and executives, business managers, and all professionals who have an interest and desire to learn these new IT and next-generation emerging technologies or have an agenda to digitize key processes within an organization to make the enterprise intelligent.

Not only does this book provide insights into the tools and technologies, but readers will have an opportunity to leverage the industry-specific use cases and examples discussed for each of technology area and apply them at the enterprise, which will help the reader contribute to the digital goals of the enterprise and make an impact through the knowledge gained by reading this book.

This book is useful for those who are absolute novices and want to equipped themselves with the latest technological trends; it will be equally intriguing to those who are more advanced in the learning curve to gain the practical insights into the implementation and usage of the technology. The book is not for someone looking for a deep-dive into the technical and coding aspects of the technology.

Organization Of This Book

As new technologies and business disruptions are reshaping business, such as Facebook, Airbnb, and Uber, this book explores the background, theory, and practical applications of major emerging technologies surrounding our ecosystem and provides a contextual meaning for the digitalization, what it means for the business, and how to adapt and get on board with the ever-changing and fast journey.

This book has been structured with the following sections and topics:

Part I, "Introduction," introduces the concept of digital transformation and its associated digital themes that an enterprise can adapt based on its industry to make itself intelligent.

Part I contains the following chapter:

Chapter 1: Digital Transformation

This chapter provides an overview of the digital transformation and its importance for the survival of the enterprise. It also discusses the factors, impact, value drivers, implementation methodology, and some of the emerging digital themes across business functions and industries that can be leveraged by the enterprise to innovate, create new business models, and become intelligent.

Part II, "Collaborative Methods and Tools," provides an insight into the tools and methodologies that are used in the digital era to implement and collaborate with the emerging technologies. The environment and ecosystem are very different now, and everything needs to be implemented and deployed faster, with the ability to meet the ever-changing customer preferences. These tools provide an accelerated path towards the adoption of these emerging technologies and digitization within the enterprise.

Part II contains the following chapters:

Chapter 2: Design Thinking

This chapter provides an overview of the design thinking process, which helps the enterprise to become creative and innovative to solve problems in collaboration with the users. It discusses the methodology and different tools and techniques that can be used at various stages of the process along with use cases to make the enterprise intelligent.

Chapter 3: Agile

This chapter provides an overview of the agile framework, its features, principles, and some of its benefits and challenges as applied in a project environment. It also discusses the methodology that is appropriate for the enterprise and the tools that are available to help the enterprise follow an agile strategy and become intelligent.

Chapter 4: DevOps

This chapter provides an overview of the DevOps methodology as a collaboration between the development and the operations teams. It also discusses the

DevOps maturity level, enablers, and some of the typical processes across the development life cycle that are potential candidates for DevOps use cases to make the enterprise collaborative and intelligent.

Part III, "Intelligent Technologies," provides an end-to-end storyline on how an enterprise can accelerate the digital transformation through the adoption of new technology that is relevant for the enterprise. The business functions rely on digital technologies to stay relevant, compete, and perform. Every enterprise wants to become intelligent, and these technologies provide that edge and help them navigate the journey.

Part III contains the following chapters:

Chapter 5: Robotic Process Automation

This chapter provides an overview of robotic process automation and its ability to automate business processes to reduce costs and have limited dependency on IT resources. It also discusses the implementation methodology and some of the typical processes across business functions and industries that are potential candidates for automation to make the enterprise efficient and intelligent.

Chapter 6: Internet of Things

This chapter provides an understanding of Internet of Things technology, explaining how the data from the connected world is harnessed, transmitted, stored, and analyzed. It also discusses the IoT architecture, implementation methodology, and some of the typical applications and use cases across industries with future day-in-life scenarios that can make the enterprise connected and intelligent.

Chapter 7: Artificial Intelligence

This chapter provides an understanding of artificial intelligence technology and what is causing enterprises to move towards it. It also discusses the various technologies and services offered by AI solutions, the implementation methodology, and some of the typical processes within functional areas and industries that are potential candidates for deploying AI to bring operational efficiency and make the enterprise intelligent.

Chapter 8: Machine Learning

This chapter provides an understanding of machine learning technology, the mechanics and challenges, and the rationale for enterprises to move towards it. It also discusses the key steps that should be taken to build a machine learning model, the implementation methodology, and some of the typical industry solutions and use cases for deploying machine learning to predict future outcomes and make the enterprise intelligent.

Chapter 9: Blockchain

This chapter provides an overview of blockchain as a distributed ledger technology along with its benefits to the enterprise and a detailed understanding of the architecture supporting it. It also discusses the implementation methodology and some of the typical applications and use cases for deploying blockchain to securely transfer information with trust and make the enterprise intelligent.

Chapter 10: Drones

This chapter provides an overview of the drones technology, various types of drones, and its ability to capture visual data for further processing. It also discusses the risks imposed by this technology, its application, and some of the typical use cases across business processes and industries where drones have the potential and ability to make the enterprise intelligent.

Chapter 11: Virtual Reality

This chapter provides an overview of the virtual and augmented reality technology and its ability to create a computer-generated immersive experience for a user or augment new layers of information in the real world. It also discusses the architecture and technology components required, commonly used platforms, and some of the typical processes across industries that are potential candidates for AR/VR use cases to make the enterprise intelligent.

Chapter 12: 3D Printing

This chapter provides an overview of the 3D printing technology, the steps required to execute the printing process, some of the benefits and challenges around the technology, and the application areas. It also discusses the methodology for adoption and some of the typical use cases across industries to make the enterprise intelligent.

Chapter 13: Big Data

This chapter provides an overview of the big data technology, its ability to enable agile business decisions based on information visibility, and analytics capabilities. It also discusses the technology components and the architecture involved along with the use cases and opportunities across industries to make the enterprise intelligent with data-driven insight.

Chapter 14: Analytics

This chapter provides an overview of analytics, the various categories such as descriptive and predictive capabilities, and the components that can be leveraged. It also discusses the methodology and various tools and techniques that can be used along with the use cases and opportunities across industries to provide meaningful insights and make the enterprise intelligent.

Part IV, "Digital Infrastructure," highlights the importance of infrastructure services such as networking, computational power, and cloud functions that are required to support innovation and facilitate the delivery of intelligent technologies. It also provides a perspective on the integration and collaboration tools that an enterprise can leverage to communicate and connect the applications with each other and with the outside world.

Part IV contains the following chapters:

Chapter 15: Cloud Computing

This chapter provides an overview of the cloud deployment models, cloud computing attributes and benefits, the cloud transformation and migration framework, the enterprise's roadmap and strategy to move to cloud-based applications, and some of the typical use cases that trigger an enterprise to take the transformation journey to the cloud and make the enterprise intelligent.

Chapter 16: APIs

This chapter provides an overview of the APIs that act as building blocks to allow enterprises to leverage the data and services in the digital ecosystem. It also discusses the architecture, business strategy, roadmap, and API development life cycle to help the enterprise integrate and become intelligent.

Part V, "Product Review," provides an overview of SAP Leonardo – a path towards digital transformation and making intelligent enterprises. With the onset and launch of SAP Leonardo, SAP provides the platform for any capability of digital transformation the such as robotic process automation, artificial intelligence, machine learning, big data, and Internet of Things, using the SAP Cloud Platform. The enterprise needs to understand each or any of these capabilities and prepare a business case that is relevant for its business, and this section of the book will enable them to understand the product.

Part V contains the following chapter:

Chapter 17: SAP Leonardo

This chapter provides an overview of the SAP Leonardo framework that connects the enterprise's business processes with emerging technologies, people, and things. It also discusses the architecture, application, and some of the typical use cases across business processes and industries where SAP Leonardo uses a combination of intelligent technologies, digital platform, and an intelligent suite of applications to deliver an intelligent enterprise.

ACKNOWLEDGMENTS

I would like to take this opportunity to thank my parents, who have always supported me in my decisions and helped me achieve my goals in life. My upbringing has been instrumental in all walks of my life and helped me to accomplish the things that I have achieved in life today. I respectfully dedicate this book to them.

I would like to convey my heartfelt thanks to my wife, Rajni, and my children, Rishab and Arush, for all their love and support, which made it possible for me to complete this book on time along with my full-time consulting career with a hectic travel schedule every week. There have been several occasions and weekends during which I wasn't able to provide time to my family and friends because of my engagement and perseverance to accomplish this feat. Without their patience and tolerance, I wouldn't have been able to write and complete this book. A special thanks to the team at Wiley, who provided me with this opportunity and have been very supportive throughout the writing of this book.

I would also like to extend my gratitude to all my readers who took an immense interest in purchasing this book.

Emerging technologies are still evolving and some of them are quite new, for which I have taken a lot of time and effort to ensure that the quality of the book remains high and meets your expectations. My goal is to provide the readers with the right level of wisdom on any of the subjects discussed in this book to become confident and take the conversation to the next level.

DIGITAL TRANSFORMATION

PART I
Introduction

CHAPTER 1

Digital Transformation

*T*his chapter provides an overview of the digital transformation and its importance for the survival of the enterprise. It also discusses the factors, impact,
value drivers, implementation methodology, and some of the emerging digital
themes across business functions and industries that can be leveraged by the enterprise
to innovate, create new business models, and become intelligent.

Digital Transformation

Innovation and emerging IT technologies are changing at a very fast pace; the
question is – are the enterprises ready to keep up with the pace, jump into the
race to digital transformation, and become intelligent in the process?

Before we proceed, let's understand the term "digital" as used in the
context here. It refers to the power of collective information that is generated
in the ecosystem and the technology that keeps the customers connected
with the business resources. Digital transformation involves the usage of
new technologies to drive significant improvements in all business segments. This includes capitalizing on new opportunities as well as effectively
transforming existing businesses and technology that enable them. Digital
transformation is the state of how promptly an enterprise can cater to the
changing customer demands and turn the technology into business outcomes
and value.

New IT is about reinventing the enterprise's business by leveraging the
exponential power of digital to drive new levels of operational efficiency,
innovate new products and services, build new sources of growth and revenue
models, be agile in the workplace, and provide personalized customer
experience.

The typical barriers for an enterprise to unlock the power of digital transformation include complex business processes, highly customized solutions,

3

stringent policies and practices, business units working in silos within the enterprise, lack of proper infrastructure, the gap in skill sets, and multiple and disparate architectures in the ecosystem.

To overcome these barriers, the digital transformation needs to be driven by the people in conjunction with the business strategy and technology providing the requisite support. Some of the key questions that the enterprise needs to ask and get answers for before proceeding with the transformation are as follows:

- How shall I adapt to new digital trends?
- How shall I identify new opportunities and business scenarios?
- How shall I get started?
- How shall I attract new talent from the market?
- How shall I incorporate change management?
- How shall I convince the stakeholders to approve the idea?
- How shall I internally fund and govern digital transformation projects?
- How shall I help the employees and business partners get connected through digital means?

Digital transformation enabled by cloud-based applications and supported by emerging technologies will become the central nervous system of the intelligent enterprise of the twenty-first century.

What Causes Business Disruption

In today's world, smartphones have become a commodity used by almost everyone. This is a perfect example of disruption, as this device has disrupted thousands of businesses and enterprises. Before the invention of the smartphone, there were cameras to take pictures, alarm clocks for wake-up, navigation systems in cars for guidance on the road, and video recorders to shoot recordings. Now, all these functionalities and more have been combined in one device and millions of enterprises that manufactured or traded these products as part of their business got disrupted. They either went out of business or changed their line of business.

Smartphones enabled various applications and empowered the consumer to order a taxi, book airline tickets, check the menu of a restaurant, or make a doctor's appointment just by sitting at home, as smartphones have the capability to connect with people and systems all around the world. This innovation has led businesses to become increasingly complex as the individual consumers have now become exponentially powerful with the tools at their disposal. A consumer in today's digital and connected economy can perform tasks that only large enterprise could do some years ago.

If enterprises want to outpace the disruption that is ongoing in the entire world, they need to equip themselves with technology that will help them adapt to the change quickly.

Factors That Influence Digital Transformation

An enterprise would need the cloud computing platform to run a successful digital transformation, as the cloud provides a scalable, flexible, elastic, easily accessible, and cost-efficient platform to run the business. Without the cloud layer, the enterprise would not be able to achieve the required automation and orchestration for the next layer, known as the data layer, that comprises big data and analytics.

Both structured and unstructured data from the internal ecosystem and the external environment is getting streamed into the enterprise's database, which might be a rational database, a relational database, or nonrelational data sets. This data needs to be transformed into essential business insights so that it can be consumed by the sales, marketing, customer service, R&D, and various product divisions to make informed and smart decisions. In order to get the information, the user needs to access it through the devices layer known as mobility.

In the post–personal computers era, users have the flexibility to work on several devices such as mobile or tablets simultaneously from any location, and this is further intensified with wearable devices such as smart watches, smart tags, and smart glasses from augmented reality. In order to connect these devices and collect the data, the enterprise needs the network layer supported by the Internet of Things (IoT).

Through the use of sensors and other devices, this layer creates a vibrant marketplace by connecting the employees, partners, suppliers, vendors, customers, and the general public with the enterprise business processes. It has been designed for internal and external collaboration to optimize the business processes and create new business opportunity.

All the key elements of digital transformation such as cloud, mobile, data, networks, and connectivity act as building blocks that aid digital transformation for all businesses. The technology is available for the enterprise to adopt and enable new insights, new innovations, and new ways to interact within and beyond the business. The CIO needs to embrace and adopt these changes quickly within the enterprise to stay relevant in the business; otherwise, the professional gets transferred to a purely nonstrategic operations role.

Methods

The enterprise needs to follow one or more of the following methods and practices to rotate to the new IT revolution:

- Design Thinking
- Agile Approach
- DevOps
- Lean Practices
- Quality Engineering
- Automation
- Behavioral Development
- Data-driven Innovation

Technologies

The enterprise needs to adopt one or more of the following technologies and architectures to execute the digital transformation:

- Robotic Process Automation
- Internet of Things
- Artificial Intelligence
- Machine Learning
- Blockchain
- Big Data
- Cloud Computing
- Augmented Reality
- Wearables
- Analytics
- Natural Language Processing
- Deep Learning
- Microservices/APIs
- User Interface
- SaaS, IaaS, PaaS
- S/4HANA
- Quantum Computing

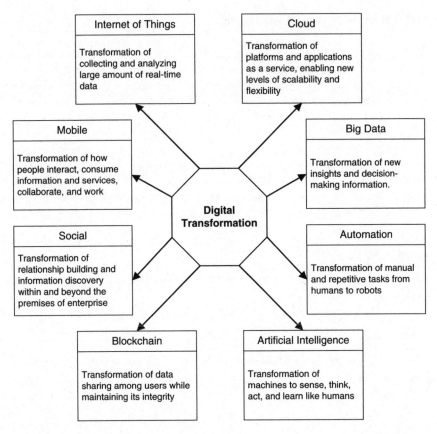

Figure 1.1   Digital transformation key drivers.

- Bioengineering
- Cyber Defense
- 3D Printing
- Identity Management

The enterprise needs to recruit the right talent or train the existing resources to use the methods, tools, and technology to successfully deploy digital transformation. Not to mention, the change management and cultural shift that will happen in parallel during the transition. Some of the key drivers that an enterprise should leverage during in its digital transformation journey are depicted in Figure 1.1.

Digital Transformation Impact

The digital transformation mapping is the first step where the enterprise needs to identify and prioritize digital opportunities and then plan to execute the initiatives that will address the current needs. This requires creating a business case for change and assessing the impacts of digitalization on the business to ensure that correct decisions and actions are taken towards the long-term goals of the enterprise.

Digital transformation mapping helps enterprises to create a roadmap for transforming themselves into intelligent enterprises by identifying which digital technology components are a perfect fit within the ecosystem. The following impacts of digitization are evaluated thoroughly, and serve as an input towards determining the transformation mapping.

Enterprise Capabilities

The enterprise needs to evaluate its existing capabilities and the new digital competencies required for transformation.

Technology

The enterprise needs to evaluate its existing technology and infrastructure landscape and see if it is ready to respond to the disruption created by the new technology.

Innovation

The enterprise needs to evaluate its current business model and see if the digital innovation brings in a new revenue stream.

Operational Efficiency

The enterprise needs to evaluate the areas of operational efficiency and improvement through the use of digital technology and then prioritize and focus on those areas.

Growth

The enterprise needs to evaluate if there are any new business opportunities or growth to an existing business that can result through the digitization.

Customer

The enterprise needs to evaluate if there will be any effect on how the enterprise runs its business with its customers after incorporating digital technology.

Competition

The enterprise needs to evaluate its competitors in the same industry on how they are incorporating the digital trend and what the response strategy of the enterprise should be. Any new player entering and disrupting the market with the aid of digitization needs to be considered as well.

Value Drivers

Here are some digital transformation activities that an enterprise needs to undertake driven by value drivers and potential opportunities.

Time to Market

This helps the enterprise to get incremental sales by reducing the time to launch its product in the market. Some of the transformational activities to achieve this feat are listed below.

- Adopt agile project implementation methodology to accelerate the delivery of the product.
- Improve the predictability of the development life cycle.
- Implement standardized DevOps processes for better team cohesion.
- Improve the performance of release planning.

Innovation

This helps the enterprise to get incremental sales by innovating and adding new products in the portfolio. Some of the transformational activities to achieve this are listed below:

- Draw a visionary product roadmap.
- Transform the role of the product owner.
- Continuously adjust to the customer's new requirements and feedback.

- Aim to improve customer satisfaction for product success.
- Establish DevOps culture within the enterprise.
- Enhance DevOps communication and alignment within multiple cross-functional teams.
- Increase forecast accuracy of delivery to end users.
- Increase timeline planning accuracy for future upgrades and releases.

Quality

This helps the enterprise to get incremental sales by providing quality products and deliverables, leading to higher customer satisfaction, fewer rejection rates, and repeat purchases. Some of the transformational activities to achieve this are listed below:

- Enhance quality effectiveness.
- Establish, standardize, and enforce code guidelines.
- Remove code that does not comply with the standards.
- Systematically conduct code guidelines.
- Drive developers towards self-quality management.
- Reduce the sprint timeline with less rework and waste.
- Automate the test efforts to minimize human errors.
- Improve the testing quality.

Operational Efficiency

This helps the enterprise to reduce operational and research and development expenses. Some of the transformational activities to achieve this are listed below:

- Adopt agile practices and prioritize using business value.
- Monitor and measure the output per resource.
- Enhance value delivered by the IT team to automate the operational processes.

Digital Implementation Methodology

The digital transformation involves strategic decision-making capabilities, innovation platform, technological capabilities, organizational capabilities, project management, and stakeholder engagement from the enterprise. Below is the methodology with implementation phases that has been proven at multiple enterprises for their digital transformation enablement.

Opportunity Assessment

The enterprise should conduct the following activities during this phase:

- Identify the enterprise's strategic objectives.
- Assess the enterprise's industry trend.
- Assess the enterprise's competitors and entry barriers.
- Assess the customer's demands.
- Brainstorm innovation ideas as applicable within the enterprise.
- Conduct innovation and new business opportunity workshops.
- Evaluate the data requirements.
- Evaluate the enterprise ecosystem.
- Evaluate the technology and application landscape requirements for the digital transformation.
- Assess the current organizational structure and operating model of the enterprise.
- Identify the stakeholders supporting the transformation.

To-Be Enterprise Model

The enterprise should conduct the following activities during this phase:

- Identify the new IT business model that would support the digital transformation for the enterprise.
- Identify the strategy and governance model for the transformed enterprise.
- Assess the target technology requirements.
- Conduct the change impact analysis.
- Identify the vendor and products with the selection criteria.
- Create the to-be organization structure and operating model for the enterprise.
- Create the transformation roadmap and get it validated by the stakeholders.

Mobilization

The enterprise should conduct the following activities during this phase:

- Develop a business case supporting the transformation.
- Map the current business processes, operations, and systems with the target structure.
- Prepare the pilot program for the new IT implementation.
- Identify all the security requirements around the new technology.
- Assess the knowledge and skills required for the program.
- Ensure stakeholder engagement and two-way communication channels.
- Set up the PMO office and mobilize the project team.

Design

The enterprise should conduct the following activities during this phase:

- Design innovative products using digital tools and technologies.
- Develop the key performance indicator metrics and scorecard.
- Refine the prototype model to achieve the implementation objectives and timeline.
- Create the technology blueprint and architecture document.
- Create the implementation project plan.
- Define the organizational structure and critical business processes.
- Create a detailed transformation roadmap for the development activities.

Implementation

The enterprise should conduct the following activities during this phase:

- Streamline activities using digital solutions such as cloud, mobile, analytics, automation, etc.
- Plan to continuously improve the prototype and implementation.
- Develop the coding.
- Conduct the unit and integration testing of the new technology.
- Ensure it passed the user acceptance test.
- Ensure any changes to the code are approved by the change control board.
- Ensure that the expectations of the stakeholders are met.
- Ensure on-time project delivery maintaining the quality standards.

Customer Engagement

The enterprise should conduct the following activities during this phase:

- Test the product with the customers and take feedback for improvisation.
- Engage the customers through a digital medium such as social media or a personalized message on mobile.
- Make the products available online and at stores to cater to the full supply chain spectrum.
- Address the queries of the customers using digital tools such as chatbots and self-service payment options.

Transition

The enterprise should conduct the following activities during this phase:

- Assess the digital infrastructure status for the entire ecosystem of the enterprise.
- Transition the service to the shared services or the IT team depending on the enterprise organization structure.
- Launch the technology for the transformation.
- Implement change management with the transition of organizational roles and responsibilities to support the new IT.
- Deploy the training courses for the business and IT users.
- Improve operational efficiency and effectiveness through the deployment of a digital platform and supporting tools.

Emerging Technology Heatmap

In order to become intelligent, the enterprise needs to evaluate all the emerging technologies against industry trends, business relevance, technical feasibility, and the overall ecosystem. The enterprise should then identify and classify those emerging technologies into the following:

Immediate Deployment

Those that have the highest priority and biggest impact and should be implemented right now. Based on the current situation, some of these emerging tools, technologies, and methods include the following:

- Artificial Intelligence
- Big Data Analytics

- Internet of Things
- Smart Sensors
- Robotic Process Automation
- Cybersecurity
- Chatbots
- Agile Development
- Cloud Computing

Short-term Deployment

Those that have broad application and should be on the horizon to be implemented in the next one to three years. Based on the current situation, some of these emerging tools, technologies, and methods include the following:

- Predictive Analytics
- Fraud Detection
- Machine Learning
- Natural Language Processing
- Identity Management
- Industry-Specific APIs
- Blockchain
- 3D Printing
- Industrial Robots
- Simulation Modeling
- Connected Home
- Design Thinking
- Edge Computing
- User Experience

Long-term Deployment

Those that should be considered as part of the enterprise's long-term technology strategy and roadmap to be implemented in the next three to five years. Based on the current situation, some of these emerging tools, technologies, and methods include the following:

- Activity Streams
- API Orchestration

- Behavioral Analytics
- Bioinformatics
- Content Analytics
- Equipment Telematics
- Smart Contracts
- Solar Power Generation
- Augmented Reality
- Autonomous Vehicles
- Intelligent Process Automation
- On-Demand Business and Technology Services
- On-Demand Scalability
- Virtual Reality
- Drones

Emerging Digital Themes by Industry

Every enterprise within a specific industry needs to define its emerging digital themes that they would like to implement as part of the digital roadmap for the future. This would require understanding the business trends within the enterprise's industry, current technology trends, product or service innovations, IT architecture with its integration into the enterprise's ecosystem, organizational strategy towards industry disruptors, and the roadmap towards a successful implementation. Some of the key emerging digital themes by industry are listed below:

Consumer Packaged Goods

There will be a need for the consumer packaged goods companies to drive growth and profit simultaneously by managing the volatility in the market caused by potential disruptors through digitalization. Consumers are rapidly changing their expectations towards products and services, and the enterprise needs to cater to their demands for survival in this competitive market.

The enterprise needs to identify which emerging technologies should be considered as enablers for them to become intelligent. Some of the key digital themes that are emerging from the consumer packaged goods industry and technology trends are listed below for the enterprise to leverage and ride on the digital innovation journey:

Engage the Digital Consumer

The enterprise should be able to understand, connect, and engage with the consumer in new ways. It should develop competencies to understand consumer needs and create its target customers. It should build the infrastructure to manage the increasing communication channels through social media more effectively. The enterprise should aim to provide personal experiences and not just personalized products to maintain long-term customer loyalty.

Data-driven Insights to Action

As the number of sources generating the data continues to multiply with the Internet of Things, the amount of data generated from the environment continues to increase exponentially. The enterprise needs to develop an architecture to monetize the data asset by embedding analytics into the business process while also developing predictive capabilities.

Flexible Architecture

Create a front-end user interface which is simpler and more convenient for consumers to use while improving and connecting it to the supply chain capabilities at the back end. The enterprise needs to create operational efficiency while increasing customer satisfaction and build agility into the system to adjust processes around consumer needs more quickly and cost-effectively.

Connected Ecosystem

The enterprise needs to develop a communication system to allow customers, suppliers, employees, and other business partners to interact more effectively with the business. It's prudent for the enterprise to focus on core competencies and outsource noncore activities to increase competitiveness and decrease the cost to serve all its partners.

Core Operations to Be Efficient and Scalable

The enterprise needs to invest in enterprise resource planning (ERP) with an in-memory platform to support increased data volumes from its core operations. Leveraging the shared services to centralize business functions is one of the means to maintain efficiency with room to expand for growth.

Banking

The combination of changing customer behavior with frequent use of digital channels and wallets, disruption from new entrants such as bitcoins or PayPal services, new regulations on capital requirements, and competition from other industries such as retail businesses launching their own credit cards are all leading to a structural change in the banking industry never seen before.

Enterprises need to identify which emerging technologies should be considered as enablers for them to become intelligent. Some of the key digital themes that are emerging from the banking industry and technology trends are listed below for the enterprise to leverage and ride on the digital innovation journey:

Industry Convergence

The current industry convergence is bringing many industries such as retail, telecom, travel, etc., together with banking, which is opening the door for new ways of doing business, new revenue opportunities, and a complete refinement of customer services and offerings. The banking industry needs to quickly adapt to these changes to face the new competitive world of financial transactions and payments from bitcoins, PayPal, etc.

Personalized Conversations

The banking enterprise needs to ensure very personalized and relevant interactions with customers so that they remain loyal and want to use the same bank for all financial needs. This is to combat competition from other banking and financial services institutions.

Customer Delight and Experience

Banks should provide a seamless front-end interface to customers so that they can have interactions across all digital channels using their mobile devices for an unprecedented experience.

Connected to the Ecosystem

The enterprise needs to create an ecosystem such that all the products and offerings are embedded and linked to other industries.

Becoming Digital

Banks need to implement the requisite tools and capabilities to enable a digital culture inside the banks and with the outside world while interacting with customers and suppliers, which would redefine exchange of information, data transparency, trust, and ease of doing business.

Compliance

Banks need to implement new policies in collaboration with the regulatory authorities to comply with the new digital age while offering advice and guidance so that there is full transparency to the customer and the sensitive customer data is protected across boundaries.

Be Agile

Banks are generally very conservative in nature, and in this era of digitization they need to change the way of working and transform from a risk-free delivery approach to agile methodology with rapid design and implementation of new products and services.

Life Sciences

The life sciences industry is going through a significant change, with mergers and acquisitions, consolidation of multiple platforms and instances, predictive healthcare from sensor-based real-time data, and expansion of the supply chain.

Enterprises need to identify which emerging technologies should be considered as enablers for them to become intelligent. Some of the key digital themes that are emerging from the life science industry and technology trends are listed below for the enterprise to leverage and ride on the digital innovation journey.

Expansion of Business Networks

The enterprise needs to change the way in which the patient's, doctor's, and insurance provider's data is being shared within the organization and within the ecosystem. The enterprise needs to develop the product insights and open the business model to interact with partners leveraging cloud, networks, and mobile strategies such as participating in the supply chain collaboration platform and next-generation track and trace serialization of medicines.

Shorten R&D Cycle

The R&D process in the life sciences industry can be accelerated by increasing efficiency and minimizing false starts using analytics and artificial intelligence technologies. Natural language processing and artificial intelligence can quickly match patients to clinical trials by scanning protocols and recommending trials for patients based on their clinical records. Big data can provide other lifestyle attributes to consider when matching. AI can accelerate R&D by scanning and analyzing clinical and chemical data to predict molecular interactions of potential compounds without having to conduct real-life experiments.

Utilize the Data from IoT and Connected Devices

The Internet of Things and connected devices provide new information within the enterprise that should be combined with the existing data to get more meaningful insights. The enterprise needs to focus on the development of the IoT capability within the business process to harness the right data.

Improve Operational Efficiency

Automation and artificial intelligence technologies can help improve the efficiency of operations at the enterprises within the life sciences industry by automating back-office administrative tasks such as reporting to regulators and payers, which helps to complete tasks with greater speed and accuracy. Automation and chatbots can also manage the increasing volume of direct consumer inquiries. Adding AI capabilities like natural language processing broadens the set of tasks that can be automated such as processing and acting upon unstructured data inputs like physician notes.

New Communication Platform

The enterprise needs to create a new communication platform so that the responses of the customers can be heard. This capability will allow the enterprise to understand how products are perceived by physicians and patients so that corrective action can be taken to maximize sales effectiveness.

Build Analytics Capability

The enterprise needs to leverage the new data from the environment and the existing data streams to build advanced analytics capability that would combine patient, physician, practitioner, and business partner to generate new information flow for improved decision making.

The enterprise can also set up channels to engage directly with people using their treatments, share information to help maximize treatment effectiveness, identify adverse effects, and scrutinize increases in drug prices.

Protect Information

The growing volumes of personal health information from electronic health records, clinical trials, health monitoring wearables, and connected devices all present a security risk for the healthcare ecosystem. It is of paramount importance that the enterprise only allow authorized access and use of personally identifiable data from clinical trials and consumer interactions. Enterprises must protect against both external cyberattacks and potential misuse of data by employees. Intellectual property protection is also critical, especially as more biologic and genomic treatments are developed.

Remote Patient Care

The emerging technology and changing consumer preferences will enable delivery of virtual care at scale, with an increasing level of personalization. The increasing use of sensors and wearables by patients to track their health gives providers the data they need to assess and advise patients remotely. This pool of remotely captured data also provides the foundation for applying bioinformatics and genomics to deliver personalized care and attention. As patients become comfortable with digital experiences and sharing their data, virtual care will become an expected, cost-effective, and convenient part of the healthcare experience.

Energy and Utilities

The energy and utilities industry is going through turbulent times, with aging infrastructure, rising costs, the complexity of operations, disruption in demand from new technology, competition from new entrants in the value chain, and changing customer behavior and expectations.

The enterprise needs to identify which emerging technologies should be considered as enablers for them to become intelligent. Some of the key digital themes that are emerging from the utilities industry and technology trends are listed below for the enterprise to leverage and ride on the digital innovation journey:

Intelligent Grid Operations

The enterprise needs to utilize analytics to predict and improve outage response, optimize voltage and power, and integrate distributed sources. The use of real-time analytics and mobile would help field operators with better directions and improve communications with consumers and coworkers.

Digitize Assets

Physical assets are digitized using the Internet of Things that generates useful data. Sensor data can help identify capital assets that require maintenance, need plant operations monitoring, and require energy usage optimization in consumers' homes. As the use of Internet of Things technologies matures within the enterprise, it will be essential to develop a strong connectivity infrastructure that can reliably handle a web of diverse sensors. It will be equally important to have robust tools for storing, sharing, and analyzing generated data.

Demand Optimization

The enterprise needs to optimize demand by integrating consumer data, grid management technology, and analytics tools. The data from smart meters and device management would support the operations and deployment.

Improve Forecasting

Energy and utilities are capital-intensive industries where advanced analytics can help enterprises predict consumption patterns and manage the supply.

Big data can also help to analyze the market and to predict the demand for raw materials, which is one of the biggest variable costs of production. Predictive maintenance technologies such as simulation modeling can be used for creating a simulated version of the equipment and modeling virtual wear and tear to help maintain uptime and ensure consistent supply.

Streamline Operations

Traditionally, the energy and utilities enterprises have aging and fragmented technology environments. Robotic process automation provides an opportunity to automate user actions on existing systems with minimal technology integration, business disruption, or investment. It can improve operational efficiency and accuracy, initiate the process of enterprise digitization, and provide a foundation to gradually apply artificial intelligence and machine learning to perform more sophisticated tasks.

Customer Interaction

With mobile, social media, and connected homes as new interactive channels, the enterprise should find avenues to interact with the customer through this digital medium and utilize the data generated through embedded customer analytics.

Utility enterprises can prepare for the future and further engage customers by adopting technologies that support a growing ecosystem of alternative energy generation, private grids, and smart buildings.

Asset Management

As utilities are a heavy asset- and investment-based industry, the enterprise can effectively use the information in cloud-enabled advanced analytics to evaluate conditions and optimize asset planning, investments, and reliability.

Safety

Safety in the energy and utilities sector concerns both physical safety among workers in the plant and securing critical infrastructure from hacking and cyberattack. For physical safety, workers can be replaced by robots in dangerous conditions. For cybersafety, new technologies and security standards need to be adapted to stay ahead of hackers. Advanced analytics can be also be used to predict and detect suspicious or unauthorized behavior, and blockchain can be used to store critical operational data to maintain its integrity.

Improved Life of a Field Worker

The mobile solutions powered with analytics can not only improve the back-office operations but also improve the planning and scheduling, logistics optimization, safety, and effective utilization of field workers in managing the work and solving customer problems in a timely way.

Retail

The retail industry is the greatest disruptor from the digital transformation, as it can continuously engage customers with tailored content and offerings across omnichannels by providing customers with an enhanced user experience. Streamlining order management and omnichannel fulfillment are some of the key benefits of digital enablement, as it simplifies and tracks the supply chain process.

Some of the key digital themes that are emerging from the retail industry and technology trends are listed below for the enterprise to leverage and ride on the digital innovation journey:

New Products and Services

The retail enterprise needs to invest in new product development, expand its range of products for a better shopping experience, be agile in bringing new products to the market quickly, and keep its merchandise available for sales through extended partner networks such as online portals and new retail formats.

Personalized Customer Experience

The enterprise needs to provide a personalized and enhanced customer experience to maintain loyalty and repeat customers through all sales and marketing channels. Customers should have the flexibility to place orders through their mobile devices and track them until delivery with a seamless return, if a customer is not satisfied with the product.

Simplify Supply Chain

The enterprise needs to simplify the manufacturing and supply chain operations to enable fulfillment from all available channels and increase alliances with business partners in the extended supply chain network.

Empower the Workforce

Change the operating model within the organization with the evolution of new roles introduced as a result of the enterprise adapting to the market disruption. Empower the employees with the knowledge to provide more value-added services to the customer through apps.

Drive Operating Model Efficiency

The enterprise needs to implement the advanced planning and analytics tools to increase efficiency by using the consumer data in a responsible way with a proper data governance model in place.

Software

The software industry is going through a major transformation that will impact the ecosystem, architecture, and the way software is written, delivered, and funded.

Some of the key digital themes that are emerging from the software industry and technology trends are listed below for the enterprise to leverage and ride on the digital innovation journey:

Innovate New Products

The enterprise in the software industry needs to integrate the solution offerings with the new business model and launch new and innovative products based on the technology trend such as cloud-based solutions. The focus needs to be around bundled solutions to deliver business outcomes rather than on certain features or functions enabled by the software.

Subscription-based Model

The enterprise needs to keep pace with the changing times by allowing multiple and flexible purchasing options from a onetime purchase to monthly subscriptions based on total usage of hardware or software capacity.

Create an Ecosystem

In this digital age, the enterprise needs to provide open source technology and forums for the external vendors and developers to enrich software and services beyond the traditional boundaries to modify the software code. This would facilitate the creation of communities to support and give way to the best-of-breed technologies.

Adoption of Enterprise Software

The enterprise software providers will need to simplify, adjust, and adapt their software solutions based on the requirements of digitally informed customers. This might include simplifying user interfaces, processes, consumption models such as payment based on the number of users or hours, and seamless integration with the current ecosystem to ultimately drive broader adoption.

Enable the Workforce of the Future

The enterprise needs to digitize its internal operations with mobility, robotics, IoT, predictive analytics, and automated workflow. This would enable a cultural shift from a labor-driven organization to a digitally enabled accountable workforce.

Oil and Gas

Some of the digital impact in the oil and gas industry has been on the usage of IoT for predictive analytics, a connected workforce using mobile solutions, data-backed real-time decision making using big data solutions, and an integrated supply chain using enterprise social collaboration with business partners.

Some of the key digital themes that are emerging from the oil and gas industry and technology trends are listed below for the enterprise to leverage and ride on the digital innovation journey:

Capital Project Delivery

The enterprise needs to achieve faster time to market to be competitive by implementing capital project management, using agile methodology, engineering data management solutions on the cloud, and digitizing engineering drawing information for faster, accurate, on-demand access by users, leading to on-time and on-budget project delivery.

Predictive Maintenance

The enterprise needs to leverage new IT solutions to make intelligent decisions on production, predictive maintenance, and asset management by deploying sensors to assets such as pipes, units, tanks, etc.

Data-driven Insights

With the Internet of Things, the amount of data generated from the ever-increasing use of sensors would continue to explode. The enterprise needs to develop architecture, embed analytics into the business processes, develop predictive capabilities to improve operational efficiency, monetize and leverage the asset.

Connected Logistics

The enterprise needs to incorporate an integrated supply chain solution supporting suppliers and customers that can optimize all functions from demand forecasting to finished product delivery in real time.

Manufacturing

The world is currently facing a massive change in the industrial manufacturing space after the inception of the internet and mobile technology. Some of the emerging technologies to be considered in transforming the business of industrial products include enablement of workers and machines to seamlessly work together, production automation, agile delivery, and resource optimization to meet tomorrow's challenges.

Some of the key digital themes that are emerging from the manufacturing industry and technology trends are listed below for the enterprise to leverage and ride on the digital innovation journey:

Data Analytics

The rise of industrial IoT has enabled enterprises to extract information from physical assets. The data from IoT devices along with advanced visualization software can be used to create simulated models of the physical assets that enable enterprises to execute potential scenarios and gain insights. Artificial intelligence can be leveraged to further exploit the data provided by IoT sensors. Data from across the supply chain can be analyzed to predict maintenance issues before they occur and optimize raw material usage to accurately forecast inventory and production management.

New Tools

Digital tools such as virtual and mixed reality enable the faster, cheaper, and more effective design of products by providing platforms to interact with products in a real-world environment before they are built. Changes can be incorporated quickly and easily before the manufacturing process. The manufacturing techniques are changing as 3D printing advances beyond prototyping to assembly-line quality, which helps to minimize the parts necessary to be sourced through the supply chain and replace the parts on an on-demand basis.

Automate Production

Robots have evolved to independently perform complex physical tasks which were only performed by humans through enhanced communication. IoT and connected devices enable machine-to-machine communication, and voice and text interfaces enable more natural communication with humans. Autonomous vehicles extend this independence beyond manufacturing by providing a means for the transportation of goods or supplies between machines. Automation is not just limited to the factory floor; back-office tasks like sending and processing invoices or booking journal entries can be automated through robotic process automation.

Optimize Resources

Optimizing the use of resources is one of the key cost-effective measures taken by the enterprises in the industrial products sector. Traditionally, prototyping require building physical products, which would eventually be disposed of, but augmented and virtual reality remove these necessities, as design and feature updates are made digitally. Simulation modeling with AI enables the ability to test the environmental impact of products operating under various conditions, and predictive analytics can help to optimize allocation across supply chains to minimize waste and transportation costs.

Conclusion

Most of the large and successful Fortune 500 enterprises have innovated and grown their businesses over many decades by industrializing the practices and policies that have made them successful. In this era of digital revolution, with new competitors and business disruptors, agility and adaptation to the new technology become critical for the enterprise to survive. Often, the very systems, policies, and practices that have enabled past success stories are now inhibiting that agility. Digital transformation within an enterprise is not easy, as it requires changes to practices, policies, technology architectures, talent, and organizational culture.

The new IT organization needs to be designed to react quickly to changes in business and technology environments by adopting a flexible organizational structure, talent strategy, and generative culture. In the new enterprise structure, the CEO (chief executive officer) sets the long-term vision and strategy, the CIO (chief information officer) enables the technology while optimizing the costs, the CTO (chief technology officer) delivers business innovation with operational efficiency, and the CDO (chief digital officer) provides the agility and technology to support the customer's preferences and needs.

PART II

Collaborative Methods and Tools

CHAPTER 2

Design Thinking

*T*his chapter provides an overview of the design thinking process, which helps the enterprise to become creative and innovative to solve problems in collaboration with the users. It discusses the methodology and different tools and techniques that can be used at various stages of the process along with the use cases to make the enterprise intelligent.

Design Thinking Overview

The emerging technology and its ease of use have changed the needs and behavior of the external market and customers. With the change to the ecosystem happening so fast, it's difficult to create a model from past experience and refer it as part of the solution for the future work that we undertake. Design thinking is the tool that focuses primarily on the customer requirements, takes all the external environmental factors into consideration, and provides multiple options for a solution that can be tested and refined to perfection to reduce risk and increase the probability of success.

Understanding Design Thinking

Design always starts with humans, their needs, values, desires, thoughts, and what they have in their mind to achieve the end goal. The design thinking concept is built on the designer's perspective, their reasoning style, and how they think and act when identifying problems and generating solutions. Thus, design thinking involves a collaborative approach with multidisciplinary teams to create a diverse array of viewpoints, which are subject to many interpretations resulting in innovative solutions and outcomes. It's a conglomeration of human principles, technological feasibility, and business capability.

Design thinking is a human-centric approach to innovate, create opportunities, and solve problems by integrating technology with requirements. The process requires the collaboration of new ideas, observation of problems, rapid prototyping, business analysis, and industry expertise to create an atmosphere of innovation, add value to the enterprise, and improve customer experience.

It's a new way of solving problems that requires the following characteristics:

- User-centric: The empathy and deep understanding of the user's motivation and behavior through direct observation and research play a big role in the solution's success.

- Collaborative: Various departments and functions within the enterprise need to collaborate to effectively develop and deliver the solution.

- Creative: The problem is reframed and looked at from different perspectives which help consider many solutions to the same problem rather than having a biased solution.

- Prototype-driven: The tangible representation of the problem is solved and presented to the users to get early feedback.

- Iterative: The feedback from the users is incorporated into the solution, retesting of the solution is carried out, and lessons are learned from early failures and applied to the next potential problem to prevent its recurrence.

Key Applications

Some of the key design thinking applications include:

- Provide innovative products or services and improve customer experience across multiple channels for existing and new businesses.

- In this era of fast change and digital disruption, design thinking helps create new business models, remain innovative, aid digital transformation, and define business strategy and a roadmap for the future.

- Improve repetitive and people-driven processes such as operations, customer service, and human resources by using iterative problem-solving methods with the users.

- Incorporate user experience, feedback, and customer pain points in the design.

- Accelerate the process of gathering business requirements through user observations, rapid prototyping, collaboration, and workshops that help users to visualize the solution early in the process.

Why Are Enterprises Moving to Design Thinking?

Key drivers such as social, mobile, and cloud computing have caused exponential changes to the external market environment such as providing a plethora of products and service options to the customers, leading to transparency and changing customer behavior and expectations.

While enterprises are faced with new competitors and digital disruptors that are emerging all the time, it is all the more imperative to provide an extraordinary customer experience to remain competitive. Design thinking is an organized way of solving problems by combining previous knowledge with new insights, building a prototype by trying things out quickly, and testing with real people in the real world to reduce risk and time to market.

The fast pace of technological innovation coupled with connectivity and instant access to data has made the future very difficult to predict. This has led to the growing need of design thinkers in the enterprise who want to maximize ROI on large digital transformation projects by emphasizing customer experience improvement as the key element for success. Design thinking is a proven problem-solving process that has been used at enterprises for quite some time to create an opportunity for innovative solutions by rethinking new services and systems instead of just improving them.

Design Thinking Methodology

Design thinking involves multiple stages during the process, and in all the stages it's visually appealing so that people are engaged during the process. People use diagrams, pictures, posters, live prototype models, videos, photos, etc., to visualize the problem, understand the context, and contribute towards the solution. Design thinking methodology involves the following implementation phases:

Discover

This phase involves understanding the core problem that needs to be solved. Some of the activities that an enterprise conducts during the discover phase include collaborating with the team, conducting extensive research on the topic, understanding the behavior and requirement of the people involved in the process, knowing the context of how the problem arose, and sketching and highlighting all the components related to the subject of investigation.

In the discover phase, the design thinking team needs to gather human insights and create meaningful solutions for the users. Learning about the users for whom the solution is designed and their needs is the key, and to accomplish this feat, the enterprise needs to leverage the following to get the insights:

- Human Insights and Open Data: The human insights are discovered by gathering and analyzing data and insights collected from conducting interviews, observations, experiments, and research with the customers and the community at large.

- Innovation and Emerging Trends: New business and pricing models, trends from peer organizations within the same industry, open data sources such as social media, and new technologies provide insights to innovation and emerging trends.
- The Existing Data Within the Enterprise: Evaluating quantitative data related to the target market segment, industry data, and competitor data provides insights into the enterprise structure.

The complete perspective on insights and data leads to new, innovative opportunities and ensures that the right problems are solved. The end goal is to build a solid foundation to understand what problems are worth solving and gather insights that will help us design solutions.

Conduct Workshop

This phase involves conducting workshops to brainstorm ideas and synthesize learnings and point of view from the discovery phase. Some of the methods and activities that an enterprise uses while conducting workshops include personas, journey maps, and blueprints.

Define the Problem

Traditionally, whenever a problem comes up, we have the tendency to jump right in and start solving it. Design thinking is a little different; it involves a deep-dive working session to understand the gravity and root cause of the problem before making a decision about whether it's worth the time and effort for the enterprise to solve it.

The enterprise needs to leverage the following while defining the problem:

- Information: Gathering and analyzing all the information collected during the discovery phase.
- Category: Organizing the data into categories so that similar issues and problems are grouped together.
- Understanding: Generating a deep-dive understanding of the problems based on the categories identified, findings, and themes that will help us generate new assumptions.

- Assumptions: Generating assumptions while defining the problem and creating initial ideas for the solution.
- Problem Description: Expressing the details of the problem that the team is trying to resolve and address.

The end goal is to create the problem statement that would not only define the problem but also generate the highest impact, if solved.

Potential Options

Instead of solving a problem with a known solution or prior knowledge, design thinking explores all the ideas from basic to crazy ones to solve a particular problem or generate an opportunity. The ideas are then discussed, merged, sorted, and assessed to sketch potential propositions.

Design thinking is not about coming up with the right idea, it's about discussing and gathering a broader set of potential ideas and possibilities by thinking beyond incremental changes and reimagining new solutions, business models, value propositions, and markets based on untapped insights and new assumptions. The enterprise needs to complete the following while generating potential options:

- Create a nonjudgmental, uplifting environment where the thinkers feel free to share such concepts with each other without constraint to generate a large volume of ideas.
- The team needs to challenge, rethink, and reshape initial ideas that could include fresh start-up ideas, new technologies, market trends, digital, and regulatory impact.
- Create a framework to rank and prioritize these ideas for the next phase to build solutions and assess impact.

The end goal is to generate a wide range of related and unrelated ideas, prioritize them, and articulate the assumptions that require validation during the prototype phase.

Prototype

In a traditional working environment, the solutions are proposed in an office without validating with the customers on their experience. In this phase of the design thinking, prototypes are generated from various ideas. Each idea is evaluated before finalizing the right solution. Some of the methods and activities that an enterprise uses while creating a prototype include storyboards, sketches, and models ranging from visual sketches to interactive simulations.

The enterprise needs to leverage the story that has been learned throughout the process to give shape to a high-impact solution while creating a prototype.

The enterprise needs to visualize ideas using various techniques, starting with low-fidelity prototypes, mock-ups, and functional prototypes that users can actually use. It can also use methods that help articulate the new value proposition of the ideas and validate whether it resonates with the users. The enterprise needs to do the following when creating a prototype:

- Design experiments and make ideas tangible so that they can be shared with the users and stakeholders.
- Validate assumptions and measure results.
- Build a prototype using various techniques such as a wall of Post-it notes, a device or appliance assembly, a role-playing activity, or even a storyboard – something tangible which a user can interact with.
- Identify the list of assumptions that need to be true so that the solution can solve the problem.

The end goal is to develop a functional prototype, ideally a minimum viable product or service that is ready to be launched in the market, once validated by the users.

Test

In this phase of the design thinking, various ideas are tested using prototype models and the learnings from each of the prototypes are noted. After a number of iterative cycles, the final solution is accepted after being validated with the customers and actual end users.

Implement

This phase involves deployment of the finalized solution with continuous feedback and refinement and releasing new iterations at the scheduled date. Some of the activities that an enterprise conducts during this phase include documenting the process, the rationale, and the results.

The enterprise needs to do the following activities while creating a document postimplementation to summarize all activities carried out during the design thinking process:

- The proposition that started the conversation to solve a particular problem

- Discovery from the research and all the ideas gathered from the workshop
- Building a working prototype to test the idea and assumptions
- The recommended proposition, users, features, etc., with key insights from the process

Once a prototype has been developed and the results and journey documented, the end goal is to make a decision to pilot a product with real users to understand how the product is perceived, act upon the feedback and insights, optimize the solution, and make investment decisions to launch the product at scale and grow with new opportunities.

Tools and Techniques

Some of the tools and techniques used during each phase of the design thinking sessions are listed below:

Discover

The following tools and techniques are used during the Discover phase:

Mind Map

A mind map is a hierarchical diagram that is used to organize information in a visually appealing format that shows all the relationships and dependencies. The objective of this tool is to identify target users, market segments, and relevant data regarding the problem to gain insights that will aid in solving the problem or fill an information gap.

A mind map is used to carry out the following activities:

- Define a central theme or problem that needs to be examined.
- Gather participants to explore relevant connections to the theme including relevant topics, other users, and existing data.
- For every new connection, the team decides its importance as to whether it can be considered as a primary connection to solve the problem.
- Once all possible connections have been listed, the team needs to prioritize all the primary connections and brainstorm what further information is needed to move to the next step.

Start-up Scan

Start-up scan is a means to help enterprises identify new products or services, disruptive business models, current market trends, emerging technology, and innovative solutions to remain competitive.

Interview

The purpose of interviewing the stakeholders is to understand the what, how, and why for the actions taken and the individual behavior towards achieving an outcome.

Some of the key activities during the interview process include

- Establish key themes that need to be explored in detail with stakeholders' opinions on the subject.
- Create a dialogue guide with questions to explore with the interviewee.
- Set up interviews with any potential stakeholders.
- Conduct interviews and ensure all insights and discussions are documented.
- Evaluate interview insights and segregate the themes that can be carried over to the next level of discussion.

Empathy Map

The objective of creating an empathy map is to collaborate all the observations to get deeper insights into a particular problem. It's a visual representation of the users' attitudes and behaviors in order to understand the problem from the users' perspective so that an effective solution can be created to meet the goals of the users.

Some of the key elements during the creation of the empathy map include:

- See: Describe the user's daily experiences including the interaction of the users with people, involvement in activities, and exposure from the surrounding environment and marketplace.
- Say and Do: Describe the user's attitude with all the actions and verbal communication with others and the behavioral changes.
- Hear: Describe what the user is hearing from the messages received from peers, boss, family, and friends and how this is influencing the decisions and impacting the thinking process.
- Think: Describe the implications and the meaning of what the user conveyed in the message by considering both the positive and negative thoughts.
- Feel: Describe the feeling of the user, including what makes the user feel good, bad, worried, anxious, excited, frustrated, and challenged.

Observation

This is a process where the users or products are observed to gain further insights. The objective is to verify if the users complied with the actions that were promised and capture workarounds, pain points, and activities that are difficult to articulate.

Open Data Source

The large volumes of unstructured data such as social media messages, call center transcripts, chat records, search, etc., are open for everyone's access, usage, and distribution and can be tapped to create a clear understanding of the customers and their requirements. This also includes deeper insights provided by thematic analysis using natural language processing.

Social Media

This involves collecting aggregated data and analyzing comments across multiple platforms such as Facebook, Twitter, YouTube, etc., to understand the user's sentiment and belief for a particular theme, brand, or product.

Conduct Workshop

The following tools and techniques are used while conducting the workshop phase:

Workshop

The objective of conducting a workshop is to gather the team together at a common place to discuss a common problem and encourage the participants to find a solution.

Some of the key activities while conducting a workshop include:

- Define an agenda including the introduction of the team members and their roles and responsibilities for the project or towards solving a particular problem.
- Clarify the scope of the project or the problem so that all participants have a clear understanding.
- Align expectations from the participants and explain the key objectives.
- Outline the end result that needs to be achieved as part of the successful outcome.
- Explain the timelines to achieve the desired outcome.
- Outline the approach of the project or problem.
- Establish the project management office and governance activities such as weekly sponsor meeting, stand-up meetings, theme meetings, and other key stakeholder engagement and communication requirements.

Define the Problem

The following tools and techniques are used while defining the problem during the design thinking phase:

Personas

Personas provide the character and structure of the target users along with their associated characteristics, behaviors, and attitudes.

Some of the key directions when creating personas include the following:

- The interviews, observations, workshops, and research that have been conducted need to be utilized to create the personas with different attributes of the users.
- The objectives, goals, requirements, pain points, and other insights of the users need to be accounted for in the personas.
- It's a good practice to group the customer segments based on similarities such as role, title, gender, location, etc.
- Provide and finalize the persona template to have consistency during the process.
- Personas will vary in terms of granularity of the information and requirements collected, but creating five to seven personas for a problem is quite common.

Problem Statement

The problem statement describes the issue or problem that needs to be addressed, improved, or solved based on the understanding of the users facing the problem.

Some of the key characteristics of a problem statement include the following:

- Is focused on the problem
- Provides deep-dive insights into the problem
- Provides the challenge of whether it is worth solving the particular problem based on its significance and the impact created by the problem
- Informs criteria to evaluate competing ideas to aid in solving the problem
- Is discrete and provides solutions to a specific product or user

User Journey Map

The user journey map is a visual representation of the entire process that a user experiences when interacting with different touch points. It's a series of steps outlining the entire sequence of functions and activities required to be executed by the user to move to the next step.

- Provide a communication medium of how the future state or the end vision would look.
- Use same-color Post-it notes to map the customer's step-by-step journey.
- Use other colors to identify major pain points and the user's behavior.

Potential Options

The following tools and techniques are used while gathering all the ideas during the design thinking phase:

Brainstorming

Brainstorming is a group creativity process to gather a large volume of ideas that are contributed by the users spontaneously to solve a specific problem.

Some of the key characteristics of a brainstorming session include the following:

- Provide the problem to the user whose solution has been targeted.
- Write one idea per Post-it so that all ideas can be collected with ease.
- The judgment for some ideas can be deferred while prioritizing the list of ideas.
- Encourage wild and outside-the-box ideas, as they may ignite a great idea for someone else.
- Bring in diverse perspectives and knowledge on the topic.
- Focus the conversation on the relevant topic.
- Encourage one conversation at a time to prevent any distortion.
- Collect and present all the ideas visually to make quick decisions.

Prototype

The following tools and techniques are used during the prototype phase:

Role-Play

Role-play is a technique where the participants assume the role and characteristics of the users to test highly interactive experiences. This method helps to gain more insights into touch points and user journeys.

Some of the key characteristics of a role-play session include the following:

- The conditions such as the attributes for the product or user need to be set up to test the real-life experience.
- The entire end-to-end story needs to be enacted to get insights for any corrective action.
- A few scenarios with different variables need to be tested to check how various experiences can affect the functionality of the product or service.

Storyboard

A storyboard is a visual map in the form of a sequence of illustrations or images that depicts the entire vision and flow of how the users connect and interact with an experience. It can be used throughout the entire project life cycle to highlight and sketch a visual representation of human-centric problems at every stage of the process.

Test

The following tools and techniques are used during the testing phase:

Test Cards

Test cards are used to test the hypothesis so that the idea can be successfully implemented when designing an experiment.

Some of the key characteristics of a test card include the following:

- Determine the name of the test to be performed, the due date, and the participant responsible for executing the test.
- Describe the hypothesis that needs to be tested, with the critical level.
- Outline the entire process in the design and check if the hypothesis is correct or needs to be revised.
- Define the data elements and their reliability.
- Indicate the duration of the test until its successful outcome.
- Define the measurable criteria to validate if the tested hypothesis passed or failed.

Implement

The following tools and techniques are used during the implementation and documentation phase:

Lean Canvas

Lean canvas is a business plan on a page that helps to take a snapshot of a participant's thought process and identify assumptions. It focuses on identifying and documenting a problem, its solution, and all other attributes that help in the resolution of the problem and provide competitive advantages to the enterprise.

Some of the key attributes in a lean canvas include the following:

- Problem or issue
- Existing workaround
- Future solution
- Value proposition
- Customer segment that is affected
- Channels
- Key metrics
- Cost structure
- Revenue model
- Any barriers

All attributes may not be filled on the canvas at once, but the users can document and make notes as the process evolves.

Use Cases

Design thinking can be used to solve challenges in various business processes and functions within an enterprise. Some scenarios and real-life case studies on design thinking are described below that have facilitated the transformation to an intelligent enterprise.

1. Case Study: Use Design Thinking to Redesign the Customer Service Experience for Both Customers and Sales Representatives
   - Scenario
     - A global automobile giant wanted to improve the quality and efficiency of customer support service.
   - Approach
     - The enterprise gathered a cross-functional team of representatives and software experts to design new software for the sales representatives based on collaborative effort.

- A learning space was created for the representatives so that the software designers could observe and learn about their requirements in detail.
- A working prototype of the new system was created in the learning space where the representative could use and provide feedback for improvement.
- The representatives were given incentives to use the prototype as part of the testing process where the technical team asked questions and captured feedback and the software team made immediate changes as part of the iterative testing and implementation.

- Results

  - The enterprise learned that the people were key in successfully implementing a process and its design.
  - Rapid prototyping and an iterative approach ensured that the problem was solved correctly.
  - Customer service improved significantly, leading to a change in customer satisfaction as revealed by the survey.

2. Case Study: Identify Innovation Opportunity for a Consumer Packaged Goods Company

   - Scenario

     - A major consumer packaged goods company wanted to use design thinking to identify innovation opportunity for its various product lines.

   - Approach

     - A workshop was conducted to explore how emerging IT technologies could be leveraged to create new, innovative product lines.
     - Various design thinking tools and methods were used to generate ideas.
     - A brainstorming session was used to explore all facets of the problem and generate a wide range of ideas from various perspectives to bring innovation to the enterprise.
     - Prototyping – using paper, Legos, and string, the participants created a prototype representing new products for the new generation.

   - Results

     - It helped the enterprise design new offerings with enhanced customer experience across various product lines for existing and entirely new businesses.

Conclusion

The design thinking concept has been built on being innovative by integrating the needs of the people, the feasibility of the technology, and the viability of the business. It's a unique approach to collaborating with multiple teams, analyzing data, identifying the right challenge, thinking of customers' needs, and redesigning the customer service experience.

Design thinking is used to solve challenges in various disciplines such as defining new business models in the a fast-changing, disruptive world, bringing an innovative solution, improving the customer experience and offerings, enhancing human-intensive processes, and improving the requirements-gathering process to design an IT solution.

CHAPTER 3

Agile

*T*his chapter provides an overview of the agile framework, its features, principles, and some of its benefits and challenges as applied in a project environment. It also discusses the methodology that is appropriate for the enterprise and the tools that are available to help the enterprise follow agile and become intelligent.

Agile Overview

Agile is a framework with a set of principles and methodologies to implement systems and software development. Its foundation is built on the principle whereby the requirements and solutions are developed in collaboration with cross-functional teams with incremental improvements over time aligned with the expectations of the users. It helps in continuous improvement and encourages rapid and flexible response to changes that are essential for the business.

In recent years, the digital platform has also evolved to bring more modularity and agility into the overall transformation undertaken by the enterprise. Agile requires a change in the enterprise culture, project principles, and values to build the software.

Salient Features

Some of the salient features of an agile framework are listed below:

- All functional teams are organized as Scrums to iteratively develop, test, and document the results of the application. The Scrum Master facilitates the scrum teams for any decisions and resolutions.
- Shorter time frames called Sprints are used to configure or develop small and focused parts of the solution.
- The requirements and other features are broken down into small pieces with a detailed level of functionality called User Stories.
- The list of all themes, user stories, project requirements, and features are collected as part of solution validation and documented as a

prioritized list known as a Product Backlog, which is owned by the Product Owner.

- Each iteration involves a cross-functional team working in all functions including planning, design, configuration, development, unit testing, integration testing, and user acceptance testing.
- A working component of the product or software is demonstrated to the end users and stakeholders at the end of every increment step or sprint cycle.
- It reduces the overall risk of the project with early testing and defect detection and helps to adapt to the changes quickly.

Key Principles

The agile methodology works on the following key principles:

- Leadership Commitment: The adoption of agile requires a top-down commitment to the change; it requires enterprise leaders who are dedicated to seeing it through and to onboard their teams.
- Pilot Approach: Create evidence and learnings through a small pilot deployment and then leverage this experience to prepare and plan the agile project.
- Empowerment: Encourage a sense of ownership and accountability from the business and product owner.
- Team Interaction: Increase real-time interactions at the team level to solve business issues and risks.
- Collaborative Approach: Use storytelling and a joint estimation approach to get collective buy-in from the team on timelines, effort, and expectations.
- User Stories: Business requirements and gaps are captured as user stories with acceptance criteria for traceability and reduction in the number of solution deliverables.
- Robust Release Planning: Engage in a collaborative effort to build a robust release plan.
- Working Software to Playback Scenarios: Prioritize the build of demonstrable working software to play back business scenarios rather than producing documentation.
- Product Backlog Maintenance: The scope of the project is governed through business-led decision making and solution ownership, and all future and nonpriority build items are put under product backlogs.

- Shift-Left Testing Approach: The testing effort is shifted left in the project life cycle so that the defects are discovered early, which reduces the defect rate in each subsequent test cycle.
- Minimize Documentation: Create a minimum number of documents that have business value and improve the quality by using business process management tools to automate the document creation.

Benefits

Some of the benefits of adopting agile include improved efficiency, reduced risk, high quality, and increased collaboration, as described below:

- There is an improvement in the quality of requirements, resulting in a reduced defect rate, fewer assumptions, and overall higher-quality product and deliverables.
- The probability of delivering a viable product within the estimated timeframe is substantially increased.
- The agile methodology creates a motivating project culture and environment, which improves its adoption.
- It provides a higher level of collaboration, results in reduced frustration, and increases the feeling of ownership from the business.
- The agile framework thrives with the use of automated testing and DevOps procedures.
- The final product is closer to what end users envision due to the frequent feedback loop and playback demo sessions with business.

Challenges

Some of the challenges of adopting agile include the following:

- Rigorous and ongoing planning is required to plan resources, sequence integrated work, and design the work in a dynamic environment.
- Planning and execution in small sprints require more experienced resources, and the overall implementation cost does not decrease.
- A variable and recurring scope change decision process and backlog maintenance require a high-level trust relationship between the internal cross-functional teams and the vendors.
- Product owners need to be strict gatekeepers of scope in order to prevent unmanaged scope creep.

Agile Methodology

Software implementations using an agile method will vary in size. The agile structure of the project may vary based on the program size and structure at the enterprise to account for building the code, testing, deployments, and maintenance. Some of the commonly used agile methodologies are described below:

Iterative V-Model

This is the traditional delivery model with an agile flavor to it. It uses selected agile practices such as early testing, product demonstration, shift left, development objects backlog, etc., to make the project more flexible. In this method, the overall approach is not different from standard project execution methodology with business process configuration, phased implementation, and transitions.

The methodology is illustrated in Figure 3.1, where multiple cycles of development-build-test are executed.

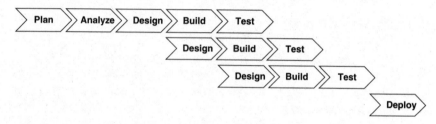

Figure 3.1   Iterative V-model delivery method.

Sprint Based

This is an iteration-based methodology which is leveraged when the scope is mostly finalized but the details are not yet fixed, thus requiring flexibility. It is a valid method for projects where several intermediate releases are planned. It is executed based on a backlog of elements to implement, which are addressed by different teams working in parallel for each release.

The methodology is illustrated in Figure 3.2, where the design, build, test, and demonstration of the software are defined as various sprint cycles by the single delivery stream. Integration testing is executed in the sprints while the user acceptance test is executed after the completion of the sprint cycles.

		Review	Design	Review	Design	Review	Design		
Plan	Analyze		Sprint1		Sprint2		Sprint3		Test	Deploy
		Test	Build	Test	Build	Test	Build		

Figure 3.2   Sprint-based delivery method.

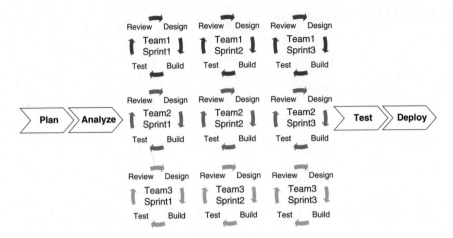

Figure 3.3   Scaled agile-based delivery method.

Scaled Agile Based

The scaled agile method is applicable at a program-level execution or within the entire IT department of the enterprise. This methodology is generally used for longer-duration projects to justify the long list of prerequisites that need to be met along with the continuous involvement with various teams in the enterprise. The main principle behind this method is to establish several agile teams to work in parallel and regularly contribute to the progress of the program by individually releasing the built and tested components. Scaled agile projects can leverage the important ratio of an offshore workforce to have a balanced mix of onshore–offshore resources.

The methodology is illustrated in Figure 3.3, where the design, build, test, and review are carried out in parallel as various sprint cycles by multiple delivery work streams. Integration testing is executed in the sprints while the user acceptance test is executed after the completion of the sprint cycles.

Agile Tools

Listed below are some commonly used tools that support the agile approach during any project implementation:

Project Management Tools

The purpose of using the project management tools is to facilitate the execution of the agile approach during the project life cycle including planning, tracking, work allocation, sprint and product backlogs, reporting metrics, and some other agile practices.

Some of the agile project management tools include the following:

- Atlassian Jira
- Rational Team Concert
- CA Agile Central
- Version One
- Atlassian Trello

Continuous Integration Tools

During the build phase of any agile-based project, continuous integration is an extremely essential development practice that includes configuration, integration testing, version control, and integration with other build tools.

Some of the agile continuous integration tools include the following:

- Jenkins
- Worksoft
- Atlassian Bamboo
- SAP ChaRM (Change Request Management)

Project Collaboration Tools

One of the key principles of working in an agile-based project is that the teams work in collaboration. This is sometimes a challenge in the case of distributed agile projects. Agile projects also involve collaboration with external partners and system integrators. The use of collaboration tools such as shared calendar, e-mail, messaging, and group chats helps the team improve internal collaboration as well as establish a solid partnership with external partners.

Some of the agile collaboration tools include the following:

- SharePoint
- Atlassian Confluence
- Skype for Business
- Cisco Webex
- Polycom

- Liferay
- Jabber

Automated Testing Tools

It is not possible to effectively complete the manual testing on time and within budget in an agile sprint cycle. Building a suite of automated scripts to perform functional testing is the most desirable approach, which includes test script maintenance, testing data, test execution, and test verification.

Some of the agile automated testing tools include the following:

- Worksoft
- Unified Functional Testing
- SoapUI
- Rational Functional Tester
- FitNesse

Conclusion

The transition to an agile model for project implementation and delivery requires upfront investment in change management and significant commitment from leadership within the enterprise, but it definitely provides a better return on investment in the long run.

Agile is the most appropriate tool to use during the following circumstances:

- The enterprise has uncertainty about the requirements and needs some flexibility.
- The enterprise is in the midst of a transformation, and time to market, along with the ability to react quickly to the customer, product, and market changes, are the priority.
- The enterprise needs to validate the minimum viable product and check the progress of the development before fully committing to the deployment of new technologies in its ecosystem.

CHAPTER 4

DevOps

*T*his chapter provides an overview of the DevOps methodology as a collaboration between the development and the operations teams. It also discusses the DevOps maturity level, enablers, and some of the typical processes across the development life cycle that are potential candidates for DevOps use cases to make the enterprise collaborative and intelligent.

DevOps Overview

DevOps (Development and Operations) is a software development methodology that optimizes collaboration, integration, and communication between software development and IT operations. The objective is to shorten the software development life cycle by delivering faster with more predictable features, fixes, updates, and releases, thus reducing the overall time to market with higher quality and lower operating costs. DevOps is used in more than 30% of active application development projects worldwide, and the number is expected to increase as we move forward towards more digitization.

DevOps applies agile and lean principles to maximize the speed of its delivery of a product or service, from a conceptual framework to release into the production environment. It's quite relevant during the digitization, where speed to market and continuous improvement are key to successful transformation. The typical DevOps software development life cycle is depicted in Figure 4.1.

Key Principles

DevOps extends the agile principles by making the IT development team work in cohesion with the IT operations team in the same way that agile has attempted to bring the IT development team to work closely with the business teams. Some of the key principles of DevOps are listed below:

- Team Cohesion: Strong collaboration between business, developers, testers, and IT professionals is required for quick release of small and frequent changes.

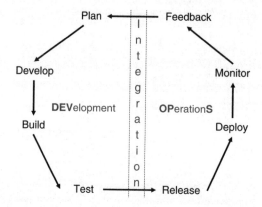

Figure 4.1   DevOps software development life cycle.

- Automation: The process of releasing software must be repeatable and reliable through the automation of tasks involved in releasing the software.

- Version Control: A strong version control process is necessary not only for development code but also for configuration items.

- Early Testing: Environment configurations, infrastructure, etc., must be tested early and often during the software life cycle to prevent delays at a later stage.

- Continuous Improvement: Teams must consistently evaluate and update their practices, processes, tools, environments, and configurations to improve on a continuous basis.

Current Challenges

Digital and mobile applications are changing very fast and need to be responded accordingly for their short feedback cycles. The current IT operating models are not designed to cope with today's high-growth business environment. Some of the challenges include the following:

- IT enterprises spend less time in designing and building the software and more time in testing, deploying, and releasing the software, as the decisions are made early on without input from quality assurance and operations.

- Delivery is not keeping pace with the growth and changes in the business.

- A high number of errors in production are causing business downtime, as the process is manual.
- IT Development and IT Operations have different objectives and work in silos without much coordination.
- The roles are separate, with developers writing the code, quality analysts testing the code, and operations specialists deploying the code in the system.

DevOps Benefits

DevOps involves continuous development where the code is written and committed to version control. It is then built, deployed, tested, and installed in the production environment using automated tools for continuous integration, test, and delivery.

Some of the benefits of using a DevOps approach to deployment include the following:

- Accelerated time to market using streamlined delivery.
- Continuous improvement of delivery.
- Testing early, resulting in risk reduction at a later phase of the project.
- Ability to build the right product by incorporating the change.
- Improved productivity and efficiency via automation.
- Reliable and more frequent releases by using automated code quality and testing tools.
- Improved product quality by testing early using test automation tools.
- Improved customer satisfaction.
- Ability to deliver in small increments.
- Resolving operational challenges and achieving sustainable cost reductions.
- Cohesive team environment.
- Maintaining security, governance, and compliance by automating policies and using configuration management methodology.
- Innovating and improving the products at a faster pace with the increase in frequency and pace of code release.
- With frequent deployments, developers receive real-time feedback about the quality and are able to respond immediately. When the quality issue is identified early in the process, it reduces the risk of defects across the life cycle.
- By removing bottlenecks such as manual testing or environment set up from the software life cycle, teams are more productive and can deliver new functionality faster with improved response time to business needs.

Market Trends

Some of the key market trends involving DevOps include the following:

- The drive to a DevOps approach usually comes from the top management including CEOs and CIOs across the development and IT operations teams to provide competitive advantages by delivering the business results at a faster pace.

- The frequency of deploying cloud and mobile applications is increasing, and enterprises need to offer a better customer experience to differentiate themselves from their competitors.

- DevOps is now being used as a mainstream strategy by many large global enterprises rather than a traditional niche strategy used by large cloud providers.

- DevOps continues to be an important trend in application services where enterprises are adopting a DevOps approach across the applications as part of adopting the digital solution.

DevOps Enterprise Maturity

In this digital era, DevOps helps the enterprise to enable both agile and digital transformation initiatives which are long-term and strategic solutions. Enterprises of all sizes – large, medium, and small – are at varying levels in their transformation journeys and their successful implementation is measured as the DevOps maturity level within the organization.

Listed below are some of the phases of DevOps maturity depending on the stage of the transformation at the enterprise.

Phase 1: Waterfall Approach

The first phase starts with a traditional waterfall method where all the business requirements are gathered and finalized before the development team can start their work. The time taken to write the code for the software to work spans several months, with significant time thereafter to integrate. This is quite ineffective and slow in today's market, where the consumer demands and preferences are changing at a very fast pace and the enterprise needs to cope with the pace to stay competitive.

Phase 2: Iterative Approach

In this phase, the development team uses iterative cycles to execute the project using an agile methodology and approach. With iteration comes quick feedback and turnaround of the code to be integrated into the system. It's a collaborative effort to decrease the time to market but is only effective within the development team and not across the enterprise.

Phase 3: Automated Testing Approach

In this phase, the development team and the testing team work together to execute the automated test scripts after every build so that the code gets validated and is ready for deployment. The code gets integrated continuously with a proper quality check done early in the process through automated testing.

Phase 4: Collaborative Approach

In this phase, the operations team and the development team work collaboratively in a perfect DevOps model. The code is validated and then deployed using automated tools in all the environments from development to production. Enterprise strategy and culture shift need to work in harmony to achieve this level of collaboration.

DevOps Enablers

DevOps can be enabled across all phases of the project life cycle starting from the creation of an idea through operations to the development. Listed below are some enablers and capabilities that can help the enterprise in the DevOps adoption and realize a quick return on the investment:

Continuous Integration

Continuous integration is considered to be a DevOps software development practice where the developers take ownership and merge their code changes to integrate into a central repository on a continuous basis using a version control system.

Once the code is integrated, continuous integration enables them to automatically build and run unit tests on the new code so that the errors can be known and addressed early in the process. Some of the key benefits of continuous integration include:

- Reduce effort with an automated build and testing process.
- Code with higher quality.
- Find the bugs more quickly.
- Improve software quality.
- Reduce the timeline to validate and release new updates.

- Allow more emphasis on innovation rather than just code fix.
- Reduce risk with last-minute build surprises.

Continuous Testing

One of the essential tasks for an enterprise is to automate the testing process in order to meet high quality expectations and end-to-end test coverage on various devices and platforms.

Automated regression test scripts help the enterprise save significant time during every build till deployment and ensure the quality standards are maintained in the code, which would otherwise be reflected in the test failure. Some of the key benefits of continuous testing include:

- A significant reduction in the effort to develop and maintain test scripts.
- Reduction in test execution time.
- More test coverage in terms of functionality and systems.
- Higher accuracy of executing test scripts.
- Lower operating costs, as fewer testers are required during the automated execution of scripts.

Continuous Delivery

Continuous delivery is a DevOps software development practice where any code changes are built, tested, and then automatically prepared to be released in the quality assurance and testing environments prior to production.

The process involves automated unit, load, and integration test execution across multiple environments and applications. Depending on the criticality of the application, there can be multiple testing environments before moving the code manually into production.

Continuous Deployment

Continuous deployment is an enhancement of continuous delivery where the final stage of deployment is also automated such that the code is moved to the production environment automatically without any explicit approval.

This makes the entire deployment process automated, reliable, and repeatable, resulting in significant reduction of deployment time with faster release cycles and updates to the customer. Some of the large enterprises such as Amazon, Google, Facebook, etc., release code changes to the production environment every second, and without the automated continuous deployment process, this would not be possible.

Continuous Monitoring

The metrics, indicators, and logs are continuously monitored by the enterprise to keep track of the impact on the user's experience based on the code changes in the application. The enterprise captures, collects, categorizes, and then analyzes the data and logs generated by applications to understand the impact on the users and gain insight into the root cause of the problem based on the changes made.

In today's world, continuous monitoring becomes ever more important with the expectation of service availability 24/7 and an increase in the frequency of application and infrastructure updates. Setting alerts at a particular threshold or performing real-time analysis of the data helps the enterprise to proactively monitor the services to customers and resolve any performance issues.

Continuous Communication

The principle behind DevOps is to automate the software delivery process by collaborating and sharing the responsibilities between the development and the operations teams. This requires a cultural change within the enterprise along with enhanced and seamless communication between the team members.

The teams use various communication channels such as chat messaging, a project tracker, or any web-based collaborative platform to set governance around sharing information. This enhances coordination among developers, operations, and other teams and avoids conflict and escalation.

Continuous Feedback

The DevOps software development life cycle as shown in Figure 4.1 illustrates that once the code is deployed, customer feedback is taken continuously to improve the quality of the product.

Feedback provides the requirements of the customer on a real-time basis and helps the enterprise to modify the code, improve the software or the product with fixes, and incorporate new features. The objective of every product or code release is to meet the customers' expectations and preferences and make them fully satisfied with the product.

Adoption by Industry

IT organizations and executives are under tremendous pressure to incorporate digital transformation using various tools and processes to make the enterprise intelligent.

The DevOps approach can transform development and operational practices and enable enterprises across industries to improve their time to market through more customer-centric application development, user-friendly interfaces, and operational efficiency of the development teams.

In this new era of transformation, IT executives are computing success in business terms and expecting DevOps teams to use business metrics to gauge their progress and success. Listed below are some of the industries with use cases in DevOps adoption:

Retail

Some of the potential and real-life use cases for the adoption of DevOps in an enterprise within the retail industry include the following:

- The retail and wholesale industry wants to differentiate its relationship and communications with customers.
- Consumer goods enterprises are rushing to update their customer relationship models and technology platforms to enable such experiences, and DevOps can support and expedite the process.

Manufacturing

Some of the potential and real-life use cases for the adoption of DevOps in an enterprise within the manufacturing industry include the following:

- Manufacturers are trying to gain operational efficiency and data insights by incorporating emerging technology into their business processes.
- Combining technology with manufacturing yields positive results for customers, which then allows manufacturers to start the process of software-based improvement.
- In the manufacturing industry, the adoption rate of DevOps within the enterprise is quite high but the culture, process, and agility that go with the DevOps process have not been matured yet.

Media and Entertainment

Some of the potential and real-life use cases for the adoption of DevOps in an enterprise within the media and entertainment industry include the following:

- Traditional media distributors and enterprises have reinvented their business model by providing rich multimedia digital content that delivers immersive customer experience through a variety of devices.

- Though the industry is a great cultural fit, the DevOps adoption is weak, as it lacks automation tools and a frequency of releases strategy.

Utilities

Some of the potential and real-life use cases for the adoption of DevOps in an enterprise within the utilities industry include the following:

- Enterprises in the utilities industry are undergoing a rapid transition in their service delivery models caused by the explosion in the number of devices through the Internet of Things and the explosion in data usage through Big data.
- The industry is currently involved in solving the problem of scaling data consumption and gathering insights from connected devices and sensors where DevOps can play a major role to expedite the process.

Financial Services

Some of the potential and real-life use cases for the adoption of DevOps in an enterprise within the financial services industry include the following:

- Financial services and banks need to reinvent themselves to compete with the financial technology enterprises that are changing the industry rules and causing disruption with innovative products backed by emerging technology.
- DevOps offers key benefits in detecting fraud, time to market for bringing new products and services to customers, and scalability to reach the masses.

Healthcare

Some of the potential and real-life use cases for the adoption of DevOps in an enterprise within the healthcare industry include the following:

- The lack of DevOps adoption within the healthcare industry is caused by stringent healthcare regulations, long budget approval cycles, and dependence on manual audit practices.
- Enterprises are slowly embarking on the DevOps journey with a mind-set towards collaboration within teams, cultural shift, and automation caused by increasing cost pressures and changing customer preferences.

Use Cases

DevOps use cases are certain scenarios where the enterprises have achieved greater business agility and lower costs using the DevOps approach. Let's study some scenarios along with real-life case studies to see how the usage of DevOps was facilitated to result in efficient and intelligent enterprises.

1. Case Study: DevOps in a System Integrated Project by a Large Retailer
   - Scenario
     - A large retailer started a systems integration project with a varied technology landscape to create new applications to deliver integrated business-to-consumer (B2C) and business-to-business (B2B) services.
     - The enterprise needed environments that efficiently supported the software delivery life cycle and allowed an agile approach to include multirelease, and multiproduction support.
   - Approach
     - The enterprise provided tools in the cloud for design and implementation.
     - The enterprise automated the provisioning of environments and provided ongoing support.
     - The delivery approach was to use continuous integration, automated testing, and automated quality gates.
     - Traceability was captured from requirements to delivery tasks, requirements to test cases, code to delivery work and defects, and other DevOps components.
   - Results
     - The project went from having no DevOps capabilities to the code being automatically pulled from version control, built, and deployed into automatically created test environments within a few weeks.
     - The enterprise was able to save significant cost in the build, testing, and deployment effort by implementing a DevOps approach.
2. Case Study: Automate Manual Activities and Reduce Time to Market for a Major Telecommunications Enterprise
   - Scenario
     - A major telecom was spending a lot of time during development and testing on manual activities. The solution delivery process was often slow and a high proportion of the incidents in test and production resulted from human errors in the manual release of the software.

- The enterprise wanted to move to a lean and automated software development process that would reduce time to market while improving the environmental quality and stability.

- Approach
  - Implemented an automated and efficient software configuration management process.
  - Enabled repeatable processes and improved efficiencies across the software development life cycle.
  - Adopted agile development methodology.

- Results
  - The enterprise was able to significantly reduce the cost of software configuration management and the cost of quality associated with configuration and deployment.
  - The enterprise saved a significant number of man-days with the new delivery model and automated life cycle development based on agile and DevOps principles.
  - The enterprise was able to respond to changing market conditions in a faster and more agile manner.

Conclusion

With demand on software developers increasing and IT under pressure from businesses, customers, and other stakeholders, there is a need to deliver like never before by finding a way to work more productively and increase the quality of outcomes. DevOps is about establishing that industrialization.

DevOps is also a key enabler and proponent of agile with its ability to move rapidly and efficiently through the development life cycle. To achieve all this, DevOps establishes a rigorous process for all phases of software development to help deliver more predictable, agile, efficient, and standardized processes with higher-quality outcomes at every stage and phase of the development life cycle. DevOps is transforming how software enterprises operate, taking performance and scalability to the next level.

PART III

Intelligent
Technologies

CHAPTER 5

Robotic Process Automation

*T*his chapter provides an overview of robotic process automation and its ability to automate business processes to reduce costs and have limited dependency on IT resources. It also discusses the implementation methodology and some of the typical processes across business functions and industries that are potential candidates for automation to make the enterprise efficient and intelligent.

Robotic Process Automation (RPA) Overview

Robotic process automation (RPA) is the use of technology to emulate the step-by-step activities that a human user would perform on a computer. This technology is leveraged to make the enterprise intelligent and efficient by automating the business and IT processes that are repetitive, rule-based, and use structured data as inputs. RPA involves the use of software "robots" that can easily be configured with minimal technical expertise and can be quickly trained and deployed to automate manual tasks.

RPA was initially designed for blue-collar jobs to execute administrative and monotonous work, but with time, it has now evolved as a catalyst for innovation to do advanced analysis of unstructured data using natural language processing. A further advanced version of RPA is known as intelligence process automation (IPA), which utilizes new IT technology such as artificial intelligence and machine learning to automate some of the business and computational decision making that were typically done manually by human beings.

Understanding RPA

Robotic: Robots, or "bots" for short, are virtual workforces that can perform activities which are configured and predefined in the RPA tool. They are triggered and start the activity when they receive an electronic input and have the capability to work between various applications simultaneously. They are nondestructive, with the capability to mimic human user actions.

However, the robots are only as smart as their programming with specific scenarios and do not have the cognitive power of artificial intelligence or machine learning. Though RPA is best suited for standardized and repetitive processes, the bots are capable of independently performing human-like activities such as interpretation, decision making, and taking action.

Process: The value proposition of RPA is that it can execute multiple business processes across applications that involve electronic input and output, are standardized, do not have a lot of exceptions, and are repetitive in nature to free up human resources from nonmotivating tasks. RPA can also be applied to the consistent execution of those statutory and compliance processes where the risk and cost associated with human errors are very high.

Automation: Robots do not have human needs such as sleep and can work 24 hours a day on various processes. RPA can automate those activities which are manually performed by humans by interacting with the user interface of existing applications. An intelligent enterprise would have a number of robots waiting to be triggered by specific processes.

Why Are Enterprises Moving to RPA?

Robotic process automation will be one of the game changers in the coming years, as it will have a huge impact on the workforce and how business will be carried out. The study shows that more than 50% of existing jobs would be automated in the next 15 years, with intelligent machines to exceed the number of humans in the job market by 2035. Some of the benefits of implementing RPA within an enterprise's business processes are listed below:

- Reduce processing time to execute a particular job.
- Avoid any human errors in the process, which, in turn, increases the quality of output.
- Humans usually work only 8 hours per day, while the intelligent machines are available 24/7 and are capable of processing around the clock.
- Reduce operating costs, as the recurring cost after the implementation of RPA is minimal.
- Business will be more process-driven than human-driven.
- Increase employee satisfaction, as they will be engaged in more value-added, innovation, strategy, and business development activities rather than the usual time-consuming and monotonous tasks.
- Robots work with existing IT architecture and ecosystems with no requirement for any complex system integration.

- Increase compliance and reduce legal costs by providing an audit trail of the rule-based processes.
- The bots are highly scalable and can be easily deployed based on the seasonal demand.
- RPA technology is deployed on top of the application and, thus, there is no change required in the enterprise's existing ecosystem.

Perfect Candidates for RPA

RPA is oriented towards the automation of processes. Processes that are perfect candidates for RPA have the following characteristics:

- Highly manual
- Rule-based with no human judgment
- Repetitive in nature
- High volume to warrant the investment
- Minimum exceptions
- No frequent change in rules or process steps
- Limited natural language interpretation
- Digital trigger
- Systems not scheduled for upgrade in the near future
- Standardized, well-defined, and documented processes
- High probability of human errors

Automation Capabilities

Robotics is the first step towards becoming an intelligent enterprise. The use of cognitive intelligence is the next step, which refers to the ability of a system to learn how to interpret unstructured content and use the analytical capability to derive and present interpretations in a structured manner, the way humans behave.

The world of automation has evolved over time, and listed below are the functionalities in the order which progresses from simple rule-based automation to complex judgment-based automation:

1. Robotic Process Automation
   - Rule-based scripting of individual tasks
   - Best suited for repetitive, rule-based tasks that rely on structured data

- Executes multistep processes through the use of structured data and processing rules
- Assists human staff members with their activities
- Increases efficiency of the existing workforce
- Helps to consolidate information and provide a consistent customer experience
- Assists in streamlining work and optimizing processes
- Replaces most of the back-office function

2. Cognitive RPA

- Next level of automation
- Best suited for complex, multisystem dependent processes
- Application of computer vision and artificial intelligence techniques to automate complex processes
- Use of speech recognition and natural language processing to automate perceptual and judgment-based tasks performed by humans
- Large-scale unattended processing
- Must respond to fluctuations in system response, unknown events, unanticipated business scenarios without interruption
- Considers security, scheduling, audit, and exception management
- Use of analytics tools to make predictions and recommendations

3. Intelligent Enterprise

- The highest level of automation
- Completely redefines the way an enterprise works by integrating with artificial intelligence, natural language processing, and machine learning techniques
- Aids or replaces subjective decision making based on large data samples
- Capable of handling unstructured data and making decisions based on learning past patterns and experience
- Interprets contextual information and provides consistent reasoning
- Assists in the streamlining of processes and routing of inquiries
- Allows human-like reasoning to be applied in larger volumes (e.g., transaction monitoring, fraud identification, call filtering)
- Learns and adapts over time, becoming as independent as human counterparts but with fewer errors

Key Players in the RPA Space

Each enterprise needs to evaluate the right vendor and product for its automation requirement based on the capabilities offered by each of the RPA tools.

Listed below are some of the leading vendors/products along with the primary capability offered on the market:

RPA Tool	Automation Capability
Blueprism	Rule-Based Automation
Automation Anywhere	Rule-Based Automation
UiPath	Rule-Based Automation
Openspan	Rule-Based Automation
Winautomation	Rule-Based Automation
Redwood	Rule-Based Automation
IBM Watson	Cognitive Automation
WorkFusion	Cognitive Automation
IPSoft	Cognitive Automation
Jacada	Voice and Digital Automation
NICE	Voice and Digital Automation
SpiceCSM	Voice and Digital Automation
Nuance	Natural Language Processing
Cortana	Natural Language Processing

Enterprise RPA Attributes

With so many vendors providing different RPA products and services on the market, it's important for an enterprise to evaluate all the products and choose the ones that have the capability to meet the requirements of the enterprise. Listed below are some attributes that the enterprise can look for in the bots and the accompanying software:

- Products
    - Software robots to automate any process end-to-end, supported with cognitive capabilities that learn as they work and analytics that can help with constant improvement.
    - Offers a software platform which is robust, highly scalable, powerful, and flexible.
    - Designed to provide organizations with a business-owned and IT-supported virtual workforce.
    - Central management of robots and analytics dashboard for insights and utilization.
    - Offers text and voice-based human-machine interfaces and interactions.

- Compatibility
  - The software works with legacy systems, supports any application, and is fully compatible with SAP, Citrix, Java, .NET, HTML, etc.
  - Requires no integration to the supported application.
  - Capable of pulling data from different types of files and sources.
  - The software can read and write any type of document.
  - Ability to host software on the desktop or server, private or public cloud, or a hybrid.
- Cognitive Capabilities
  - Uses visual/image recognition technology to see screen elements just as humans do.
  - Uses machine learning for semistructured processes that typically need expert decision making.
  - Natural language processing for analyzing natural written language.
  - Asks for human assistance when it encounters something it cannot understand and will learn from those escalations to continuously improve its ability to automate similar tasks in the future.
- Security
  - Multiple bots to share architecture with central control.
  - Ability to deploy globally with data privacy regulations to keep data within country boundaries.
  - Architected for enterprise-level security, compliance, support, and auditability.
  - Security to ensure only authorized personnel of the enterprise can access or manipulate data.
  - High levels of flexibility for both encrypting the stored data as well as securing the communication between various resources.
- Automation Process
  - Process steps are recorded for functions so that the bots can follow these steps and execute the tasks.
  - Workflow manager has the ability to create the workflow for multiple bots and link them via a task chain.
  - Bots understand the data and objects on the screen, making it somewhat robust in application changes.
  - Ability to record multiple activities at once.
  - Prebuilt connectors that can easily integrate with various applications within the enterprise.
  - Visual interface to allow business users to easily drag and drop process activities, with a minimal learning curve.

- Robots can be scheduled, placed in queues, triggered, set at predetermined times, initiated by humans, or actively monitor databases to activate.

- Scalability
    - Executes unlimited business processes with a single bot for greater scalability.
    - The software supporting the bot to have built-in objects and libraries that the enterprise can reuse in order to support scaling up of processes, and automation can be scaled up or down according to business needs.
    - Provides flexibility to adjust the number of resources assigned based on business demands.
    - Software to offer four levels of integration – UI, API, OS, and database—to support scaling up automation based on the enterprise's needs.

- Exception Handling
    - When changes occur in the automated process, error handling to provide the users with multiple handling options.
    - Can easily track the errors, provide alerts, and recommend changes to processes.
    - Controls for exceptions to be configured easily, including notifications as needed.
    - Change in the process to flag and notify the administrator and then continue or terminate depending on preset rules or administrator action.

- Implementation
    - Can be hosted either on-premise by the enterprise, by a managed service provider in partnership with the RPA vendor, or on a public cloud such as Microsoft Azure or Amazon.
    - Automatically handles software maintenance and is compatible with any version upgrades.
    - The model should be flexible and utilize the SaaS-based platform.
    - Any changes made to automation scenarios in the bots as a result of application version updates, process changes, etc., are saved to the server and immediately available for the bots to execute. This makes change management easy.

- Centralized Control and Analytics
    - The control room to provide visibility and control from a single, centralized dashboard to schedule, track, verify, log, organize, and

report on all automation activity, allowing the enterprise user to maximize the benefits of automation.

- Bots to capture all content-level information so that every action of all bots would yield real-time process statistics and operational analytics for the digital workforce.
- Bots to help optimize processes and provide RPA reporting.
- Enterprise users to track KPIs and cost savings through automation and monitor individual worker and entire workforce performance.

- **Audit Trail**

  - Audit trail to monitor all the users and bot activities through the control center.
  - Displays both scheduled and failed tasks.
  - Any failure is documented for future audit needs.
  - Detailed log sheet provides a time-stamped history of every action and decision that is taken.

- **Training and Support**

  - The RPA vendor to offer in-house, on-premise, and via an online portal.
  - The technology should be user-friendly so that no SME support is required to create bot process flows.

- **Pricing**

  - Annual license fee with additional bot licenses varies depending on the requirement.
  - Consider per-transaction and usage-based licensing model.
  - No additional charges for the server component or any centralized functionality.
  - Maintenance to be included in the pricing or clearly stated, if charged additionally.
  - The enterprise owns IP for automation developed by them using the bot software.

Enterprise RPA Architecture

The enterprise needs to prepare a technical architecture of bots that would help to create an ideal landscape for automation and scalability. The bots can be hosted, developed, and uploaded at the enterprise's own IT center or they can be controlled, executed, scheduled, and maintained through an interface.

The design for building the bots should be thoroughly analyzed into the automated parts and components requiring manual intervention. This can be very useful in defining governance structure by the clear separation of roles and their corresponding owners.

The requirements and the level of automation would dictate whether an enterprise should go for:

- Assisted bots that require a human interface to trigger the process, and can be useful in complex automation scenarios, or
- Unassisted bots that do not require a human trigger and have the capability to perform the tasks on their own. These are used in the enterprise to automate the entire process with no manual intervention. In this case, the implementation would be very lengthy, as all rules need to be incorporated within the bots along with exceptions handling capability.

Some of the possible architectures that can be considered by the enterprise for building bots are described below:

- Simple Architecture
  - One bot runs on one computer or server and is operated and controlled by a single user. This bot can be used for simple automation for low-volume processes.
- Regular Architecture
  - Multiple bots run on one server and can be controlled by multiple users. These bots can be used for complex flows, scheduled tasks, and large-volume processes. The dashboard is created and placed at a central location to control and track the bot activities.
- Distributed Architecture
  - Multiple bots run on nested and multiple servers and are operated by various users. These bots can be used for very complex and large-volume processes in parallel. The dashboard is managed and controlled centrally to track the bot activities.

There are multiple considerations that the enterprise needs to evaluate before embarking on the journey to RPA. Some of the additional RPA components that need special consideration while building the architecture are as follows:

- Infrastructure
  - Hardware components such as application servers, database servers, and virtual desktops.
  - Software components such as operating systems.
  - Hosting the bots on-premise; in the cloud such as Microsoft Azure, Google Cloud, Amazon Web Services, etc.; or split between one or more platforms as part of the hybrid solution.

- Service providers that will manage and support hosting in any environment.
- Software to Develop RPA
  - Business users identify the processes, which are then developed using RPA-specific software such as UiPath, which follows the instructions to carry out an automated process.
  - Hosted on virtual desktops.
  - It is useful but not mandatory for this software to have access to the downstream applications involved in the automation process.
  - Will not create, delete, edit, or migrate any data within the downstream applications, thus has no impact on the existing ecosystem.
- Software to Execute RPA
  - Executes the processes created by the RPA development software such as UiPath Robot.
  - Hosted using virtual desktops.
  - One robot can perform only one process at any given time but can perform multiple processes sequentially, which can be triggered by manual or automated scheduling.
  - Must be able to access the downstream applications involved in the automation process including network access and security privileges to perform the tasks.
  - May create, delete, edit, or migrate data within the downstream applications dependent upon the process that it is executing.
- Software to Manage RPA
  - The software is installed as a control layer on top of the bot execution layer.
  - Hosted using an application server.
  - Enables the user to centrally control all robots and processes within the RPA platform, allowing robots to be assigned to processes and processes assigned to queues and schedules.
  - Also provides exception reporting and load monitoring.
  - Access to the downstream application is not required but requires access to the robot execution layer.
  - Will not create, delete, edit, or migrate any data within the downstream applications.

Enterprise RPA Model

An enterprise needs to create an operating and engagement model for the implementation and maintenance of RPA within its organization.

Operating Model

The enterprise should take into consideration the following elements that comprise the functioning of the operating model:

- Organizational Setup and Strategy
  - Set up an RPA center of excellence to facilitate the journey for automation.
  - Define a roadmap for future automation.
  - Define the RPA strategy in line with the digitalization strategy of the organization.
- People and Culture
  - Form the stakeholder to sponsor and support the implementation.
  - Create a communication plan to ensure the free flow of information between business analysts, RPA developers, and IT.
  - Establish and present the culture of a continuous improvement process.
  - Provide RPA training to the employees to work under the new environment.
- Process
  - Establish an implementation process including analysis, selection, and implementation.
  - Define test cycles and a maintenance plan.
  - Create a business case to justify the benefits of RPA.
  - Establish change request management for the program.
- Technology
  - Define procedures for selecting one or more RPA providers.
  - Keep pace with the market and follow the RPA trends and developments.
  - Deploy bots along with their maintenance schedule.
- Governance
  - Define the tasks, responsibilities, and roles within the RPA framework.
  - Document a release process during process changes.
  - Secure the implementation process as well as the operational work through the defined escalation process.
  - Set up reporting for analysis and action (for example, service including KPIs, implementation status, identification of RPA potentials).

Engagement Model

There are various ways an enterprise can implement the RPA model either by itself or by partnering with a service provider. Here are some possible engagement models that an enterprise can leverage for the RPA engagement:

- In-house Model
  - The enterprise purchases and owns the bot licenses.
  - The enterprise establishes a center of excellence and builds up the resources and skills over time to manage the bots.
  - The enterprise would retain control of the capability that it builds.
  - The enterprise devotes both the time and investment needed to develop the internal resource capability and become self-sufficient.
  - Involves recruitment and training fees to build the skill set.
- Joint Service Model
  - The enterprise purchases and owns the bot licenses.
  - The service provider's RPA resources implement and deliver process automation.
  - The service provider's control team operates, maintains, and runs the automation services on behalf of the enterprise.
  - The enterprise retains ownership of licenses and infrastructure.
  - The enterprise takes the leverage of the service provider's experience and skills across multiple technologies.
  - A flexible and usage-based service fee based on a percentage of the transaction price or fixed price model.
- Managed Service Model
  - The service provider purchases and owns the bot licenses.
  - Infrastructure can be owned either by the enterprise or by the service provider.
  - The service provider's RPA resources deliver and run process automation on behalf of the enterprise.
  - The flexible pool of bot licenses is available at no minimum investment, which provides the ability to ramp up bots to deliver processes during seasonal peaks.
  - Full access to the service provider's propriety tools and industry-leading best practices and methodology.
  - A flexible and usage-based service fee based on variable transaction price or fixed price model.

Enterprise RPA Implementation Methodology

The best approach for an enterprise to implement any new technology is to start small and quickly assess what works and what does not based on the enterprise's business, learn from its mistakes, leverage the potential, and finally scale up across all business units or product lines. Below is the methodology with implementation phases that has been proven at multiple enterprises for their RPA implementation projects.

Discovery

The enterprise should identify the processes that are suitable for RPA and conduct the following activities during this phase:

- Assess the business units that are to be considered in scope for the project.
- Identify business processes that are standardized and repetitive.
- Create a heatmap for processes with RPA potential.
- Conduct workshops to derive RPA efficiency and feasibility where robotics can be utilized.
- Understand the enterprise structure and the skill set of the employees to support this project.
- Prioritize the business processes that are potential candidates for automation and can provide a quick ROI.
- Ensure the business is ready for the approach including the change management aspect, training for its business users, and getting the sponsorship.

Proof of Concept

The enterprise should identify those processes that can easily be automated as part of the proof of concept and conduct the following activities during this phase:

- Assess the enterprise's function and identify the opportunity for automation to show the stakeholders that this technology can be leveraged and scaled up.
- Select only the simple to medium-complex processes as part of the proof of concept to demonstrate the functionality.
- Identify value through deep-dive sessions with collaboration and engagement with the business.
- Create interest and awareness about this new technology and how it can be beneficial to both the users and the enterprise.
- Demonstrate the automated process in the testing environment.

- Generate consensus on the proof of technology and its integration with the existing applications.
- Develop the RPA architecture that can become a part of the ecosystem.

Implementation

Based on the lessons learned from the proof of concept and identified processes that can be automated, the enterprise needs to build a business case for a go-no-go decision to move forward on the RPA journey and build an RPA center of excellence within the internal IT organization to support the technology. The enterprise should conduct the following activities during this phase:

- Evaluate and select the vendors and tools that are suitable for the enterprise.
- Develop a high-level RPA implementation project plan.
- Identify all the activities, staffing requirements, timeline, and cost for the automation.
- Conduct a financial business case and investment appraisal for approval of funds to support the project.
- Procure all hardware and software as per the design.
- Prepare the automation design flow.
- Develop bots, perform testing, and move it to the production environment.
- Build the new robotics operating model for the enterprise.
- Make the robots present on all necessary machines as RPA implementation is rolled out across businesses.
- Update the operational tools, procedures, ways of working, and behavior towards the new technology.
- Build the change management plan and policies for the enterprise.

Pilot

The enterprise should always deploy the RPA for a particular business process or for all business processes for a specific business unit to establish the new technology. The enterprise should conduct the following activities during this phase:

- Execute and validate the RPA solution for a simple business process within the enterprise as a pilot kickoff.

- Establish the delivery and run the operating model and the technology platform for the RPA.
- Deliver process automation along with exception handling capability.
- Identify risks and gaps in the implementation plan during the pilot phase.
- The automation of specific business processes should be up and running to establish credibility.
- Evidence of the automation benefits should be established with the stakeholders.

Scale and Sustain

After the deployment, the enterprise should now be running the RPA solution in the production environment. The enterprise should start thinking of how to scale the RPA to other processes and businesses and conduct the following activities during this phase:

- Establish a center of excellence and hand over support to the RPA team.
- Establish structured organizational change and capability transfer.
- Realize benefits for the existing bots and build the bots for other processes and capabilities with the goal to generate higher value within the enterprise.
- Assess the new career path of employees, their new roles, and redeployment strategies as part of a successful automation implementation.
- Establish ongoing benefits realization and key performance indicators tracking.

Potential Automation Opportunities

There are various business processes and areas within the enterprise where the application of RPA can quickly result in the realization of value. Some of these areas within the ecosystem of the enterprise which have the potential for automation have been described below:

- An enterprise usually comprises multiple systems where the opportunity for automation is to access various programs, find records based on a set of rules, and then compile that information for further analysis by humans.
- Complete the data entry by getting the records, navigating through multiple screens within the same system.

- Get the data from various systems and perform data cleansing, computation, and formatting based on predefined rules.
- Validate the data in various systems by identifying the fields based on the defined parameters and dependencies.
- Extract data values by leveraging optical character recognition (OCR) technology and then input the data in a particular field.
- Send automated e-mail notifications along with an attachment, if required, on completion of a task or at a predefined time.
- Access APIs and extract time-consuming reports at a preset time.

RPA Opportunities by Industry

Robotic process automation comprises the software configuration and design of "robots" as a digital workforce for the future that requires little IT knowledge to operate and can be quickly trained and deployed to automate manual tasks. Each industry is unique by itself and so are the business processes within that industry. Let's analyze some of the industry-specific business processes where RPA can be leveraged for a quick ROI, reduction of error, and cost of operations.

Healthcare Industry

The healthcare industry is an ever-changing industry undergoing rapid growth while facing challenges in becoming more streamlined and efficient. Major operational challenges include rising costs, fast-changing demographics, and increased attention to customer experience and efficiency.

Healthcare involves providers, physicians, patients, and pharma companies that require a large volume of paperwork to be accounted for, documented, exchanged, and analyzed. Many of the operation functions like admin, payroll, HR, and research can be easy, effective, and efficient with RPA.

RPA is playing a key role to help cut costs, bringing value to customer care, and driving high-quality patient care.

RPA has wide application in the healthcare industry. Some of the applications or processes for automation in the healthcare industry where RPA is best suited with respect to cost efficiency, value creation, and business benefit include the following:

- Insurance Claim Processing: Currently, the customer service team member manually keys the information into the system for the insurance purchased online and the claims received by mail. Due to manual errors with data entry, the claims are being sent to the wrong system queues, leading to further delays. This can be automated using the optical character recognition capabilities that can reduce the manual data processing elements of the insurance claims process. RPA could also be leveraged to automate the workflow related to the insurance claim processing, which would expedite and improve the accuracy of claims.

- Patient Info Records: In the public health system, during the course of the treatment, a patient's health details are recorded and updated in multiple systems using various types of medical software. The systems that are used by physicians contain similar details but all need to be updated over the course of treatment. Furthermore, retrieving information from another application would require the nurse or doctor to log out of one application and into another. Automation could help these systems interface with each other and automatically update based on input entered into one of the systems.

- Physician Referrals: Currently, the onboarding and referral process for surgery is quite a manual paper-based process. Referrals are manually documented by the patient's referring physician and sent via fax to the hospital. These are then manually entered into the system and patients are notified by post or telephone call when their surgery is scheduled. At present, there is a large backlog of names on the register that needs to be reviewed. The manual component of the process creates massive delays and incorrect processing of the information. Automation could enable a more accurate, timely process.

- Medical Supplies Inventory: Currently, the inventory management of medical supplies for a specific hospital ward is a manual process performed by the nursing staff of that ward. There is no automated inventory management capability to track when supplies are critically low, and no ability to forecast based on numbers of current and incoming patients. RPA processes could enable automated inventory management and forecasting capabilities.

RPA is essential in streamlining back-office processes, eliminating paperwork, and reducing the amount of time it takes to process files. However, RPA goes far beyond these simple tasks. It helps healthcare providers not only reduce costs and gain efficiency but also increase the quality of patient care and the amount of time spent with the patients.

Financial Services Industry

In a challenging and competitive market, financial institutions are looking to automate a wide range of activities without the need for complex programming or systems. Currently, RPA is playing a pivotal role to automate all repetitive, business rule-driven work to rapidly reduce costs, improve controls, quality, and scalability, and operate 24/7. In the financial services industry, RPA is best suited for automating tasks like cross-system manual processing, bulk data updates, reconciliation activities, reporting, document verification, and tasks with a combination of high transaction volumes and complex regulation, among others. RPA has also proven itself as a method to reduce outsourcing or offshoring of financial operations.

RPA can perform tasks at a high speed and provide a uniformly high quality of work while freeing up people involved in compliance functions. RPA has changed the way financial institutions are addressing mundane process execution while harvesting business benefits.

Some of the potential processes for automation in the financial services industry include the following:

- Credit Card and Loan Processing: Some of the key difficulties around credit card and loan processing result from manual data gathering and searches, rekeying data, and inputting compliance assessments. Many of these transactions are paper-based and could be improved by optical character recognition and system automation. Further complications result from a lack of real-time reporting and information distributed across multiple systems.

- Payments and Funds Management: Manual processing of payments, funds management, and transfer can lead to potential human errors and lack of timeliness. RPA can be set up to automate and enable the initiation, settlement, and reconciliation of payments, transfers, and funds management.

- New Client Initiation: The client's onboarding process is the first interaction with the enterprise, and as such, it's important that this process be seamless and timely to create the first impression and retain the client. Once the customer data is received, it is reentered into another system, which involves duplication of data processing. As there is a lack of system interfaces in this process, the data needs to be rekeyed at other stages throughout the process, thus delaying the onboarding process due to human error.

- Compliance: Adherence to regulatory compliance and ensuring that systems are defect free is essential in the financial services industry. In many enterprises in the financial services industry, a good portion of the a manual element is involved in the process, which leads to potential defects and compliance errors being undiscovered for a longer period of time. Greater automation in the testing process can ensure defects are detected much earlier and lead to more accurate results.

RPA has been instrumental in helping financial institutions achieve cost efficiency, capitalize on operational resilience and efficiency, deliver significant and sustainable value in short timeframes, and reduce overall operational risks. Overall industry statistics show that introducing RPA within an enterprise helped to achieve 45% manual work automation, have 100% audit trail, and attain ROI goals faster than a traditional ERP deployment. It is estimated that around 45% of financial services tasks will be completed by robots in the next 15 years.

Energy and Utilities Industry

In this era, the energy and utilities industry is positioned as the most important and highly sought after by modern society. This sector is overwhelmed with manual processes, which can lead to a high margin of error. Embracing RPA can take utilities companies and cooperatives to the next level.

The prime reason for the need of RPA is the massive amount of transactions handled manually, which occur every single day in this sector. RPA is capable of providing process efficiency and improving turnaround time across many services transactions.

RPA in the energy and utilities sector has wide application. Some of the potential processes for automation in the energy and utilities industry include the following:

- Control Center Processes: Automation has the potential to expedite control center processes. Currently, there are many human and manual intervention steps involved in the monitor, control, and optimization of generator/transmission performance. RPA could be used to automate decisions on how to proceed when a system alert is generated. This would be based on a more advanced form of RPA where the system can make decisions based on information gathering and past decision making.

- Compliance: RPA can automate some of the compliance processes around ensuring that the notice periods for power disturbances are issued, that the response rate to new customers happens in a timely manner, and that existing customer inquiries are addressed on time – as regulated by the National Electrical Code. Automation could enable the system to generate alerts for reminders, as well as autogenerate notices to ensure compliance requirements are met.

- Claims Workflow: RPA has the potential to automate customer claims and hardship tests. Claims such as high-voltage incidents are often paper-based, so there is an immediate need for digitization and automation of the claims workflow. There is a lot of human intervention in the way of processing and thus the potential to automate these processes is imminent.

RPA provides cost efficiency, value creation, and business benefits to the energy and utilities sector. RPA has delivered 60–70% efficiency improvement and a projected 50% potential reduction in headcount in certain cases.

Telecommunications and Entertainment Industry

One of the complexities of the telecommunications industry is that it involves large volumes of operational processes.

RPA can support telecom providers by managing their back office more easily and dealing with large volumes of repetitive and rule-based operational processes. Managing the customer experience is one of the major priorities of the telecom industry, as customer satisfaction drives the success of telecom companies. RPA capabilities help telecom providers to improve data communication, reduce costs, and improve operational efficiency. This allows telecom companies to improve their customer service. Operations of telecom providers include database management, invoice and purchase order processing, IT and infrastructure services, and customer interaction. Telecom providers are able to boost their own workforces and streamline their operational processes using RPA, which in turn allows them to deliver higher-quality services and customer experience.

RPA has wide application in the telecom industry. Some of the potential processes for automation in the telecommunications and entertainment industry include the following:

- Leads Management: Automation can expedite and streamline all the steps around making the product or service ready for sale. Specifically, leads management can be automated to ensure that sales information and forecasting is captured correctly, that leads are assigned to the right sales staff, and that client leads are prepopulated based on existing data, thus enabling leads to turn into realized opportunities.

- Minimize Disruption: Automation can simplify the ordering and activation process. Some of the key issues in the telecommunications industry are the inconsistency of quotes, order loss, and activation causing disruption to its customers. Automation can ensure that invoices for similar products and services are automated based on historical sales and invoice data, that orders are put into the right ordering system queues, and that service activation is automated and performed remotely to minimize disruption to the customers.

- Issue Resolution: Issues experienced around the resolution of a problem are generated from a lack of system automation for key service management and IT operational processes. Automation could expedite the incident management and service request processing times to better meet KPIs and improve reporting on and response to service availability issues and security threats.

- Customer Usage and Billing: Telecommunications companies face the challenges around the usage of cash due to lack of a consolidated view of usage and billing across key customer accounts. The existing systems do not provide a holistic view of usage and billing, leading to multiple bills being sent to a single customer with improper tracking of usage. Automation can remove the manual element and help automate to retrieve the data and solve some of these common issues.

RPA helps the telecom industry to achieve higher levels of scalability, reduce costs, and improve operational efficiency, data communication, and transmission.

RPA can be used not only to automate back-office processes but also to drive front-office improvements for customers.

Processes involving more complex reasoning and human interaction, such as developing customer relationships, can also be partially automated.

Public Sector Industry

The government sector is moving into an era of robotics process automation, which allows software robots to automate basic business applications and processes.

RPA benefits can be found in numerous processes in the government sector, which can enhance the speed of business processes, improve quality, and increase visibility. RPA is useful for government revenue functions, tax functions, local citizen services, and customer contact centers, among others, which can be automated and assimilated into enterprise multichannel service desk platforms. Implementing RPA results in quicker turnaround time and quality improvement for services to citizens. RPA is helping government employees focus on more value-adding areas, making better use of their skills, as most of the monotonous work is taken care of by software bots.

RPA has wide application in the government sector such as IT operations in various offices and customer relationship management. Some of the potential processes for automation in government include the following:

- Immigration Applications: The current immigration application process can be greatly improved by automating the entire process. Most of the existing processes are manual due to various systems and paper-based forms. Some of the checks performed on applications require human-based decision making. There is potential to automate checks, generate alerts for incomplete information, and automate the process to ensure applications are progressed throughout the process queue.

- Identity Management: RPA has the potential to significantly improve identity management and fraud detection across multiple government departments. Currently, each department within the government performs its own identity checks for each interaction. Automation could enable a single identity across government departments using existing information to process applications. Automated security alerts to appropriate personnel and systems could also be enabled to improve the fraud detection process.

- Back-office Processes: Automation has the potential to expedite processes such as Medicare and disability welfare applications. Although currently many of these can be processed online through the MyGov online system, there is a lot of potential for automating the back-office processes. For example, customers can upload images and documents online, but in the back end, these need to be verified by a person. The process of checking information and progressing the application to the next process step has the potential for automation.

- IT Operations: Automation has a lot of potential to improve IT operations. Automation could vastly improve the IT refresh processes for a system such as MyGov. There is also a lot of potential to automate problem resolution processes such as enabling automation and artificial intelligence to match the right information to customer requests.

It has been observed that RPA has delivered 50% efficiency improvement, as the bots performed tasks in 50% less time than the current team. It has been instrumental in improving accuracy, standardization, customer service, and employee satisfaction, as they are free from mundane processes and can focus on more interesting, value-adding activities.

Shared Services Industry

Shared service and global business services (GBS) organizations typically contain many rule-based, repetitive, but business-critical processes supporting different departments in the enterprise.

Shared services and GBS should consider RPA because of its ability to unlock value by lowering process delivery costs, auditability, and expanding a virtual workforce to cover 24/7 availability.

Implementation is easier because organizations don't need to make significant updates or changes to underlying applications.

RPA can help increase productivity, reduce turnaround time, and free capacity for employees to work on increased value-added tasks.

RPA has wide application in shared services. Some of the potential processes for automation in shared services include the following:

- Finance and Accounting: RPA could be used to track real-time inventory levels, generate alerts, and create an order. It can enable invoice processing to be automated. RPA can automate all the steps from sales through purchase by ensuring information is directed to the right systems. Usage and billing are automated using usage reporting and by consolidating billing data across multiple systems. RPA can be deployed in the cash application process to automatically clear open receivables by applying the payments received.

- HR Services: Automation could be used to onboard a new employee and support time and attendance management. RPA could enable easier tracking of benefits administration such as leave, superannuation, and insurance. RPA could enable automation around the collection, organization, and storage of all pay-related information, and the ability to automate the transfer of data between the timesheet and pay system.

- IT Operations: RPA has the potential to automate a lot of the IT service management operational processes. RPA can be used to automate fraud detection by scheduling repetitive scans and by automating the data analysis process. RPA can automate the collection of and reporting on data around customer interaction with the marketing channels.

RPA is generally seen as a way for companies to free employees from the burden of repetitive, high-volume tasks in the back office that can be fully automated.

RPA can reduce turnaround times by 200–300% in major procurement, finance, HR, and other internal shared services, which might include highly complex rule-based processes.

RPA Opportunities by Function

The enterprise's journey to robotic process automation should be undertaken as a step-by-step transformation in all the business functions with a focused vision, governance, and a controlled scope. Some of the processes and subprocesses within a business function where an enterprise can look for automation opportunities are listed below. Most of them are labor-intensive, require accessing multiple systems, are repetitive, or can be audited for compliance periodically.

Record to Report

RPA can be implemented in the finance function for the following processes:

- General Ledger Accounting
  - Initiate and post journal entry (JE).
  - Capture and extract data from applications and enter it into JE lines.
  - Route JE for approval to designated personnel.
  - Automate approval for JE based on a threshold amount.
  - Post JE in general ledger on approval.
  - Auto-accrual of unpaid invoices.
  - Develop financial forecasts by gathering data from various systems within the enterprise.
- Bank Reconciliation
  - Have access to the bank website and obtain a bank statement.
  - Match checks and deposits against a list that is cleared by the bank.
  - Prepare journal entries for adjustments.
  - Archive bank reconciliations attachment.
- Accounts Receivable
  - Use the cash application process to clear open AR.
  - Match lockbox fields to get a higher clearing rate.
  - Update customer master record in all applications when there is a change in the source system.
  - Run periodic credit checks.
  - Calculate and generate a customer invoice.
  - Write off aged invoices.
  - Generate and send dunning e-mail.
- Intercompany Accounting
  - Review intercompany account balances at period end.
  - Match account balance variances to transaction history.
  - Prepare journal entries for adjustments.
  - Archive intercompany transactions attachment.
- Fixed Assets
  - Calculate and record depreciation expense.
  - Prepare journal entries for adjustments.
  - Print/save fixed assets register.
- Management Reporting
  - Extract data from multiple applications and input it into report fields.
  - Generate management report.

- E-mail management report to requestor.
- Archive/index management report for a user group.
- Period End Close
  - Reconcile accruals, GL, and bank accounts.
  - Close subledger and accounting period.
  - Run standard period-end reports and statements.
- Consolidation
  - Preview financial statements of all in-scope entities.
  - Create preliminary consolidated financial statements.
  - Offset intercompany transactions and eliminate account balances.
  - Run standard period-end reports and statements.
  - Archive/index period end reports.

Procure to Pay

RPA can be implemented in the materials management function for the following processes:

- Manage Vendor Master
  - Update vendor information in systems.
  - E-mail feedback to the requestor.
  - File vendor information and feedback.
- Create and Submit Requisitions
  - Automate workflow while submitting the requisition request.
  - Validate data entered into requisition.
  - Notify approver for requisition approval.
- Manage Requisition Approvals
  - Route requisition to designated approver.
  - Automate approvals within a certain threshold.
  - Notify requestor once approved.
  - Archive requisition.
- Create Purchase Orders
  - Initiate/submit purchase order request.
  - Validate data entry into required fields.
  - Release purchase order to designated approver.
  - Archive created purchase order.
- Manage Purchase Order Approvals
  - Receive new PO requests in the system.
  - Match PO information to requisition form.

- Validate vendor master file information.
- Automate approvals within a certain threshold.
- E-mail requestor the newly approved PO.

- Submit Purchase Orders to Vendors

  - Submit PO to vendor contact.
  - Archive submitted purchase order.
  - E-maill requestor the newly submitted PO.
  - Receive order confirmation from the vendor.

- Process Goods Receipts

  - Validate quantity and description to match with PO.
  - Validate receipt matches with vendor invoice.
  - Close PO line and submit an invoice for payment processing.
  - Archive receipt.

- Manage Invoice Collection and Entry

  - Receive/verify approved invoice.
  - Check/verify invoice for required data.
  - Create invoice batch.
  - Index invoice with PO/non-PO purchase or prepayment.
  - Save and close invoice batch.

- Manage Electronic Invoicing

  - Receive electronic invoice from the vendor.
  - Capture data from the electronic invoice.
  - Match invoice against PO and receive report.
  - Route invoice batch to the responsible person for approval.
  - Review/verify approved invoice.
  - Archive electronic invoice.

- Validate and Handle Invoice Data

  - Capture, extract, and validate invoice data.
  - Save and close invoice batch for handling.

- Conduct Matching and Handle Approvals

  - Validate goods receipt note (GRN) or delivery note information to match with PO.
  - Validate invoice information match with PO.
  - Notify requestor for more information if matching step fails.

- Submit Transactions for Processing

  - Submit approved invoices for payment processing.
  - Validate and approve accounting entries.
  - Update accounts payable subledger.
  - Create an approved invoices batch for payment.

- Run Payment Process
  - Validate and deliver the batch to the payment processing agent.
  - Input data into the payment form.
  - Submit payment run.
  - E-mail draft payment report to AP/GL reconciliation.
- Generate Standard Reports
  - Obtain transaction data from the system.
  - Capture/extract/validate data and input it into report fields.
  - Generate standard report.
  - Categorize or index report for specific user group.
  - File report and e-mail report to the requestor.
  - Archive report.

Order to Cash

RPA can be implemented in the sales and distribution management function for the following processes:

- Review Customer Applications
  - Route customer application to the responsible person for review.
  - Automate approval for customer applications meeting guidelines.
  - Route approval to the responsible approver for customer applications outside of guidelines.
  - Notify requestor after application approval.
- Maintain and Manage Customer Data
  - Extract new customer data from maintenance requests.
  - Consolidate and sync customer data from multiple systems.
  - Notify requestor after customer data is updated.
- Investigate New Customer Credit
  - Compile new customer data files for credit analysis.
  - Submit recommended customer credit for approval.
  - Automate approvals for credit within a threshold.
  - Route approval to the responsible approver for special cases.
  - Notify requestor once new customer credit is approved.
- Manage Customer Credit Exposure
  - Calculate customer credit exposure periodically.
  - Validate customer credit exposure against credit limit.
- Create and Manage Customer Orders
  - Capture/extract order data from systems or PDF orders.
  - Automate approval for orders within a threshold.

- Route customer orders above the threshold to respective approver.
- Notify customer after order approval and processing.

- Create Initial Sales Quote

  - Validate if the customer exists in the system.
  - Look up customer quote data in pricing sheet and populate initial sales quote.
  - Route quote for approval and update quote status.
  - Finalize quote and prepare to convert the quote to a sales order.

- Process Order

  - Capture/extract order data and input it into the order form.
  - Acknowledge and confirm the order with the customer.
  - Send order out for fulfillment.

- Manage Inventory and Shipping

  - Perform inventory check.
  - Extract order data and shipping information.
  - Coordinate with logistics department for shipping.
  - Notify customer once the order has been shipped.
  - Update inventory.
  - Archive shipping requests.

- Process Returns and Exchanges

  - Receive and index return or exchange request.
  - Route return or exchange request for approval.
  - Issue reimbursement/exchange, if the request is approved.
  - Notify customer of return approval.
  - Update inventory once return/exchange is processed.

- Manage Rebates and Chargebacks

  - Calculate rebate or chargeback.
  - Automatically approve rebate or chargeback calculation.
  - Route rebates/chargebacks above the threshold to the respective approver.
  - Settle rebate or chargeback against the transaction.
  - Archive rebates/chargeback requests.

- Handle Customer Inquiries

  - Classify inquiry and gather inquiry data.
  - Route customer inquiry to the responsible person.
  - Automate response to routine customer inquiries.

- Send response for nonroutine customer inquiries.
- Archive and close customer inquiry.

■ Generate Customer Invoices

- Autogenerate invoices based on order parameters in the system.
- Automate approval for invoices within a threshold.
- Route invoice for approval to a responsible person.
- Release invoice to the customer for payment.
- Archive invoice.

■ Manage billing

- Autogenerate billing based on customer payment profile in the system.
- Validate invoice and billing account details.
- Distribute bill to the customer for payment.
- Archive customer billing.

■ Post Receivables to the General Ledger

- Autogenerate receivable entries when billing is sent to customers.
- Autopost accounts receivable journal entries below the threshold amount.
- Post accounts receivable entries to GL.

■ Manage Cash Applications

- Log on to bank online portal and download transaction breakdown.
- Capture lockbox payment and remittance data.
- Apply/match cash receipt to invoice.
- Create and post journal entries to offset AR against payments received.
- Match cash receipt to bank reconciliation adjusting items.
- Update bank reconciliation adjusting item list.

■ Conduct Aging and Bad Debt Analysis

- Perform an aging analysis.
- Generate aging and bad debts estimation report.
- Generate journal entries to adjust bad debt provision.

■ Capture and Register Customer Complaint

- Capture complaint data and input it into the form.
- Classify/index customer complaint.
- Route customer complaint to the responsible person.
- Automate response to common complaints.

Financial Planning and Analysis

RPA can be implemented in the Planning and Budgeting function for the following processes:

- Standard Budget and Forecast Preparation
  - Collect relevant performance data and future growth indicators.
  - Perform detailed budget/forecast modeling to create an initial budget/forecast baseline.
  - Route budget/forecast for approval.
- Standard Variance Analysis
  - Capture/extract actual data from systems and various data sources.
  - Generate initial budget versus actual analysis report.
  - Update forecasting and underlying key assumptions.
  - Share report and variance analysis findings.
  - Archive/index budget versus actual report.
- Data Gathering and Validation
  - Pull unstructured data into a predefined form.
  - Gather previously created reports and analysis.
  - Extract/organize data and perform data validation.
  - Create a data set and preliminary report template for further analysis.
  - Populate data to predefined columns in preliminary decision support reports.
  - Include maintenance in the pricing or state it clearly, if charged additionally.
  - The enterprise owns IP for automation developed by them using the bot software.

Use Cases

RPA use cases are certain scenarios where the goals and objectives of an enterprise are addressed to automate certain business processes to save costs and make the operations more efficient. Let's study some scenarios along with real-life case studies to see how the journey to robotic process automation can be facilitated to result in an intelligent enterprise.

1. Case Study: Automate the Process to Reduce the Days to Bill Bulk Products to Its Customers for an International Oil and Gas Company

- Scenario
  - An integrated oil company with businesses across refining, retail, energy marketing, and trading.
  - Key processes in scope for the automation project include billing, goods issue, vendor setup, vendor invoice processing, goods receipt, and payment.
- Approach
  - Most of the bulk billing invoices were billed with two-day payment terms.
  - In case of valid dispute due to incorrect billing caused by pricing, quantity, taxes, etc., the two days are counted started from the date of revised invoice receipt by the customer.
  - The enterprise analyzed last six months data to arrive at the root cause of the errors causing incorrect billing.
  - Implemented controls to minimize the number of incorrect billings.
- Results
  - Reduced the average days to bill from five days to less than two days.
  - Early cash flow resulted in $2M benefits in the cost of working capital.

2. Case Study: Automate Low-Risk Customer Approval Process for a Major Bank
- Scenario
  - A major national bank wanted to automate its credit card account opening process for online applications where income verification was not required.
  - The bank designed and implemented an automated process which reduced operating costs and completion time for opening the account.
- Approach
  - The standard time to activate an item on the highest-volume credit card account opening queue was very slow even when no customer interaction was required.
  - The queue was operated by five offshore FTE (full-time equivalent) at a very high cost.
  - Manual errors led to downstream complaints.

- Results
  - Reduced offshore FTE cost significantly.
  - Reduced processing time on average process cycle, which improved from four hours to five minutes.
  - Automated 98% of transactions through the process.
  - Customers had a direct beneficial impact with faster, more reliable access to opening credit card accounts.

Conclusion

The path to an intelligent enterprise starts with rule-based robotic process automation. The next step for the enterprise is to move to cognitive RPA, where certain AI techniques are applied to automate complex processes. The enterprise can then move towards implementing virtual agents and advanced analytics to predict and provide a recommendation. The next step on the ladder is to automate and execute machine-based processes, following which the enterprise can leverage AI to redefine its processes and become intelligent.

RPA provides significant improvements in accuracy and cycle time and increased productivity in transaction processing by transforming the way we think about and administer business processes, IT support processes, workflow processes, remote infrastructure, and back-office work while eliminating people from dull and repetitive tasks.

CHAPTER 6

Internet of Things

*T*his chapter provides an understanding of Internet of Things (IoT) technology
   with how the data from the connected world is harnessed, transmitted, stored,
   and analyzed. It also discusses the IoT architecture, implementation methodology, and some of the typical applications and use cases across industries with future
day-in-life scenarios that can make the enterprise connected and intelligent.

Internet of Things Overview

IoT is the fourth-generation technology after the development of mainframes,
personal computers, and mobile computing. IoT, in simple terms, is computing with the shared environment at a massive scale.

A consumer IoT takes a normal consumer device, connects with the
internet, and adds new functionality to make it a smart device for better and
enhanced consumer experience.

An industrial IoT connects assets and equipment to physical sensors
to monitor activities and bring in operational efficiencies. Data is collected
real-time for on-the-fly optimization to reduce inefficiencies in the usage and
processes.

Some of the industries where IoT will have its major impact include automotive, electronics, retail, utilities, energy, banking, insurance, healthcare, and
agriculture.

Understanding the Internet of Things

The Internet of Things describes the ecosystem of physical devices embedded with sensors, software, electronics, and network connectivity that enable
them to communicate among themselves and with cloud services to gather
and analyze the data and provide meaningful insights about the physical world
(Figure 6.1).

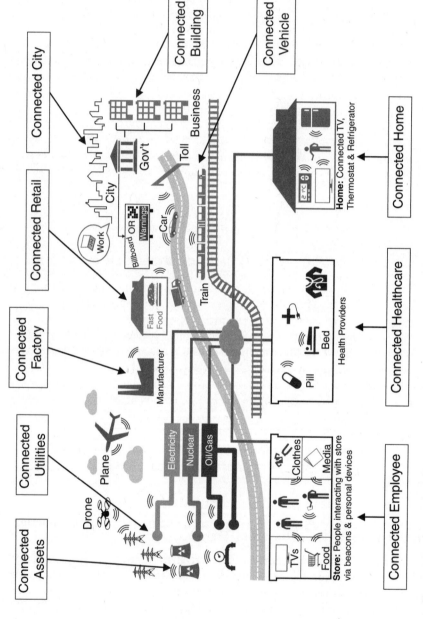

Figure 6.1 Connected world.

The most significant value proposition for adopting IoT-based solutions is the fact that they have the ability to turn raw data into actionable information that can help enterprises gain operational efficiency, create new revenue streams, create customer delight, and optimize product performance.

The percolation and deployment of IoT in the industrial economy are less than 10% at present, and there is a huge opportunity for enterprises to ride the growth and create new service and revenue opportunities. The industrial IoT revolution will start with operational efficiency and cost reduction, with a gradual move towards creating new products, and finally generating demand based on automation and catering to specific needs.

Market Pulse

The Internet of Things is one of the top-growing technologies, with spending to exceed $3 trillion. It is expected that IoT will grow annually at 20–25% and will have more than 76 billion connected devices in usage worldwide by 2025 from 26 billion connected devices currently. It will have deep economic impacts and is poised to create broad business disruptions across industries where companies need to reinvent their operational strategies and create new business models to take full advantage emerging from IoT in order to remain ahead of the disruption curve and be competitive.

It is expected that the global IoT device base will be seven times greater than the current smartphone base by 2020. With the growth in the number of tech companies offering an IoT platform as a solution, the cost of using their service will eventually come down due to the competition. This will increase the adoption rate of IoT, thus bringing substantial advantages to consumers.

Every organization should evaluate IoT as part of its growth strategy and should take into consideration the following:

- How will IoT impact their business?
- What product or market segment should they consider for IoT?
- Which IoT product is causing disruption to their existing business?
- What are potential new revenue opportunities utilizing IoT in the business model?
- What benefits will it bring to their end customers?
- Who are their potential competitors, and have they started offering IoT?

Even the tech companies are investing in IoT development by closely integrating the solution with artificial intelligence, virtual reality, the blockchain, robotics, drones, and 3D printing to provide an unparallel user experience. These interconnected technology megatrends are driving major disruptors across industries and sectors, thus shaping the future of IoT.

Adoption Drivers

The acceleration of the pace at which IoT will be adopted by both consumers and industrial usage will be based on the following drivers as described below:

Processing Power

In 1970, Moore's Law stated that the overall processing power for computers would double every two years, but with the rapid pace of technological development, CPU speed doubles almost every year. With cheaper processing power, it has now become feasible to install IoT as part of consumer or industrial products.

Connectivity

The IoT value chain requires the ability to connect and communicate seamlessly over the internet. With technological innovation, it is now much more affordable to deploy both long- and short-range connectivity to IoT devices. Some of the options that companies might choose for IoT connectivity include:

- **Unlicensed,** where the connectivity to the IoT device is not exclusively licensed to a particular company and hence is unreliable. Wi-Fi is the most popular in this category.
- **Low Power Wide Area,** which helps connected devices send and receive small data packets securely over long ranges with low power consumption. This technology is relatively new but offers lower cost and energy consumption, leading to longer battery life and greater reliability. This is the most preferred option, as it can easily penetrate walls and other barriers, depending on the location of the device. Sigfox, LoRa, and LinkLabs are the most popular in this category.
- **Cellular,** which provides higher bandwidth of up to 100 megabytes per second and a larger range of more than 10 miles. Though it has good reliability, it is an expensive option to choose. 4G LTE is the most popular in this category. 5G is still being developed, and it will provide speeds 100 times faster than current speed.
- **Satellite,** which provides a connection where neither the cellular nor the underground optic fiber is available. Though it has low to medium bandwidth with a wide range of more than 100 miles, it provides a reliable connection at a very high cost. National defense is the most popular use case for managing drones.

IoT Platform

Similar to a computer's operating system, it can create and manage applications, generate analytics, provide security, and store secure data from the connected devices. With the development of platforms for specific devices and industries, companies will opt for a platform-as-a-service model, which will dramatically reduce the IoT application cost and accelerate the adoption and use cases of IoT.

Big Data

A very large amount of data will be generated by more than 25 billion IoT-connected devices, and this data is of no use if it is not structured and analyzed properly. The advent of large data storage companies will increase adoption and the possibility of deploying the infrastructure and analyzing large and complex data generated by IoT.

IPv6

Internet Protocol version 6 is one of the most important innovations for internet-connected products where it allows more unique TCP/IP addresses to be created to meet the demand for such large connected devices. Some of the adoption levers for Ipv6 include higher security with end-to-end encryption capability, scalability with a unique identifier available for devices, and allowing all the devices connected to the same network to talk to each other without posing any network address translation or firewall issues.

Fog Computing

This technical innovation involves not just the processing of data close to the devices where it gets generated but also the network connection that is required to store the data from the edge to the endpoint, which could be the cloud or a data center.

RFID Technology

Radio Frequency Identification (RFID) technology is one of the key enablers of the IoT deployment. It uses radio waves to transfer data by automatically identifying and tracking the bar code labels attached to any product. It uses the following three components to function:

- Reader: It can be stationary or mobile and executes the application.
- Antenna: It is connected to the reader and generates a power field.
- Transponder: It is powered up as soon as it enters the field and the chip inside it starts the communication process.

Data Security

With more and more people using IoT devices as part of their daily routine, data security and privacy remain key barriers to adoption. Lack of robust standards, customers and device manufacturers unwilling to pay higher prices, and semiconductor companies still struggling to make profits all inhibit the growth of data security. The business can refer to the best practice guidelines on web security as laid out in the Open Web Application Security Project (OWASP) and deploy these standards in the IoT devices to reduce any breach of security risk. The security of the entire ecosystem needs to be analyzed and the devices need to be fully protected on the connected networks.

Infrastructure Requirements

Some of the technology infrastructure areas in which IoT will drive changes and innovations are described below:

- Device Hardware: Most IoT devices gather the signals of their surrounding area such as temperature, motion, light, vibration, etc., through sensors or modify the physical world information using actuators. They also use hardware components that convert the sensor signal into digital data such as analog to digital conversion, voltage to frequency conversion, signal conditioning, scaling, and interpretation.

- Data Collection: Collecting, managing, and interpreting the huge amount of data generated by sensors are key to support the analytics and provide insights to take appropriate action. Some of the considerations should include what type of physical signals need to be measured, how many sensors need to be installed, type of sensors that would be required to capture appropriate data, how fast the real-time data should be collected, and how accurate should the data be.

- Data Processing: One of the key components of the IoT architecture is the data processing that is required on the data collected from the sensors. Considerations should include the processing power and the hardware size for the data storage at the edge, which would determine the performance, functionality, useful life, cost, and the size of the device.

- Data Storage: The data retention policy along with how much data is collected, the frequency of acquiring the data, and how fast it needs to be sent to the cloud for further analysis govern the local storage space required towards the edge of the network for doing real-time computations, which ultimately results in saving time and improving efficiency.

- Cloud Platform: With the exponential data growth as collected by the IoT devices, it would be prudent for the enterprise to look for options where the data can be managed efficiently and is scalable to meet the ever-growing demands. Thus, storing, computing, and analyzing the information in the cloud rather than managing it on-premise might be the most economical solution.

- Connectivity Management: The communication from the IoT device to the cloud platform and with third-party systems is a key factor of the IoT technology stack in determining the gateway architecture. The gateway serves as a medium to consolidate, interpret, secure, and transmit the data from the sensor to the cloud.

- Application Enablement: The application enablement platform provides a critical role of linking various IoT devices to applications, and this requires a middleware platform to support scalable, consistent, secure, and cost-efficient IoT solutions for customers. It can play the role of a platform service that would enable rapid deployment of IoT applications and provide foundational services.

- User Interface: This is the actual product used by consumers or in industrial applications such as Fitbit, Nest thermostats, smart water pumps, and autonomous vehicles. The innovation could be an altogether new product for an existing or new application or converting the existing application to become smart.

Understanding IoT Architecture

An IoT architecture primarily involves a fleet of connected devices and the data that they generate. Figure 6.2 depicts the components that build up the IoT architecture framework.

The three major components of the architecture involve the following:

- Connected Devices: It's the physical hardware to capture environment data and then transmit the data to be processed.

- Connectivity: A gateway helps the data reach the central processing location for storage and analytics. This is an optional connectivity between connecting devices and IoT platforms.

- IoT Platforms: These are central cloud services that ingest all the data from the devices to store and run analytics and also explore data for higher-level applications and visualization.

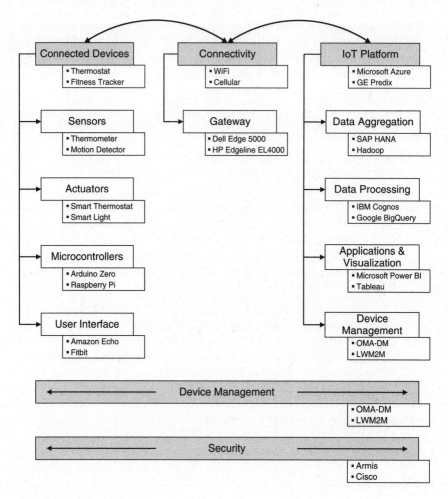

Figure 6.2   IoT architecture.

IoT architecture can be quite complex depending on the use case at the enterprise, but the following components should be analyzed and considered while designing the architecture for any IoT applications.

Connected Devices

These are the physical hardware to capture environmental data, process the data, and then transmit the data to be centrally stored and further processed. Some of the common examples include connected cars, fitness trackers, connected thermostats, and connected security cameras. These connected devices must have a power source, which could be a battery, solar energy, or a power outlet.

Sensors

Sensors are used to capture data around the world based on the changes detected in some environmental variables such as a thermometer to capture temperature readings or a motion detector to capture any movements. The quality of the sensor is measured by its sensitivity to the measured property where the captured data is not influenced by changes to other variables in the environment. Some of the factors that should be considered when choosing the sensor for the IoT architecture are described below:

- Precision and Accuracy: The sensitivity of a sensor is inversely proportional to its range. When choosing the sensor for an application, it is important to select one that has the highest sensitivity for the range of values it might get from the data.

- Environmental Conditions: Many external environmental factors might influence the readings of the sensors. Therefore, it is important to consider the working conditions of these sensors and where they will be placed. Most sensors work within a defined range of temperature, moisture, and vibrations, and if these conditions are not within the specified parameters, sensors might provide inaccurate readings.

- Size: Sensors are embedded within other electrical and mechanical components. The smaller their size, the greater their adaptability and placement options. Even the power consumption of a smaller sensor will be less as compared to that of the larger size, which directly impacts the operational cost.

- Adjustments: Some sensors need to be adjusted based on the environmental conditions under which they operate. This is due to sensitivity to environmental properties other than the measured property. An ideal sensor is only sensitive to a single property and ignores everything else in the world. There are known other properties that affect the sensor, so the sensor needs to be calibrated with the environment.

- Compatibility: Sensors can output analog or digital signals and are connected to the computing device through a serial port, I/O pins, or another specialized connection. It's important to choose the sensor that can output the signal which is compatible with the computing device.

- Add-on Software: Some environmental measurement data captured by the sensors produces a disorderly signal that needs specialized add-on software to convert and produce a meaningful output. This software is often provided by the device manufacturer and is adjusted specifically with the sensor.

Actuators

Actuators accept the digital signal and data captured by the sensor and act on it to provide a quantifiable change to its environment. For example, a sensor inside a smart thermostat captures a temperature reading from the environment and if it goes above the threshold limit, the actuator triggers the air-conditioning unit to bring the temperature back within the limit. Thus, while a sensor captures data around the world, actuators act on that data to trigger a change, which could be altering the position of the physical object or adjusting the sound, light, or amount of heat in an environment. Actuators are able to interpret the messages received and react to them, which helps in automating the systems with no human intervention.

Microcontrollers

Microcontrollers act as microcomputers on a chip which provides memory for storage, programming functionality for computation, and/or real-time operating systems designed to do a specific action. These hardware boards come in various configurations such as 8, 16, 32, and 64 bit, and depending on the nature of the application, the correct configuration of microcontroller should be used. Some of the factors that should be considered when choosing the correct microcontroller include the following:

- Computation Power: The functional requirements and its complexity determine the microcontroller's processing and computational power.
- Memory: The amount of storage that is required at the connected device depends on the criticality of the application, the size, and frequency of the collected data. The storage requirements at the edge (connected device level) determine the selection of the microcontroller.
- Energy Consumption: This is one of the key factors that should be considered when selecting the board. Typically, a microcontroller consumes around 100–150mA during Wi-Fi or Bluetooth data transmission and around 10mA during the deep sleep mode. This means the connected device can potentially last three to five years with just a smartphone battery.
- Compatibility: The microcontroller should be compatible with the sensors and actuators in terms of the availability of input/output ports.
- Cost: The cost of the microcontroller should be evaluated based on the value and solution it can provide to the overall application.
- Scalability: The architecture of any IoT project should be planned in such a way that it can be scaled up in the future depending on the new business model. Thus, the size and features of the microcontroller should be evaluated with a long-term horizon.

- Support: Experienced vendors with good customer support in handling any hardware issues and development effort should also be considered, as IoT is still in its evolution stage, and out-of-the-box support expedites the development of the application and provides a solution when a problem is encountered during the implementation.

User Interface

A user interface is commonly required in the consumer IoT space as compared to industrial IoT applications. Most of these connected devices lack screen space, ports, and graphics capability. Thus, more innovative designs are being incorporated into connected devices to make the interaction of the end users with the device a great experience.

Compact devices such as Fitbit, Google Nest, or Amazon Echo use LED lights or voice commands to communicate a message or status information, as they do not have space for keyboard, mouse, or advanced graphics processing.

With the popularity of smartphones, large screens, and ease of use, it has become the most popular choice, serving as the user interface for the connected devices through the associated app.

Connectivity

Connectivity helps the device to transmit to and receive data from other devices and/or the cloud serving as the IoT platform. Some of the considerations that should be taken into account when choosing the connectivity method during the IoT setup are listed below:

- Coverage: The distance that you need to send and receive a signal to have reliable coverage.
- Power Consumption: The power consumption during normal working conditions required to send that signal.
- Scalability: The maximum number of devices that need to be connected to a single hub.
- Threats: The environmental conditions and objects that can block the transmission of the signal.

There are several models and methods to establish connectivity. Some of the features that should be considered are described below:

- Hub/Spoke Model: The hub/spoke wide area network (WAN) model allows all the connected devices to transmit data to a central hub, which then connects to the internet. This network structure can be considered if all devices have reliable access to the hub and do not require connectivity with each other. Though this model utilizes low power protocols, it may cause communication time lags. There is always a risk – if the network of the main hub fails, all communication from all the IoT devices may fail. WiFi and Bluetooth are primary examples of the hub/spoke model. The model is shown in Figure 6.3.

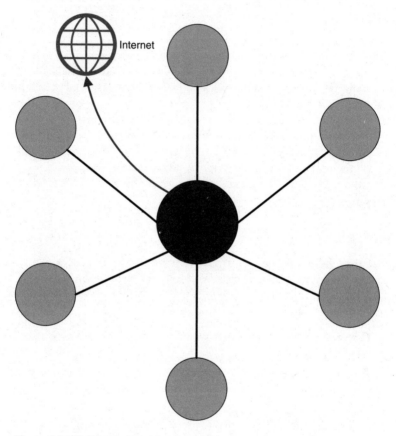

Figure 6.3   Hub/spoke model.

- Mesh Model: The mesh model allows connectivity between each of the connected devices in the same network whereby each of the devices can receive and transmit data, eventually reaching a central hub. This network structure is complex to configure but is considered quite reliable. Zigbee and Z-Wave are primary examples of the mesh model. The model is shown in Figure 6.4.
- Direct Connect Model: The direct connect model allows connected devices to have a direct connection to either a cellular tower or a

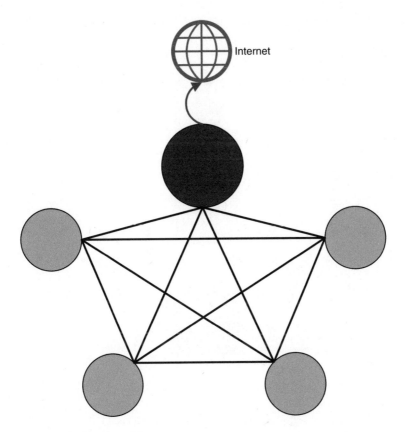

Internet

Figure 6.4   Mesh model.

satellite, which then connects to the internet. This structure is good if the services are available in the region and does incur an additional ongoing cost for the use of the network. It provides increased capacity, low battery power usage, wider geographical coverage, and reduced interference from other signals. Cellular such as 4G and satellite are primary examples of the direct connect model. The model is shown in Figure 6.5.

Gateway

A gateway is an optional hardware component that acts as an intermediary between connected devices and IoT platforms. It helps to connect the devices and sensors to the broader internet and applications so that the data can be transmitted efficiently and securely to the central processing location for further analysis.

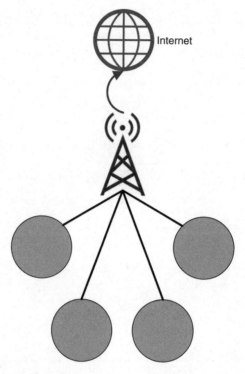

Figure 6.5   Direct connect model.

It can be an internet router, a mobile phone, or a custom-built device developed to support a particular ecosystem. The architecture of the gateway in the context of IoT setup is depicted in Figure 6.6.

Gateways can provide any of the following functions.

- Battery Life: In an application where the sensors and devices are installed in remote areas, it would require long-range connectivity such as satellite to transmit the data directly from the connected device to the cloud. This would require substantial power consumption which, in turn, would reduce the battery life of the devices. In such scenarios, gateways are installed near the devices so that the sensors and devices have to send data a shorter distance and the gateway can then transmit the data back to the cloud using a higher bandwidth connection.

- Security: The connected devices are constrained by the computational capability and power consumption and are not able to provide robust

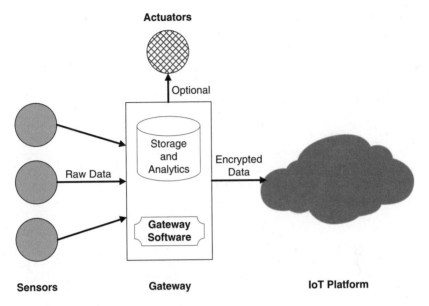

Figure 6.6   Gateway Architecture

security around the data captured from the environment. The gateways, in turn, provide data encryption before transmitting the data packets over to the IoT Platform via large wide area network. The data from the connected device to the gateway is unsecured, while from the gateway to the internet it is secured.

- Protocol Translator: Some of the connected devices are constrained by using the HTTP protocol that is used by our computers to communicate with servers. Instead, MQTT (message queuing telemetry transport) and CoAP (constrained application protocol) are commonly used lighter protocols designed for machine-to-machine applications.

Gateways receive data from the sensors in the form of lightweight messaging protocols such as MQTT and CoAP, interpret and then transmit the data using a protocol with a higher quality of service such as HTTP.

- Data Filtration: Sometimes, the sensors and connected devices generate a huge continuous data streams, which may not be required to be sent over to the cloud; moreover, it might be very expensive to send a huge data stream to the cloud due to its storage cost. Gateways have the processing capability to filter unwanted data such as when no activity has been recorded by a security camera, which helps to decrease transmission, processing, storage, and operating costs in the cloud.

- Data Storage and Analytics: Gateways can serve as a localized data buffer to prevent data loss in case of erratic connectivity from the connected devices to the IoT platform. When the gateways receive the raw data from the connected devices, they have the ability to provide meaningful insights and analytics on this data before sending it to the IoT platform.

- Localized Messaging: In certain situations such as a medical emergency or fire alarm where the actuator needs to be triggered immediately based on the sensor reading, gateways can serve as localized messaging routers between these devices.

As an example, the temperature sensor embedded within the connected device sends the temperature reading to the local gateway. The gateway has the business logic built in whereby when the temperature reaches above a particular threshold and the fire is likely to start, it sends the signal to an actuator which shuts down the motor. In such situations, there is no time for the data to be transmitted to the IoT platform for analysis, as the event is time sensitive. The gateway acts in transmitting the message to trigger a localized event.

Sensor/actuator, computing, and connectivity are some of the core functions of a connected device, while routing is one of the core functions of the gateway. When designing the overall IoT architecture, it is important to consider and segregate the functions that need to happen at the connected device, the gateway, and the IoT platform.

IoT Platform

IoT platform services offer secure and scalable public or private cloud services to capture, analyze, and present all the data from the devices and sensors to run analytics and also explore data for higher-level applications and visualization. All the scattered data from various connected devices is collected centrally at the IoT platform for computation and analysis and then from there exposed to various users and applications.

Data Aggregation

Data aggregation is the process whereby the IoT platform collects all the data from the environment and physically stores and captures it within a database in order to take actionable insights. There could be a continuous stream of data depending on the IoT application and use case which needs to be captured for processing. There is the potential to scale up to a huge volume of data with the addition of connected devices such as miles of oil pipe or agricultural land monitoring. Every data point has a timestamp, and some of the sensitive data may require this information during analysis.

Data Processing

Data processing is the core function of the IoT platform with its cloud-based services. Though gateways have both the processing and analytics capability, it is done at the localized level. The IoT platform offers the computation and processing of the metadata on a global scale so that it can be analyzed and presented meaningfully for a particular action.

The architecture for managing the aggregation, processing, and analysis of IoT data is illustrated in Figure 6.7.

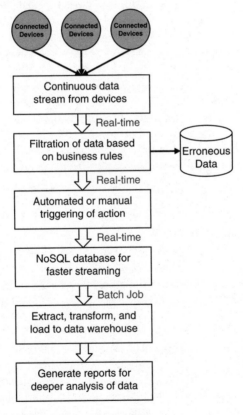

Figure 6.7   IoT data architecture.

- The data from the connected devices is first passed through the in-memory data filter, which is governed by the data acceptance business rules and guidelines. Inaccurate data should either be set aside for analysis or removed from downstream analysis such as temperature reading with an erroneous record like a string or a word that will break the analysis down the road.

- Triggers create automated actions or responses wherein a minimum threshold (i.e., data outliers) should spur immediate machine intervention. Careful consideration and controls should be applied when managing critical events by using both machine automation and human discretion.

- When it comes to triggering actions or events, it might be time sensitive. So, it's important to do it immediately before the data is stored in the database. Triggers should be generated with automated responses or actions when a minimum threshold of sensor data is reached. Careful consideration and controls should be applied when managing critical events by using either machine automation where the trigger automatically turns off an actuator or human discretion where it can send a note to a human to take a look and take appropriate action.

- The data is streamed to a low-latency, time-series NoSQL database that can commonly handle over 50,000 insertions per second in its original format. It stores 24 hours of rolling data and then the data is moved to the warehouse to avoid unnecessary storage costs. The data is captured in real time, and then on a 24-hour basis, the data is moved to the warehouse, which can then be utilized to produce analytics.

- The data is finally transferred to the data warehouse using the ETL (extraction, transformation, and loading) process via batch mode. In this process, the data is restructured and then loaded to respective tables in the warehouse. It can then be combined with other enterprise data or data-in-hub to generate reports and analytics.

- Once the data is optimized and organized in the database, business users can create queries to analyze the streaming data and generate meaningful and user-friendly reports.

Applications and Visualization

Applications and visualization constitute the user interface for analyzing the data and taking actions. There are some basic apps that come built-in with the IoT platform or can be extended by third-party applications so that they can provide a front-end interface for the users to see patterns, observe trends, and understand the underlying data captured by the devices and sensors through the dashboards in the form of charts and 2D and 3D models.

Most IoT platforms offer a direct interface to device and sensor data through an API. Some of the commonly used applications by the end users are described below:

- Management Dashboard: This is used for device management, user credentials, and notifications with an overall view and statistics of the device performance.
- Real-time Data Dashboard: This is used for analyzing the streaming data, trends, patterns, and analytics.
- Third-Party Service Integration: This feature is used to customize the dashboard based on user requirements and incorporate machine learning algorithms for advanced analytics and automation.
- Triggers and Event Processing Dashboard: This is used to provide notification to the users for appropriate action when the environmental conditions are outside the threshold limits. The actions can also be automated and notification sent to the users.

Device Management

Device management and security features are common to all the components of the architecture – devices, gateway, and the platform.

Device Management

IoT implementations require the organization of all connected devices that are deployed across vastly distributed areas to ensure they are all working properly. The IoT platforms use the device management protocols such as OMA-DM (open mobile alliance device management), LWM2M (light weight machine-2-machine) or TR-069 (Technical Report 069) to centrally control, communicate, and update the devices.

The following considerations should be made while designing the device management for the IoT ecosystem:

- Authentication: One of the features of using device management is to authenticate the device that is being connected to the cloud-based IoT platform. It needs to be ensured that the connected device is authentic, is running all the prerequisite software, passes the security test, and is working on behalf of the trusted consumer or organization.
- Provisioning: Whenever the devices are installed for the first time or added to the existing ones, they need to be enrolled in the ecosystem within the network to start functioning. Device management can automate the provisioning of these devices by checking the credentials such

as model and serial number or authenticating the certificate or key that is stored in the secured memory within the device.

■ Device Configuration: In scenarios where thousands of devices are installed such as a fleet of trucks or monitoring crops on agricultural land, device management can be very handy in providing a remote configuration option to the users. The users would be able to enable or disable any specific feature of the device such as name and location and allow changes to settings and parameters of the device. In case the device needs to be decommissioned, the user would also be able to reset to factory default configuration settings.

■ Software Updates: One of the key aspects of device management is its ability to update and maintain the device by providing for new software and/or bug fixes to be loaded on the device with minimal downtime and impact on the business users. One needs to consider the timing of the update when the devices are reliably connected to the network and the device is not streaming critical and sensitive data.

■ Monitoring and Maintenance: Monitoring the health of the device is imperative to smooth functioning and operation of the IoT ecosystem with minimum impact from device downtime. This would involve monitoring the storage capacity, networking, connectivity, and resource utilization levels.

Device management helps identify and monitor any software bugs or operational issues by querying status and automatically retrieving the error reports from the device and troubleshooting the defects or maintenance issues remotely.

Security

With all the devices being installed in this uncontrolled environment, it poses security challenges to the entire IoT ecosystem. All the devices are exposed to security threats, some of which are highlighted below:

■ Physical Devices: The security risk is that people may literally hack the device, physically tamper with it, or connect to the device in order to retrieve or destroy data or perform some malicious action.

■ Protocol: The security risk is that people may send requests through an unsecured communication protocol in order to initiate malicious actions or retrieve sensitive data.

■ Transmission: The security risk is that people may block, capture, or imitate the signal of a connected device to capture data or send a malicious signal to the platform.

In order to provide the end-to-end security of the IoT ecosystem, the full spectrum of security needs to be considered, mainly:

- Security and identity management of the physical devices.
- Security and access to the network.
- Security of the gateways.
- Security of the IoT platform in the cloud.
- Security of the IoT applications.
- Security and access management of the end users.

IoT Implementation Methodology

The enterprise needs to take advantage of the connected devices, capability and implement the IoT project using the proven methodology with implementation phases as described below:

Discovery

The enterprise should conduct the following activities during this phase:

- Assess the market for the IoT technology.
- Gain insight into IoT best practices.
- Understand the pulse of the market.
- Discover the customer need and how an IoT solution could address the challenge.
- Research market demand, competitor initiatives, and the technology required to make it possible.

Plan

The enterprise should conduct the following activities during this phase:

- Identify three to five priority use cases as applicable for the enterprise's business.
- Prioritize existing processes and customer channels where IoT can drive the most value.
- Define initiatives from top to down of IoT stack, starting with data monetization scenarios.
- Develop the value proposition for the overall IoT initiative within the enterprise.

- Develop the security framework and data model.
- Define the roadmap and roles for executing a proof of concept.

Proof of Concept

The enterprise should conduct the following activities during this phase:

- Mobilize a cross-functional IoT task force to execute on the strategy.
- Prioritize the use cases based on the business function and revenue potential.
- Build an IoT operating model.
- Create a prototype of priority use case.
- Define future processes that will impact the PoC.
- Collect feedback from target users on the design concept, business proposal, feasibility, etc.
- Measure execution against strategy through an implementation checklist and a set of predefined key performance indicators.

Pilot

The enterprise should conduct the following activities during this phase:

- Partner with technology and product vendors to launch the initial set of pilots.
- Run small-scale pilots (<30 days from design to rollout) across the priority use cases.
- Validate the technical, operational, and commercial viability of priority use cases and expand, if successful.
- Define the operating model and evaluate organizational readiness for the larger implementation and rollout.
- Complete high-level assessment and the roadmap to transition.

Development and Scale

The enterprise should conduct the following activities during this phase:

- Design and implement a full-scale solution based on pilot results.
- Develop custom hardware, back-end API integration, data model, vertical applications, and user experience.

- Test a full-scale solution with third-party services to ensure interoperability, connectivity, integration, security, and stability.
- Execute end-to-end implementation of the IoT device and commerce capabilities.
- Integrate with the enterprise's ecosystem.
- Deploy a solution and make it available for all channels and customers.
- Developing the IoT solution needs thoughtful planning to minimize risk and realize long-term business benefits. The following factors should be accounted for in designing the IoT architecture so that the solution can be scaled as per the enterprise requirements:
  - The maximum number of devices that the architecture can sustain and connect
  - The number of possible events per second that can be captured
  - The maximum number of users that can work with the data in parallel
  - The maximum number of workflows that can be executed in parallel and processed per hour
  - The number of executable rules per device and its frequency

Expand and Sustain

The enterprise should conduct the following activities during this phase:

- Scale the outcomes and platform to other businesses, new customers, or target segments.
- Use data insights to increase workforce productivity, asset utilization, and consumer adoption.
- Use existing IoT solutions to redefine processes and pilot new revenue streams and differentiation opportunities.
- Emply device and vendor management as part of the ongoing maintenance.
- Deploy ongoing improvements tracking.

New Era with Connected Devices

It is estimated that the connected device market is more than five times the total population of the world and by 2020 there will be more than 50 billion connected devices with a revenue opportunity of more than $1 trillion for the enterprises. In the new era, the connected "things" and "devices" will need to work seamlessly for the enterprise to reap the benefits of commerce through connected devices.

Connected Devices Model

In the current environment, the smartphone is connected to individual smart devices and thus the commercial transactions are done through the smartphone as per the model illustrated in Figure 6.8.

The future of the Internet of Things depicts a completely different picture where the entire ecosystem of devices is connected and they communicate with each other as per the model illustrated in Figure 6.9.

Thus, the enterprise needs to pave its path to interface with all these connected devices to tap into the new revenue model.

The connected model would include the following major processes:

- An intelligent embedded device is attached to the application, collecting real-time data.
- The data is then uploaded to the cloud.
- The data in the cloud is analyzed to get insights.
- The meaningful insights result in process optimization to increase the profitability and operational efficiency for the enterprise.

Figure 6.8   Current model of connected commerce.

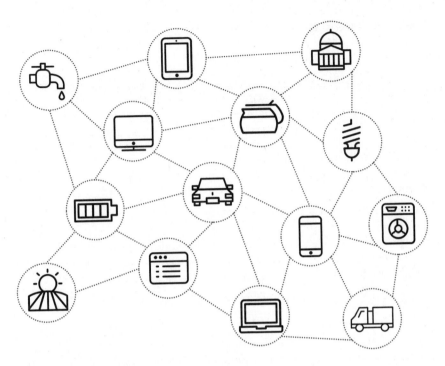

Figure 6.9 Future model of connected commerce.

Industry Solutions

The connected devices offer vertical IoT solutions across multiple industries, some of which are described below:

Connected Health

Improve the quality of healthcare service, enhance the patient experience, and optimize operational processes and asset utilization of medical equipment. Examples include remote patient monitoring, wellness monitoring, connected medical and smart devices driving research and development, major disease prevention, etc.

Connected Operations

Optimize and enhance the operational and manufacturing work processes and asset performance to enable productivity enhancements.

Examples include connected manufacturing processes for cost optimization, connected asset management for predictive maintenance, connected workers to assess productivity, connected mines to prevent mishaps, connected agriculture to improve productivity and assess watering requirements, etc.

Connected Places

Improve the use and experience of the physical places where we live, work, play, shop, and sleep.

Examples include connected homes for security monitoring, connected buildings for social events, connected cities for information exchange, connected retail for better customer experience, etc.

Connected Logistics

Expand and maximize vehicle interaction with people, infrastructure, surrounding environments, and payload.

Examples include a connected vehicle for real-time navigation, connected trains and airplanes for real-time departure and arrival information, connected freight for inventory optimization, insurance telematics for roadside assistance, etc.

Connected Commerce

Enable commerce in the IoT world and deliver a personalized trade experience when a transaction is required or initiated by an individual or device.

Examples include IoT payment through voice-enabled Alexa or through the dashboard of a car, etc.

A Day in the Life of a Consumer in a Connected World

The millennial consumer is quick to adopt new technologies in everyday life, at home, while on the road, or at work. Consumers are always looking for new technologies that can save time, simplify their everyday tedious tasks, and make life more enjoyable. In the new era of connected commerce, the commercial and payment activities are seamless, which lets consumers focus on things that really matter most to them.

Let's analyze a day in the life of a consumer with connected devices and commerce.

Ordering Daily Groceries from Home in the Morning

After getting up on one fine morning, the customer realizes that he is out of stock on coffee beans and it's time to order more and refill the stock. He uses Alexa and says, "Hi, Alexa, order my coffee beans." The voice assistance from Amazon helps the customer to order daily grocery needs and everyday purchases just by talking to Alexa and ordering the items needed. The product preferences, shipping, and payment information are already stored in the customer's profile and saved with Alexa.

Thus, the customer can leave home without even taking out a credit card from a wallet or calling anyone and get on the road to work. The coffee will arrive in three business days as per the schedule set on the profile.

Filling Up Gas in the Car While Driving to Work

The customer gets into the car and starts the drive to work but doesn't notice that the car has under a quarter tank of fuel. While on the road, the notification comes on the car's dashboard regarding low fuel level. Simultaneously the car's navigation system provides the audio message, "Your fuel level is low, would you like directions to the nearest gas station?"

In the future world, the car would be connected with the payment gateway as well as the gas station. When the customer arrives at the gas station, the car automatically detects the gas station and preauthorizes the station with the preferred credit card as set on the profile and the car automatically selects the grade of fuel as appropriate for the car. The in-car payment provides the customer with a streamlined and frictionless fueling experience, not to mention the amount of time saved at the station.

The customer just needs to get out of the car and fill up the gas tank without even taking out a credit card or making the zip code entry, thus avoiding any security breach. The customer might notice enough loyalty points for a free donut! The customer walks into the convenience store associated with the gas station and presents the digital loyalty card on the smartphone and enjoys the complimentary donut.

Ordering Office Inventory While at Work

In this case, let's assume that the customer is employed as a supply chain manager of a retail store. As a manager, he needs to ensure that the warehouse is stocked with a certain minimum threshold level of inventory and uses radio frequency identification (RFID) tags to track any inventory movement.

At any given point in time, when the material is removed from the shelf, the RFID tag captures the activity and the event will automatically place a replenishment order to the retail store's preferred supplier of that material once the stock goes below the threshold limit as set. The sensors and smart tags detect low stock and enable automatic reordering, which allows the store to keep the inventory at an optimum level.

The manager gets a text message as well as an e-mail alert on the smartphone indicating that the order has been placed with the vendor with an estimated arrival date of the material in the warehouse.

Paying the Vendors Related to Office While in Transit from Office to Home

The sensor-enabled tracking device provides the confirmation to the manager that the recent shipment of inventory has now been delivered at the warehouse. The delivery confirmation triggers a smart contract, which automatically initiates payment to the supplier of the goods.

The payment is initiated with a debit to the retail store's bank account and is processed and settled instantly over a blockchain-enabled network, directly into the supplier's bank account.

The entire transaction is completed online with no involvement required by the manager. The real-time blockchain-enabled global payments let the manager and receivables clerk spend less time on administrative and paperwork activities and more time focusing on a strategy to grow the business, bring down the costs, delight the customers, and be competitive in the market.

Paying the Personal Home Electricity Bill While Having Dinner at Home

After the day's hard work, when the customer is back at home and enjoying his dinner with family, the sensors on the smart meter in the home are working 24/7 and automatically charge the customer's credit card on file to pay the monthly bills on time and keep the lights on.

Maintaining Home Appliances While Relaxing at Home in the Evening

While the customer is relaxing at home after dinner, the sensors in the refrigerator light up, signaling that it's time to replace the water filter cartridge.

The refrigerator shops in the marketplace for the best quote on the filter and executes the purchase with the presaved payment and shipping information.

The customer receives a message on his smartwatch that a new water filter has been ordered and will be delivered in three business days. With appliances becoming intelligent so they can automatically shop and reorder parts, it provides more time for the customer to relax and enjoy the time with the family.

At the same time, it also provides an opportunity for the enterprise to tap the digital market for new sales pursuits, thus making the life of the customer simpler and free of administrative actions. The various connected devices would be able to initiate secure commerce transactions within the new payment ecosystem.

A Day in the Life of a Connected Factory Worker

The enterprise would be able to achieve a significant increase in productivity at the workplace, including factory assembly, once all the components in the ecosystem get connected through IoT technology. A day in the life of a connected worker would be as described below.

1. A worker signs into the corporate network by using a secure and uniquely generated identifier.
2. Based on the location and skill level of the worker, the most appropriate work order is generated and provided to the worker.
3. Using indoor and outdoor positioning data, the worker is guided to the job site.
4. Smart sensors trigger additional contextual and asset-specific data to help the worker carry out his duty efficiently.
5. The combination of connected asset and work order information automatically generates step-by-step digital task procedures for the worker.
6. The worker can also call in on-demand live expert help when doing the installation, maintenance, and repair that improves quality and worker efficiency.
7. The worker adds a real-time picture, voice, or video feedback to update the procedure or asset management system to assist in future repairs.
8. The worker completes and closes the work order and waits for the next job.

A Day in the Life of a Connected Hotel Staff

Let's look at a day in the life of hotel staff for the following use cases as described below using the SmartWorker Connected Hotel Staff solution fully integrated with the property management system of the hotel.

Smart Shift Preparation

In the new connected world, the following sequence of activities would take place in the shift preparation:

- The housekeeper arrives for her shift at the hotel and collects an available SmartWorker device from the docking station.
- She firmly attaches the device to a wrist strap.
- She touches her employee badge on the smart device, which then downloads her current schedule.
- The housekeeper is then able to go straight to her first task. Dynamic scheduling enables the supervisor to focus on higher-value activities to enhance the guest experience, as it removes the need for daily initial shift planning.

Smart Problem Reporting

In the new connected world, the following sequence of activities would take place in reporting a problem as encountered by the housekeeper:

- The housekeeper notices a broken door handle. By pressing the report key on the device, she is able to create a damage report using her Smart-Worker device.

- She selects the type of report and attaches a short audio recording and a picture and then continues with her remaining work.

- The maintenance team receives the report on their tablet instantaneously.

- By listening to the audio and analyzing the picture, maintenance personnel have enough information to estimate and repair the door handle. Task tracking ensures the breakage isn't forgotten about, improving hotel guest satisfaction.

Smart "Do Not Disturb" Rescheduling

In the new connected world, the following sequence of activities would take place in rescheduling any activity:

- The housekeeper knocks and enters a guest's room to find out that the room is still occupied.

- She reports that the room is occupied and moves on to the next assigned room for cleaning.

- The supervisor is notified by the SmartWorker device of the schedule change and the housekeeper's new location.

- The housekeeper's schedule is updated to incorporate the earlier postponed task at the optimal time. The system dynamically optimizes the cleaning schedule and minimizes the impact on guests with minimal supervisor input.

Smart Early Guest Check-in

In the new connected world, the following sequence of activities would take place in early guest check-in:

- As a guest tries to check in early at the hotel, the receptionist logs the request on the smart device.

- While conducting the room clean, the housekeeper is discreetly notified that her next scheduled task has changed.

- The housekeeper follows the change of schedule and cleans up the room for the waiting guest.

- Once completed, the housekeeper logs in the information, which is then communicated back to the receptionist. The receptionist is able to notify the guest that the room is ready. Real-time communication and scheduling enable the receptionist to give an exact time when the guest room will be ready, allowing the guests to plan their day accordingly.

IoT Applications by Industry

With technological advancement and innovations in IoT, a series of new capabilities and opportunities are being developed in consumer-facing applications and in improving the operational efficiency and asset utilization of the existing businesses. Some of the applications and industry use cases of IoT are described below:

Manufacturing

Some of the IoT applications and use cases that the enterprise can leverage and implement to reap the benefits and become intelligent in the manufacturing industry include the following:

Improve Asset Tracking and Maintenance

Use sensors to:

- Identify asset location
- Predict machine condition
- Detect liquid and humidity
- Monitor machine power and usage

Optimize Operations at Factory Floor

Use sensors to:

- Auto adjust based on the environmental conditions
- Activate or deactivate the machine operations

Efficient Inventory Management

Use sensors to:

- Self-direct vehicles and warehouse pick and pack
- Perform automatic quality control
- Monitor stock on shelves

- Monitor temperature and humidity in the warehouse
- Maintain a particular temperature in water pipes

Worker Health and Safety

Use sensors to:

- Identify proximity to hazardous chemicals
- Factory worker recognition with CCTV cameras
- Monitor indoor air quality level for toxic, explosive, or hazardous gases or oxygen level

Transportation and Logistics

Some of the IoT applications and use cases that the enterprise can leverage and implement to reap the benefits and become intelligent in the logistics industry include the following:

Improve Vehicle Tracking and Maintenance

Use sensors to:

- Track and monitor parcel and freight
- Optimize fleet schedule by leveraging external and big data analytics
- Minimize vehicle maintenance cost and breakdown by detecting malfunctions through vehicle conditions
- Optimize vehicle tracking and navigation by suggesting routes based on traffic congestion, weather conditions, road construction, and events information from social media
- Use autonomous vehicles to reduce road accidents through rash driving by humans
- Improve public safety by immediately detecting any toxic gas leakage and providing alert messages
- Track valuable aircraft parts and equipment to avoid losing parts and ensure timely maintenance of the fleet to increase the safety and lifetime of the aircraft

Improve Flight Experience

Use sensors to:

- Identify at airport check-in through wearables
- Track and monitor checked baggage

- Adjust in-flight seats based on tiredness of the passenger and other conditions
- Identify the levels and number of parking spots available at the airport

Improve Traffic Management

Use sensors to:

- Monitor traffic
- Detect traffic violations
- Automate parking and toll charges using license plates
- Optimize city traffic lights based on the environmental conditions

Agriculture

Some of the IoT applications and use cases that the enterprise can leverage and implement to reap the benefits and become intelligent in the agriculture industry include the following:

Improve Farming Equipment

Use sensors to:

- Identify and monitor large areas of fertile farmland
- Track and monitor tractors
- Monitor crop yield

Improve Farmer Safety

Use sensors to:

- Monitor the health of farmers through wearables
- Identify any toxic gas leakage

Increase Crop Production

Using sensors to:

- Monitor sunlight
- Monitor nutrient level in the soil
- Monitor and automate pest control
- Monitor and automate climate control by adjusting temperature and humidity level at crop warehouse
- Monitor and automate the irrigation and watering of plants
- Detect any crop damage by animals or erosion

Improve Animal health

Use sensors to:

- Monitor animal behavior and health for increase in milk and cheese production
- Review the data from health monitoring devices
- Identify the location of the animal

Oil and Gas

Some of the IoT applications and use cases that the enterprise can leverage and implement to reap the benefits and become intelligent in the oil and gas industry include the following:

Improve Operational Efficiency

Use sensors to:

- Monitor performance at oil rigs
- Deploy and monitor worker's safety
- Prevent accidents by using autonomous trucks
- Optimize the asset function and pressure levels by predicting any failures, detecting an interruption in refinery operations
- Improve oil and gas tanker conditions
- Improve the supply chain by sending the oil tankers to the gas stations by monitoring the demand through smart meters
- Monitor remotely from a central operations unit to minimize the need for site visits
- Investigate alerts triggered by underwater assets to assist in investigation and compliance through the use of drones

Automotive

Some of the IoT applications and use cases that the enterprise can leverage and implement to reap the benefits and become intelligent in the automotive industry include the following:

Improve Customer Experience

Use sensors to:

- Manage connected cars by installing infotainment for an enhanced entertainment experience

- Monitor security and theft alert
- Provide real-time traffic updates through the apps on the dashboard

Insurance

Some of the IoT applications and use cases that the enterprise can leverage and implement to reap the benefits and become intelligent in the insurance industry include the following:

Improve Customer Experience

Use sensors to:

- Study and monitor driver behavior and provide better pricing models from insurance providers
- Automate claim investigations
- Detect a fire at home or in an office building, preventing severe damage and loss of human life, resulting in a reduction of insurance premiums

Utilities

Some of the IoT applications and use cases that the enterprise can leverage and implement to reap the benefits and become intelligent in the utilities industry include the following:

Improve Power Generation and Distribution

Use sensors to:

- Study and monitor driver behavior and provide better pricing models from insurance providers
- Monitor the performance of solar power
- Optimize wind power generation by monitoring actuators and changing the pitch of wind blades
- Prevent any misuse or power theft
- Deploy preventive maintenance of wire transmission lines
- Improve failure prediction and blackouts
- Monitor demand and consumption levels to reduce peak loads
- Increase the safety of workers at power plants by detecting any radiation emission
- Analyze and monitor real-time power consumption through smart meters at the consumer's premises

Improve Water Distribution

Use sensors to:

- Monitor water quality and improve public safety by identifying any chemical and metal particles
- Detect any water leakage in real time
- Monitor water pressure in the pipeline for seamless flow to the consumer

Improve Waste Management

Use sensors to:

- Optimize garbage collection routes through GPS tracking, leading to fuel and cost savings
- Monitor the garbage level in the container to optimize pickup schedule

Consumer Goods

Some of the IoT applications and use cases that the enterprise can leverage and implement to reap the benefits and become intelligent in the consumer goods industry include the following:

Improve Retail Sales

Use sensors to:

- Autoreplenish products on the shelf
- Identify consumer behavior in the store and send coupons
- Prevent theft within the store and at a self-checkout counter

Home Automation

Use sensors to:

- Detect any intruders
- Secure the home at windows and doors by detecting motion at night
- Optimize lighting at home based on the darkness level, leading to energy conservation and lower electricity bills
- Optimize temperature settings by maintaining cozy conditions using thermostat settings

- Monitor the dryness level of clothes in the dryer and shut off the unit when dry

Healthcare

Some of the IoT applications and use cases that the enterprise can leverage and implement to reap the benefits and become intelligent in the healthcare industry include the following:

Improve Patient Care

Use sensors to:

- Help patients access real-time health records and take any preventive action
- Permit doctors to access all the medical records of patients, which will reduce the cost of redundant and multiple examinations and tests
- Monitor and track wellness and fitness
- Monitor and secure remote patient care

Use Cases

IoT use cases are certain scenarios where an enterprise connects with the environment to capture data and analyze it for new business opportunities, to enhance revenue models, or to save costs. Let's study some scenarios along with real-life case studies to see how the journey to the Internet of Things enabled the enterprise to become intelligent.

1. Case Study: Building New Revenue Streams with the Implementation of the Industrial IoT Platform
    - Scenario
        - A global manufacturer and distributor of machines for processing wood wanted to seize the opportunity for the next wave of industrial revolution.
        - The enterprise built an Industrial Internet of Things (IIoT) solution that would deliver new capabilities to its customers and build robust new services for its machinery aftermarket.
        - The enterprise wanted to improve operational efficiencies, reduce costs, and open up new revenue streams such as machine usage analysis and production process optimization by implementing connected asset management across its industrial machinery.

- Approach
  - Designed an IIoT operating model, business case, solution, and roadmap of the program.
  - The pilot solution was first implemented across eight machines at one of their customers.
  - Pilot services included preventive maintenance alerts, machine management, and manufacturing events analysis. Sensors and devices on the machines produced in-depth analytics for display on user-friendly dashboards using data visualization on mobile devices.

- Results
  - The pilot program helped the enterprise improve customer service and loyalty, reduce warranty and maintenance costs, and obtain real-time customer data and alerts.
  - The enterprise now has the ability to use performance and usage insights from the field to improve product development and add features that would be beneficial to the customer.
  - The predictive maintenance and in-depth analytics helped to improve the productivity of the machines and customer satisfaction, as it reduced machine outages significantly.

2. Case Study: Connected Assets

- Scenario
  - An integrated energy company providing gas and electric utility services wanted to monitor its assets using the IoT solution.

- Approach
  - Implemented the IoT solution for all its business units and developed a centralized monitoring and diagnostics center.
  - Assets monitored included gas turbine, generator, steam turbine, condenser, boiler pump, coolant pump, air heater, hydraulic turbine, transformer, etc.

- Results
  - One of the major alerts issued by the connected assets saved the enterprise several million dollars.
  - The solution has been able to detect and prevent hundreds of failures and breakdowns in the fleet.
  - Fan motor vents and filters were cleaned in time based on the early warning signals, avoiding any shutdown.
  - A tube leakage was bypassed and a faulty emergency drain valve repaired, saving the enterprise thousands of dollars.

- Alerts were issued on any abnormal vibrations in steam turbine bearings and boiler feed pumps.

3. Case Study: Predictive Monitoring for Vehicle Maintenance

- Scenario
  - A transit system for a major city was known for its outstanding maintenance operation. It wanted to find ways to reduce maintenance costs while keeping its reputation for excellence.
  - The goal was to spend less on costly maintenance that forced vehicles to stand idle while extending the life of its major assets, the buses.
  - The transit system was searching for an innovative solution that would allow it to achieve an even higher level of performance that could transform the future of equipment maintenance by identifying when individual vehicles required maintenance.

- Approach
  - The enterprise developed a predictive monitoring solution by deploying sensors to electronically transmit information about vehicle problems so that mechanics could fix them before there was a breakdown and the maintenance schedules could be optimized for each bus in the fleet.
  - The enterprise installed sensors on 20 buses as a pilot to gather engine and transmission operating data, which was stored in collection boxes on each bus. That information was relayed electronically to a centralized monitoring center where sophisticated statistical analytics software created a snapshot of each bus and compared its operating data to an analytic model of the bus's "normal" behavior.
  - The system provided alerts on any issues before the failure, thus repairs were scheduled on time to minimize the impact on bus service.

- Results
  - The sensors detected overheating in the hydraulic retarder, part of the bus's transmission system, allowing maintenance personnel to fix the problem before it escalated into an expensive transmission repair.
  - It allowed the transit company to extend the life of its buses by customizing a maintenance schedule for each vehicle.
  - It reduced the overall cost of ownership. For example, the system was used to identify a bus's fuel inefficiency, and when it went below the threshold limit, a tune-up of the vehicle was done to restore fuel efficiency.

- While most enterprises are focused on using data to better understand the past, predictive monitoring shifts that focus, allowing the transit company to look into the future by capturing data in real time so that it can take preventive action.

4. Case Study: Predictive Maintenance of Fleet
   - Scenario
     - A global tire company wanted to provide its corporate customers a solution for fuel efficiency and tire management across all its cars and trucks.
   - Approach
     - Sensors were installed in the tires of all vehicles so that they could be monitored remotely from a centralized location.
     - The data from the tires such as air pressure, usage, etc., was communicated from the local network where the vehicle was located to the central platform.
     - The central platform on the cloud collected the incoming data and analyzed the tires that were at risk based on the threshold limit specified for air pressure, temperature, and other attributes.
     - The fleet operators were notified when the tire pressure or temperature was outside the normal range and they were able to track and take corrective action using their mobile application.
   - Results
     - The fleet operators made more than 3% cost savings in fuel efficiency.
     - The tire manufacturing enterprise transformed itself to a new revenue model, from just a product company to a service-oriented organization, catering to customers across the globe.

5. Case Study: Service Opportunity Based on Telematics Data
   - Scenario
     - A global auto manufacturer wanted to identify new service opportunities based on sensor data and dealer reports.
     - The enterprise wanted to explore new ways to improve customer service and optimize product development through the connected car and digital mobility services.
   - Approach
     - The car sensors and dealer repair reports were analyzed in real time to predict failure and forecast the need for producing or ordering the spare parts.

- The data was also combined with the demographic pattern of the user that further enabled prediction of the future needs and preferences based on customer segments.
- New service opportunities and pricing structures were defined for the customers based on the telematics data.

- Results
  - The telematics services resulted in new revenue models.
  - The enterprise improved the vehicle relationship management such as remote diagnostics, preventive alerts, etc., that led to enhanced customer experience.
  - It also enabled the dealers to proactively target customers with specific needs to achieve a higher conversion rate.

Conclusion

IoT offers great potential for companies to grow by penetrating new markets and offering new products and services or modify their existing products to make them smarter to meet the new consumer demand.

Executives recognize the importance of IoT and its impact on building an intelligent enterprise but face challenges in allocating adequate budgets to cover the entire spectrum of IoT and make investments- in the analytics to act upon the data collected by the devices, in the technology platforms to store and analyze the data, in the security and controls of the IoT ecosystem, and in the development of in-house skills to manage all aspects of the IoT solution and architecture.

In order to facilitate this journey, the enterprise should initiate a small pilot project with a compelling use case, which could be just one small production line or just one of the products in the portfolio, and analyze the results and benefits derived from this transformation. As the data is generated in real time, within a matter of a few weeks or months the enterprise will be able to create a business case and strategy for implementing IoT within its operating environment. This will be one of the steps in the digital transformation and building an intelligent enterprise that can strive, thrive, and survive.

CHAPTER 7

Artificial Intelligence

*T*his chapter provides an understanding of artificial intelligence technology and what is causing the enterprise to move towards it. It also discusses the various technologies and services offered by AI solutions, the implementation methodology, and some of the typical processes within functional areas and industries that are potential candidates for deploying AI to bring operational efficiency and make the enterprise intelligent.

Artificial Intelligence (AI) Overview

Artificial intelligence (AI) is the technology that allows machines to interact with humans, data, and the entire ecosystem and learn from this such that they can perform more than what either humans or machines can do on their own.

We are in a period of extraordinary technological innovation that the world has never seen before, and some of the major technology revolutions include mainframe, personal laptop, e-commerce, mobile, cloud computing, big data, predictive analytics, Internet of Things, smart machines, artificial intelligence, and quantum computing. Digital disruption has caused more than 50% of the Fortune 500 enterprises to go out of business; thus, it's prudent for any enterprise to cope with the latest trend or else face the repercussions. AI is predicted to be the technology of the decade that will be most disruptive to the way businesses are run by the enterprise.

According to the International Data Corporation (IDC) Worldwide Semiannual Cognitive Artificial Intelligence Systems Spending Guide, the total spending on cognitive and artificial intelligence systems will reach $77.6 billion in 2022 at a compounded annual growth rate (CAGR) of 37.3%.

Understanding Artificial Intelligence

Artificial intelligence has the ingredients to sense, think, act, and learn. Let's understand each of these characteristics in the context of AI.

- Sense: Artificial intelligence has the acumen to see, hear, speak, smell, feel, understand gestures, recognize sounds, and process images by using input from sensors such as cameras and microphones. Examples include sensors in vehicles to recognize outside weather, image identification for insurance claim processing during an accident, speech recognition and natural language processing by Amazon Echo, emotion detection by virtual bots during a telephone conversation, face recognition for immigration at airports, etc. Neural networks are used during training to improve and refine the models to increase the accuracy over time.

- Think: Artificial intelligence has the ability to understand and analyze information and add insight to the collected data to make logical decisions and generate natural languages. It has the capability to apply intelligence to solve complex problems and take over human tasks and execute them faster and cheaper. An example includes the radar and visual sensors in an autonomous vehicle that can identify the signs and interpret their meaning so that it can drive at the correct speed where the speed limit indication is 35 miles per hour.

- Act: Artificial intelligence can take action and make decisions in the physical world based on the data, knowledge, and understanding obtained from the environment. Examples include making moves during a chess game, slowing down a vehicle based on the speed limit in an autonomous vehicle, recommending movies on Netflix based on the past history, and shutting down an air conditioner based on the temperature threshold limit setting.

- Learn: Artificial intelligence can obtain knowledge and experience from real-world examples and experiences and can improve upon its performance in terms of accuracy, quality, and consistency. The initial learning of the AI model starts with a set of training data where the underlying algorithms continuously get adjusted to make the model as accurate as possible. An example includes recognition of handwriting, where the neural network can incorporate the pixels to develop a model that can accurately identify the letters written without any human intervention, clearing open items in accounts receivable based on the customer's historical payment pattern.

In summary, AI components include computer vision, audio processing, knowledge representation, natural language processing, and machine learning, while some of the potential solutions include virtual agents; cognitive robots; text, speech, and video analytics; identity analytics; etc.

Why Are Enterprises Moving to AI?

Artificial intelligence is one such technology disruptor that has the potential to double economic growth for most major economies of the world and increase labor productivity by more than 40%. Some of the benefits of incorporating artificial intelligence as a technology within an enterprise are described below:

- Augmented productivity with fewer employees required to complete repetitive tasks and the potential to operate 24/7.
- Reduce processing and handling time to execute a particular job.
- Consistent quality improvement with the elimination of any human error.
- Optimize the use of raw materials, assets, and capital for the enterprise through analysis and recommendation of the optimal solution to the procurement and operations lead for efficient inventory and working capital management.
- Significant reduction of processing cost, making the enterprise more competitive in this digital era.

How Can Enterprises Create Value from AI?

It's important to understand the benefits that an enterprise can derive from each of the AI value levers, some of which are described below:

- Cognitive Process Automation: The rule-based robotic process automation has the capability to execute a repetitive process and do it 24/7 at consistent levels of quality. Cognitive process automation now provides the ability to automate more complex business processes involving unstructured data, adapt to changes and exceptions, execute with no human intervention, and improve performance through self-learning as the process changes or evolves with new business dynamics.

   Utilizing cognitive automation capabilities helps the enterprise drive enhanced profitability through more efficient processes, activities, and services.

   Examples include mimicking human behavior in observing existing processes, documenting them, and executing them in an automated fashion, relying only on computer vision to observe the screen and executing keyboard and mouse actions.

- Improved Decision-Making Capability: The enterprise can leverage AI capability to further improve the decision-making process traditionally governed by human intelligence.

  Leveraging AI capability helps the enterprise ride the growth trajectory by improving the quality and effectiveness of the human decision-making process.

  Examples include using natural language processing to optimize procurement decisions from unstructured data by identifying relevant web and social media content to improve the procurement strategy of the enterprise. This would involve complex self-learning natural language processing algorithms to identify relevance from over 10,000 sources and 15,000 documents to enhance predictions.

- Improved Communication: The enterprise can delight its customers and deliver a superior experience to the users by communicating personalized real-time information through AI-based systems.

  AI-enabled customer interactions will help the enterprise improve and drive growth in customer acquisition, retention, and overall satisfaction.

  Examples include engaging with customers and, based on the rewards card, making suggestions on food and other products that had been typically purchased by the customer in the past.

- Improved Products: The recent application of AI has been into developing and pioneering new products, services, and business models.

  The introduction of AI-enabled new and innovative products and services will help the enterprise accelerate growth and monetize activities with new revenue models.

  Examples include the usage of multiple home entertainment ideas and devices such as Apple TV, Amazon Fire TV Stick, Xbox, etc., that made it possible for the providers to get their content more easily to consumers, thus improving the overall entertainment experience for the customer.

- Build Trust: The enterprise can build trust with the application of AI by using it effectively with its customers and employees.

  The confidence and transparency that is built with AI can help the enterprise lower its costs on governance, prevent any business disruption during the implementation, and earn the trust from the stakeholders and society at large. The enterprise gets transformed from focusing on governance and control to true collaboration with its partners and achieving collective outcomes.

  Examples include the health department's random selection of restaurants for inspection. An AI model was deployed to scan thousands of blogs and social media sites on potential food poisoning concerns, which resulted in a higher percentage of restaurants involved in health violations.

Feasibility of Implementing AI

Artificial intelligence technology is not new; it was prevalent even a century ago, but the three vital factors that made the era of AI feasible are the availability of huge historical data, the invention of deep learning algorithms, and intense computational power.

Today, computing power is very easily accessible for any high-performance requirements. For the last 30 years, the computational power increased by 50% every year, but with the introduction of graphics processing units (GPUs), computational power has exponentially increased more than 100 times. Based on the growth and recent success with high-performance aspects of GPUs, this has increased the potential for further improvements in implementing AI solutions, as it will support faster training, more real-time responsiveness, and the ability to run/handle more complex machine learning solutions that can handle increasingly complex activities.

Listed below are some of the factors that have been instrumental in the advancement of AI:

- Availability of Computing Power:
  - The fastest computer in the world is three times more powerful and four times cheaper than what it was three years ago.
  - High-performance cloud computational processing is now available for anyone to use at less than $0.50 per hour.
- The Democratization of AI Skills:
  - Availability of skilled resources to work and develop AI solutions such that the enterprise can easily adapt the AI solutions driving significant value.
- Availability of Big Data to Train the AI Model:
  - Availability of large sets of data increases the accessibility, use, and comprehensiveness of the information produced inside and outside the enterprise. With more than 2 billion images uploaded daily, big data is used to train the machines' learning algorithms so that the model becomes adaptable to the real-life scenarios with high predictability.
- The Explosion of AI Products and Solutions:
  - Availability of various vendors developing AI products that can be quickly installed and provide near-term value.

- Increasing options to plug and play AI solutions using API services through the cloud, causing limited disturbance to the existing ecosystem.

- Higher Adoption Rate:
  - Ability to increase performance as cost decreases and learn/improve based on regular use/improvement from data have made the strategy of being a fast follower potentially outdated. Adopting AI solutions and using them in products is a faster path for an enterprise to become intelligent and remain high performing.

- Low Barriers to Entry:
  - With a plethora of vendors and products available in the market at very competitive pricing, more and more enterprises are entering the market to harness the power of AI.
  - The enterprises aren't limited by legacy systems, distribution channels, or workforce transformations.

Services Offered by AI

AI as a service is offered by various vendors and partners and includes the following services that an enterprise can utilize within its business. Some of these services include:

- Vision: Process image-related algorithms:
  - Emotion
  - Facial
  - Video

- Speech: Process spoken language:
  - Speech to text
  - Text to speech
  - Speaker identification
  - Translation

- Language: Process natural language and sentiment of human users as unstructured text and classify them:
  - Natural language processing
  - Intelligent conversation
  - Relationship identification
  - Tone analyzer
  - Language translation

- – Text analytics
- – Retrieve and rank
- – Personality understanding
- – Spelling check
- ■ Search: Make the search engine experience smarter and engaging:
  - – Web search
  - – Image search
  - – Video search
  - – Document search
  - – Word search
  - – Autosuggest
  - – News search
- ■ Customer Service: Automate the operational process to enhance customer service:
  - – Virtual agents
  - – Robots
  - – Machine learning
- ■ Data Insights: Solve complex tasks and make intelligent suggestions:
  - – Academic data
  - – Exploration
  - – Recommendations
  - – Forecasting
  - – Experimentation and innovation

AI Capabilities

The enterprise needs to evaluate and implement the right product from the portfolio of capabilities offered by artificial intelligence. Listed below are some of the major capabilities offered in the market:

Machine Learning

Machine learning is an application of artificial intelligence where the system analyzes data, identifies patterns, learns from the data, and has the ability to make decisions based on experience without any human intervention.

- ■ Some of the vendors in this space include Apple, Amazon, Darktrace, QBurst, Facebook, Google, IBM Watson, Digital Reasoning, Descartes Labs, Skytree, and Pienso.

Sample Use Cases

These systems use their intelligence to act, improve, and learn from the feedback as described below:

- Take a large set of data with normal e-mails and pre-label them as spam e-mails.
- The machine learning algorithms create a long list of characteristics or words that can be used to create a spam profile from the data set.
- The system learns these characteristics to segregate all new incoming e-mails to the spam or inbox folder.
- If a user manually labels a particular e-mail as spam, the system learns, makes changes to the spam profile, and adapts to alter its decision-making process to account for changes.

Deep Learning

Deep learning is a subfield of machine learning where the system learns multiple levels of features in unstructured data that define an increasingly abstract aspect of the data. It works similarly to how human brains process information.

- In deep learning, the computer learns to perform classification tasks directly from images, text, or sound, often surpassing the performance of humans.
- In analyzing handwriting, the deep learning algorithm would first extract lines from the pixels, then letters from the lines, etc., each level being a complex combination of the previous one.
- The objective of deep learning is to derive one algorithm that can be used to solve all problems in the artificial intelligence space – that is, one algorithm that could be used for computer vision, audio processing, natural language processing, etc.
- Artificial neural networks, which mimic the human brain, are the architecture used in deep learning.
- Deep learning is primarily used in academic institutions but some industry leaders such as Google, Facebook, Twitter, and Qualcomm are looking to leverage this technology in research and development.
- Some of the vendors in this space include Salesforce, Descartes Labs, ClusterOne, Boxx, Voysis, and Aiera.

Sample Use Cases

- Enable driverless cars to recognize a stop sign or to distinguish a pedestrian from a lamppost.

- Ability to accurately detect cancer cells in a human body.
- Detect human or other vehicles within unsafe distance by the worker while driving heavy machinery in the factory.
- Detect and locate multiple objects within an image.

Natural Language Processing

Natural language processing (NLP) is the technology whereby natural human language such as English is used to interact between human users and systems.

- Natural language comprehension extracts meaning from human speech or written sentences and decodes it to an executable task.
- Natural language generation expresses the message in a natural language such as English that a human user can understand easily.
- Some of the vendors in this space include Dialogflow, Twiggle, TaskUs, MindMeld, SoundHound, Google Cloud Natural Language, Azure Translator, and IBM Watson Natural Language Classifier.

Sample Use Cases

- Translate text or speech from one natural language to another while on a tour to a different country.
- Easy communication with systems and bots by the business users and customers who are not sufficiently tech savvy to understand coding.
- Resolve tickets using document search functionality and answering basic transactional queries from customers.

Audio Analytics

Audio analytics is the method whereby the computer acquires and processes the audio inputs such as voice samples and then analyzes them to bring business intelligence to the enterprise.

- Automatic speech recognition converts spoken words to text so that it can be analyzed using natural language processing.
- Voice recognition identifies a person using voice biometrics that are unique to an individual.
- Emotion recognition senses the emotional state and sentiment of a person.
- Some of the vendors in this space include Amazon Alexa, IBM Watson Speech to Text, Google Cloud Speech, Microsoft Speaker Recognition Clarabridge, Aspinity, OSP, Speechmatics, Nuance, Globalme, and Audio Analytic.

Sample Use Cases

- Extract the interaction with the customer and the call agent and detect hidden insights for new business opportunities.
- Provide operational efficiency by analyzing multiple voices and text interactions.
- Provide improved customer service by identifying the feelings, emotions, and sentiments through the speech recognition software. This can help enterprises maximize their interaction with customer's by understanding the contextual awareness and the tone of the speech.

Virtual Agents

Virtual agents are interactive characters that display human-like qualities and communicate in natural language with humans through speech or text in order to answer questions and perform business processes.

- Virtual agents receive requests from the users in the form of text or speech, process them using natural language processing or speech recognition technology, search knowledge repositories to formulate a hypothesis, and then provide the answers back to the users. They usually imitate human behavior.
- Virtual agents have the capability to leverage machine learning technology to improve their decision-making ability.
- Knowledge repositories and computation are usually handled in a cloud-based large-scale centralized information processing center.
- Virtual agents have found popularity in industrial applications with advancement in natural language processing, speech recognition, big data, machine learning, and cloud architecture.
- Virtual agents such as Apple Siri and Microsoft Cortana have found great acceptance from the end users.
- Increasingly well-structured and intelligent knowledge engines such as Google search capabilities and Wikipedia can act as open source knowledge repositories that can serve as sources for the virtual agent.
- Virtual agents can transform the way we interact with computers, making those interactions more natural.
- Some of the vendors in this space include IBM, Wolfram Alpha, Microsoft, Anboto, Artificial Solutions, IPSoft, Nuance, eGain, IntelliResponse, Cognitive Code, Creative Virtua, EasyAsk, Expect Labs, Evi, Icogno, NextIT, and Sherpa.

Sample Use Cases

- Provide business and technical support by helping diagnose problems and answer queries as a helpdesk function.

- Help users as personal assistants in daily tasks such as organizing calendars, sending reminders, and typing e-mails.

- Retrieve information from a webpage or a database by simply asking in a human spoken natural language.

- Analyze large amounts of unstructured data, find patterns within that data, and suggest strategies based on the information extracted.

Computer Vision

Computer vision is the technique of acquiring, extracting, processing, classifying, and evaluating digital images and videos to decompose them into a representative model from which a computer can understand and abstract any content.

- Detect an object such as vehicles, humans, product, place, etc., in an image.

- Classify an object by extracting features and establishing what an object is in the image, such as a car, bird, chair, etc.

- Recognize an object by identifying objects in an image, for example, that the person in the image is Mr. X.

- Track an object by following the movements of objects such as vehicles or humans in a video.

- Some of the vendors in this space include Cognex, Image Sensing Systems, National Instruments, Gazepoint, IntelliVision, Sportvision, Image Metrics, Microsoft Kinect, Brickstream, and ObjectVideo.

Sample Use Cases

- Detect when an individual leaves an object behind for a certain duration at a public place such as an airport.

- Assess the customer's demographics such as age, gender, ethnicity, etc., to create a profile for marketing purposes.

- Detect faces and match them against known criminals for airport security.

- Detect license plates and match them against known vehicles.

- Detect how long a vehicle has to wait at a certain traffic light.

- Calculate the average time taken for travel from point X to point Y.

Video Analytics

Video analytics leverages computer vision technology to automatically analyze live video feeds or recordings and detect events to extract meaningful information.

- Machine learning techniques could also be used to detect additional patterns or irregularities based on past incidents.
- CCTV cameras are increasingly becoming digital, with significant improvement in optics, resolution, and frame rate.
- IP networks, bandwidth, processing, and storage are making CCTV cameras part of the enterprise IT infrastructure.
- Computer vision algorithms have evolved to generate reliable alerts for operators and applications.
- Some of the vendors in this space include Cognitec, BRSLabs, CyberExtruder, VCA Technology, Digital Barriers, iCetana, Intertraff, iOmniScient, intuVision, and Verint.

Sample Use Cases

- Smart cities for governments and police.
- Transportation such as airports, train stations, public transportation, etc.
- Sales and customer-facing facilities including retail, banking, insurance, telecommunication, utilities, etc.
- Security insights such as critical infrastructure protection, police, border control, etc.

Biometric Identity

Biometric identification systems verify the user's identity by extracting, compiling, and comparing the user's unique characteristics or traits to those registered in the database.

- Biometric identification can be in the form of identifying a face, fingerprint, voice, etc.
- It can be used for mass applications with the availability of affordable sensors.
- Biometric matching algorithms are in the evolution stage.

- There is growing user acceptance of biometric systems.
- Some of the vendors in this space include Apple, Agnitio, BioID, Auraya Systems, AuthenWare, Nuance Communications, Hitachi, BehavioSec, BioCatch, Daon, DigitalPersona, Sensible Vision, and Validity Sensors.

Sample Use Cases

- Verify the identity of a user to grant access to either an office building or a restricted area such as a military base.
- Identify customers when entering a store and recommend personalized services and products to them based on their purchasing behavior.
- Identify wanted criminals in public arenas through video recording and image capturing.

Augmented Reality

Augmented reality systems use computer-generated sensory input, such as sound, video, graphics, or global positioning system (GPS) data, to enhance or supplement live images of a real-world environment, thus augmenting the user's current perception of reality.

- Use object recognition technology to detect objects in the image to augment.
- Use sensor processing to assess the best path to augment such as orientation, brightness, sharpness, etc.
- The technology is becoming popular with the increased availability of sensors and advancement in computer vision.
- Growing computational power in handheld devices.
- Some of the vendors in this space include Google, Qualcomm, Nokia, Catchoom, GeoVector, Layar, Metaio, Zugara, Wikitude, Tonchidot, and Total Immersion.

Sample Use Cases

- Link real-life objects to internet sources that provide information about those objects.
- Superimpose directions directly onto the user's view of the road on the GPS navigation.

Affective Computing

Affective computing technologies identify the emotional states of human beings through facial expression, gesture, behavior, posture, tone, interaction, vocabulary, respiration, or skin physiology, and take action accordingly.

- Sense user's emotion via sensors, microphones, cameras, and software algorithms.
- Machine learning with large data sets is used to train the system on detecting a particular emotion.
- The technology uses computer vision and language processing and runs in real time on devices and embedded systems.
- The technology is gaining momentum with the availability of cheap sensors, digital memory, and computational power.
- By detecting emotions, systems can help the enterprise to identify the needs of its customers.
- Some of the vendors in this space include Affectiva, Attensity, IBM, HP Autonomy, Affective Media, Beyond Verbal, ThirdSight, Nice Systems, CallMiner, Verint, Mattersight, Nemesysco, and Nexidia.

Sample Use Cases

- Personalize customer service based on the customer's mood, occasion, and personality.
- Allocate advertisement spending based on an emotional response.
- Identify if the customers are emotionally engaged for any brand messaging.
- Detect nervous individuals and angry behaviors during an event.
- Identify the emotional state of the driver to improve safety and driving experience.
- Monitor social media sentiment.

Enterprise AI Architecture

The architecture design of artificial intelligence would vary based on the capability and product that an enterprise chooses for its digital transformation. Listed below are some of the technology components and the major players offering them in the market. An architecture diagram of a virtual agent has also been explained from a business user perspective:

AI Technology Stack and Key Players

AI Technology Components	Examples
Infrastructure	▪ Google Tensor Processor Unit ▪ Microsoft FPGAs (field programmable gate arrays) ▪ Nvidia GPUs (graphics processing units) that offer parallel processing capabilities ▪ Field programmable gate arrays ▪ Amazon GPU Instances ▪ Intel Nirvana
Machine Learning Platform	▪ Azure Machine Learning Studio ▪ Google Machine Learning Engine ▪ Amazon SageMaker
Machine Learning Framework	▪ scikit-learn ▪ Apache Spark
Deep Learning Framework	▪ TensorFlow ▪ Keras ▪ Caffe ▪ Chainer ▪ Torch ▪ Deeplearning4j
Application Platform	▪ Alteryx ▪ H2O.ai ▪ KNIME ▪ SAP Leonardo Machine Learning ▪ IBM ▪ RapidMiner
Data Platform	▪ Azure Data Factory ▪ Dataiku ▪ Databricks ▪ Domino
AI Software-as-a-Service	▪ Amazon AI Services ▪ Google Cloud AI Services ▪ Microsoft Cognitive Services ▪ IBM Watson Cognitive Services
Intelligent Agents	▪ Robots ▪ Virtual Chatbots ▪ Autonomous Vehicles

AI Application Architecture with Bot

Based on some action words and verbs, the virtual agent is able to identify the intent of the user. The bot then maps the input received from the user to variables that can be used to fulfill, such as nouns, objects, or things. Based on the user's intention and objectives, the logical flow and response from the bot are designed.

The challenge comes in training the bots with the historical data so that the bot gets more intelligent over time. Various use cases are identified, and for each use case, hundreds of chat statements are collected and clustered to map to the correct intent.

For example, the following chat labels are mapped to the intent of "Thanking":

- Thanks for your help.
- Appreciate your help.
- OK, thanks for all of your help.
- That's all, thank you.
- That's wonderful, thank you.
- Thank you for your assistance this evening.
- You did a great job.

The clustering algorithm assigns each message to a group based on the similarity of the messages collected from various groups. This helps the bot in providing an intelligent response based on the message from the user. Figure 7.1 provides an application architecture overview of a virtual agent or bot.

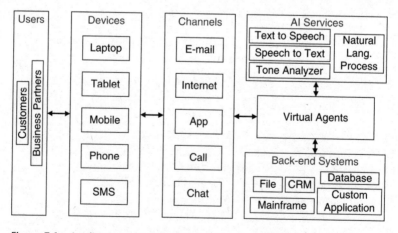

Figure 7.1   Application architecture of a virtual agent/bot.

The following example is a use case of an address change from a user. The logical sequence of steps shows the seamless conversation flow between a human and a bot. It also describes the integration with various AI services and back-end systems and the complete mechanism of how the architecture is designed by the enterprise for the functioning of the chatbots.

- User: A user uses the laptop, logs into the enterprise portal and starts the conversation with the virtual agent by typing the message: "I want to change my address on the file."
- Bot: Through the key words "change address" and using the AI services, the bot understands the intent of the user and types the message: "Do you want to change the billing or subscriber address?"
- User: The user types: "I want to change my subscriber address."
- Bot: To validate the user, the bot types the message: "Please provide your name, phone number, and existing address."
- User: The user provides the requisite information to authenticate the security questions.
- Bot: The bot checks the information as provided by the user in the back-end system where the user profile is maintained, and if the information matches, it types the message: "Please enter your new address."
- User: The user then types the new subscription address.
- Bot: The bot validates the address from the knowledge database, suggests the address in the correct format, and asks the user to validate and confirm.
- User: The user types: "I confirm the new address."
- Bot: The bot types: "Okay, your subscriber address has been changed."
- User: The user either says "Thank you" or just exits the chat window that triggers the exit of the bot conversation.

Enterprise AI Implementation Methodology

The effort to drive the implementation of AI resides mostly in the rich data repository within the enterprise, which can be utilized to make the enterprise intelligent. The methodology for AI implementation is driven by the urge to innovate and deliver high-performance AI solutions within the enterprise. The enterprise should consider the following steps when implementing an AI-based solution:

Discovery

The enterprise should identify the processes that are suitable for AI and conduct the following activities during this phase:

- Understand the goals and objectives for implementing an artificial intelligence solution.
- Analyze the current enterprise business processes and situation in detail.
- Determine possible areas of opportunity within the enterprise where the AI capabilities can be enabled.
- Define the opportunities and business case supporting the AI solution.
- Select relevant AI technologies.
- Lay out the architecture and business process for the to-be solution.
- Define pilot scope and requirements.
- Establish critical success factors for the implementation.

Data Validation

Once the AI use case has been defined and approved, the enterprise needs to ensure that it has the processes and systems already to capture and track the data with all the requisite attributes required by AI to perform the analysis and provide recommendations.

Before building the model, the enterprise should perform the due diligence and validate the source, quality, and consistency of the data to train the model.

Pilot

The enterprise should always deploy the AI solution as a pilot program with limited scope for a particular business process or application. The enterprise should conduct the following activities during this phase:

- Execute and validate the AI model for a simple business process within the enterprise as a pilot kickoff.
- Design the future solution.
- Build, test, and deploy the operating model and interfaces.
- Train and test AI agents with enough data for the model to work intelligently.
- Train the enterprise resources to the usage of the AI agents.

- Deploy the application to a selected set of pilot users to validate and check the solution.
- Validate the feasibility of the application along with the lines of the business case that was proposed for undertaking the initiative.
- Define the detailed deployment scope, timeline, resources requirement, and execution plan.
- Communicate the findings to the stakeholders to modify the model to make it suitable to the enterprise's business.

Deployment

Based on the findings from the pilot where the business users provide continuous feedback to improve the performance of the model, the enterprise needs to prepare for implementing AI on a large scale across the enterprise. The enterprise should conduct the following activities during this phase:

- Roll out the AI model to production to a wider section of the enterprise.
- Industrialize the operations.
- Deploy the functionality configured during the pilot to additional users.
- Fine-tune the operations with the adjustment required for the model to work independently.
- Understand the profitability, growth, and sustainability benefits that the enterprise can get from the AI implementation.
- Report the benefits and KPIs achieved to the stakeholders.

Scale and Sustain

After the deployment, the AI model and solution would be in operations. The enterprise should now look for opportunities to scale it to other processes and businesses and conduct the following activities during this phase:

- Monitor the model continuously for performance and quality of service.
- Update additional data sources and interfaces based on any change in the market dynamics.
- Identify new use cases that can be considered for deploying the AI model.
- Manage various environments within the enterprise's ecosystem.
- Provide ongoing support to improve the performance.

Potential AI Opportunities

There are various applications within the enterprise where artificial intelligence can be applied and can result in making the enterprise intelligent. Some of these areas within the ecosystem of the enterprise that have the potential for AI application are described below:

- Data Insights: A platform where business users can write or ask questions in natural language on the large structured data set and can get their queries answered by the system. Some of the examples include AnswerRocket, Viv.ai, Expect Labs, and Tableau.

- Video Analytics: Find patterns through the video footage captured using computer vision or CCTV cameras to mine for analytics and patterns, predict the risk, or identify key customer behavior. An example is the Video Analytics Platform from various vendors such as Siwel, IBM, IntelliVision, etc.

- Biometric Analytics: An identity management solution to recognize people based on what they have and do. One examples is the Unique Identity Service Platform from Accenture.

- Text Analytics: An application that processes high-volume unstructured text, understands the text, and provides accurate information with proper classification and grouping. Some of the examples include ExpertSystem and Intelligent Text Analytics Platform.

- Image Analytics: Extract the meaning and insights from visual data or an image and detect certain characteristics such as brand, face detection, undamaged, fully damaged, or partially damaged car in an auto insurance context; use pattern recognition such as a cancer tumor in an MRI scan, or find a damaged crop from the image taken by a drone. Some of the examples include Clarifai, Rekognition, and CloudSight.

- Documents Identification: A natural language search engine that can retrieve relevant documents from a large unstructured data set at a very fast pace. Some of the examples include retrieving the documents in the order of relevance by IBM Watson, Google search, and Bing search.

- Robotic Process Automation: Automate complex business processes using the enterprise's unstructured data for optimizing processes and predictive analytics. Some of the examples include BluePrism, Automation Anywhere, and Fusion.

- Virtual Assistant: Automate helpdesk functionality to have an intelligent conversation and solve problems related to customer requests, PC troubleshooting, or network connectivity issues. Some of the examples include Amelia, Artificial Solutions, NextIT, CreativeVirtual, and Nuance.

- Technical Assistant: The ability to learn a product manual and answer questions such as absorbing a car manual or industrial procedure and assisting a user with queries or step-by-step instructions to solve problems. Some of the examples include Amelia, Artificial Solutions, NextIT, CreativeVirtual, and Nuance.

- Domain-specific Intelligence: Use natural language to perform computation, extract data, and assist in research for a specific domain such as thermodynamics, food and nutrition, engineering, etc. One example is Wolfram Alpha.

AI Opportunities by Industry

Artificial intelligence uses the following applications in various industries for its digital transformation objective:

- Video analytics
- Text analytics
- Deep learning
- Robotics
- Virtual agents
- Biometrics identification

Let's analyze some of the industry-specific business areas and use cases where AI can be leveraged for achieving any of the following value drivers:

- Customer experience
- Increase in revenue
- Business growth
- Risk mitigation
- Operations efficiency
- Cost reduction

Automobile Industry

Auto manufacturers are focusing on artificial intelligence to improve different aspects of car automation, creating a better customer experience, and greater car safety, thereby increasing both the top and bottom line of the enterprise.

Some of the areas and use cases where AI can be applied in the automotive industry are described below:

- Car Manufacturing: Digitization has opened up an altogether new world of opportunities for car manufacturers to optimize the production process and lower the cost of operations. Some use cases include:
  - Using robots at manufacturing plants to enable record production levels at the economies of scale by the automotive industry.
  - Artificial intelligence has been effectively utilized during the crash testing of a vehicle, leading to a reduced number of vehicles being destroyed during the process.
  - Intelligent tools to support factory workers in assembling the parts, simplifying the complex process and providing alerts to the workers with any special requirements to eliminate human error.

- Driver Assistance: Watch drivers and determine if a driver is too tired or distracted by the entertainment package, thus impacting the safety of the driver. Some use cases include:
  - Assisting the driver by using cameras to extract human binocular vision images and detect the presence of other vehicles and pedestrians on the road.
  - Alerting the driver to take over the steering wheel from cruise control when the speed goes below a certain threshold.
  - Automatically applying the brakes when the vehicle in front of the driver is too close and there has been no activity detected by the driver.
  - The rear camera alerting the driver not only about the object behind the car but also about the cross traffic on both sides of the vehicle.
  - Analyzing the facial expression of the driver such as rolling back of the eyes or time spent on the closure of eyelids to detect signs of fatigue.

- Car Safety: Build safety around self-driving vehicles to avoid collisions and determine the status of a legitimate driver. Some use cases include:
  - Utilizing deep learning along with multiple sensors to recognize objects in the near vicinity, anticipate potential threats, and provide safety alerts to the driver or enable autopilot functions.
  - Using deep learning models and computer vision in autonomous cars to detect pedestrians or other objects in real time to ensure the safety of the vehicle and people on the road.
  - Using advanced AI capabilities and sensors to monitor 360 degrees around the car to handle complex real-world driving conditions and ensure the safety of the car.

- Traffic Management: AI can be used as the most reliable technology in assessing and predicting traffic conditions, based on the traffic data collected in real time from the vehicles on the road through the integrated and connected vehicle program. Some use cases include:
  - Capturing real-time traffic conditions and integrating with calendars, messages, and other apps to reroute or add destinations to the journey.
  - Making intelligent decisions to prevent incoming calls causing a distraction to the driver during traffic congestion when the driver needs to be more alert.
  - Providing recommendations to the driver based on the profile and historical preferences to spend time at some place other than being in the traffic congestion after a major event or around shopping malls.

Banking Industry

Banks are implementing AI solutions to improve the customer experience, accelerate business growth, mitigate risk, and increase operational efficiency.

Some of the areas and use cases where AI can be applied in the banking industry are described below:

- Customer Support: Bots in the front office will always be available to provide faster and efficient service to customers without a long wait to get an appointment with the bank's representative. As banking is more inclined towards serving its retail clients, automating the front office and customer-facing activities will greatly boost revenue growth while maintaining customer loyalty. Some use cases include:
  - Introducing a human-like robot at the reception area that can analyze facial expressions and behavior of the customers to provide responses.
  - Developing a virtual assistant for the online banking customers to provide immediate online support and assistance with customer needs such as activating cards, changing a PIN, reporting lost or stolen cards, and gaining access to the account balance. This reduces a considerable load on the call center volume.
  - Using facial recognition and fingerprint scan to verify the identity of the customer, who is then able to withdraw funds from the ATM without the use of a card or PIN.
  - Using the voice recognition technology to allow customers to use their voices to check credit card balances and pay bills.

■ Financial Services: The customers should be empowered to have full control of the money management process, and the technology should offer a recommendation on upgrades, new services, and investment products based on the customer's risk appetite, goals, and profile. Some use cases include:

  – Using virtual agents for conversation and answering customer questions. This saves time for customers in terms of waiting on hold for a customer service agent at a call center to answer the call.
  – Introducing an app powered by artificial intelligence so that the customers can talk to retrieve the information they ask for and make money transfers.
  – Using machine learning to analyze unstructured data and behavior patterns to offer personalized and tax-optimized investment advice tailored to live events such as a wedding, anniversary, or real estate purchase.

■ Back Office: Bots are replacing humans in the repetitive data entry back-office jobs, leading to faster processing time and cost reduction. Some use cases include:

  – Implementing cognitive process automation across a wide range of processes such as account opening, accounts receivables, fraudulent account closure, loan application, etc., leading to a reduction in FTEs and bad debt provision.
  – Using biometric verification to detect fraud and using algorithms to detect any early signs of deceitful activities, which are generally detected by humans after the occurrence of the event.

Healthcare Industry

Healthcare providers are adopting AI to improve patient treatment and satisfaction, bring operational efficiency, and reduce costs. The AI-based solution will have the ability to provide insights from various data sets including medical records, laboratory tests, clinical studies, and medical images to assist the patients in diagnosing the problem and its treatment. Some of the areas and use cases where AI can be applied in the healthcare industry are described below:

■ Patient Care: Cognitive computing and AI technology will help healthcare providers decrease medical errors, create a customized treatment plan, and recommend prescriptions with accurate medicines. It will also have the ability to provide the patients with a skilled and trusted advisor for diagnoses based on their behavioral data. Some use cases include:

- Introducing a human-like robot at the reception area that can analyze facial expressions and behavior of the customers to provide responses.
- Using cognitive computing such as IBM Watson to help doctors create personalized treatment plans for cancer patients based on the genomic information from cancer cells for that patient.
- Using virtual agents that can understand natural language, patients can now book appointments with their doctors or find information regarding any disease, healthcare topic, and vaccine.
- Using deep learning, physicians have the ability to enter patient diseases and symptoms, which then generates a range of possible diagnoses accompanied by images. This would help diagnose the patients without bias toward any recent occurrence of a similar condition.

- Hospital Administration: AI technology has the potential to improve operational efficiency within the hospital administration and internal operations and enhance patient satisfaction. Some use cases include:

  - Using algorithms to evaluate past and present trends in patient insights and create a predictive schedule for hospital nurses. This type of scheduling reduces labor costs, as the hospital would be less likely to be over-or understaffed.
  - Using biometrics identification to protect the medical records of the patients from fraud and misuse.

Consumer Goods and Retail Industry

Consumer goods and retail stores have started to deploy AI across the value chain, from sourcing, goods receipt, and back-office operations to delivery. Some of the areas and use cases where AI can be applied in the consumer goods and retail industry are described below:

- Sales and Marketing: Text analytics, machine learning, virtual agents, and image recognition can be creatively used to understand customer preferences, test advertisement effectiveness, and quickly rebalance advertising and marketing strategies to be more effective, leading to an increase in revenues. Some use cases include:

  - AI can be used in creating advertisements that can communicate the idea without being biased toward any particular religion, culture, or habit.
  - Creating an advertisement to effectively market the product based on the real-time emotion of the public on any event or incident that has an immediate impact on the purchasing pattern.

- Building an algorithm to compute how happy a customer is with the service for a repeat purchase, to identify the upcoming trend and the inventory the enterprise should buy associated with the trend, and to learn from images the style and fashion that are liked by consumers so that products can be made accordingly.
- Using image recognition by creating a fitting room where the mirror automatically recognizes the clothes carried by the customer and populates with additional colors and sizes to choose from, which immediately notifies the sales associate with just one tap on the image. The mirror is also capable of collecting data and providing analytics to the merchandising team for the goods that are frequently brought into the fitting room but not purchased by customers.

- Supply Chain Management: Robotics and machine learning are used by retailers to optimize supply chain management including real-time forecasting and inventory levels. Some use cases include:

  - Using robots that can walk around the store autonomously to recognize goods and load at the appropriate shelves, track inventory, and place orders to vendors for items low in stock. The next level would be when robots can replace humans at the cash counter and service the customers.
  - Using advanced robotics and automated guided vehicles, entire end-to-end supply chain planning can be optimized, resulting in stock accuracy, a reduction in truck loading time, and wastage elimination.

- Delivery: As many retailers are not manufacturers, the use of AI has not been as prevalent compared to organizations involved in manufacturing only. Machine learning and robotics can be leveraged to increase operational efficiency, create a safe environment and workplace, and minimize risk. Some use cases include:

  - Some of the large online retailers such as Amazon use robots at their fulfillment centers to optimize the picking, packing, and shipping process. The robots roam around the shelves to pick goods and carry them to the warehouse, which has resulted in a significant reduction of packing and shipping time, making on-time delivery to customers a reality.
  - Machine learning can be deployed in agricultural fields to monitor moisture levels of crops at various depths. The data is then sent to a web-based interface where the information can be analyzed centrally to make timely irrigation decisions, preventing the crop from getting destroyed or losing nutrients.
  - When a customer orders food online, delivering the food to the customer involves time to prepare the meal in the kitchen, time for the

delivery person to reach the restaurant and pick up the meal, and time to get the meal from the restaurant to the customer. Machine learning can be utilized to analyze the past collected data and estimate the time to optimize the cost and delivery time of every order.

- Back Office: CPG and retail organizations operate with a very competitive and thin margin due to severe competition. Text analytics, video analytics, and virtual agents can be deployed to automate repetitive processes, better manage their workforce, and reduce any loss due to theft. Some use cases include:
  - Timely response to customers has always been a challenge in the CPG industry. A machine learning model can be built and trained from thousands of past messages from customers to identify, categorize, and prioritize customer e-mails and provide an automated response with a human element to it.
  - Using facial recognition and biometrics identification on the images captured by the cameras in a store, a retailer cross-references the person's identity with a database for a possible match with past shoplifters or known criminals. The data can be explored further to identify premium customers and recommend to them product ideas and matches when they are passing through a particular aisle.

Oil and Gas Industry

The energy industry comprising oil and gas companies is applying AI in security and controls, production optimization, internal process improvement, predictive asset analytics and monitoring, and stakeholder management including customers and vendors.

Some of the areas and use cases where AI can be applied in the oil and gas industry are described below:

- Upstream: Robotics is used upstream to maximize oil extraction, provide safety measures and alerts for work in a hazardous environment, optimize oil and gas reserves, improve capital-intensive processes such as equipment monitoring, and safety checking. Video analytics, deep learning, virtual agents, and natural language processing are also used to enhance operational efficiencies. Some use cases include:
  - Robots are deployed to monitor equipment and carry out safety checks at remote locations where it is extremely difficult for humans to work in adverse weather conditions. The sensors, cameras, and wireless communications allow centralized monitoring of the infrastructure by a worker from a safe location.

- Robots help in gathering meteorological data from the sea to assist in oil and gas exploration and production efforts.
- Predictive analytics are used to provide insights when the equipment requires maintenance even before a breakdown, resulting in huge savings by preventing a complete halt in operations.

- Midstream: Robotics is used midstream for inspection of assets in difficult situations and environments, resulting in cost savings and process optimization. Some use cases include:

  - Drones can be deployed to inspect pipelines both on land and in water to provide alerts on any maintenance issues for proactive action.
  - Robots are used to inspect oil, liquefied petroleum, and hazardous chemical storage tanks from a safety perspective. This reduces the exposure of humans to adverse and unsafe conditions, resulting in time and insurance cost savings.

- Downstream: Text analytics is used by downstream retail stores to derive insights and customer satisfaction, while video analytics is used at gas stations to track any fraudulent activity and maintain security. Some use cases include:

  - Surveillance systems powered by AI and video analytics can be used by the oil and gas downstream companies for security at their retail locations. They also help to keep track of any fraudulent customers based on historical data records.
  - Biometric security systems can be deployed at highly sophisticated plants to prevent any security threats caused by misuse of access cards.
  - Fingerprinting is getting replaced by codes for employees to access secure areas and records at gas stations, as this results in the reduction of the crime rate.

Insurance Industry

Insurance companies are adopting AI to maximize the customer experience, offer new products, accelerate business growth, increase operational efficiency in claims processing, and build competitive advantage through pricing strategies. Some of the areas and use cases where AI can be applied in the insurance industry are described below:

- Underwriting: AI systems can be used to perform research and combine, improve, and present required information to underwriters so that they can concentrate on core underwriting activities. Some use cases include:

- Using artificial intelligence techniques and rules engine to automate the underwriting of life insurance applications and create operational efficiency by following the underwriter guidelines.
- Combining machine-learning techniques and data analysis to assess the creditworthiness of the borrower and provide instant loan decisions, resulting in a lower default rate for the enterprise.
- Deploying virtual assistants to help the insurance agents get the quotes for some of the complex products without waiting in the queue for the call center agent.
- Deploying sensors on devices such as helmets to monitor data and prevent workers from getting injured on the work site. This helps maintain the risk for workers, which affects the underwriter's decision-making process

- Claims Management: Artificial intelligence can be applied to automate the claims data management process and detect any potential fraud when a customer applies for a claim. It can also help to evaluate the damage based on the overall trend and fast-track the claim to the customer. Some use cases include:

  - Deploying drones to inspect disaster sites with no manual intervention and processing the claims faster.
  - Using artificial intelligence to recognize and check all critical documents required to process a claim that has been received, which streamlines manual tasks and the decision-making process, leading to more efficient claim processing.

- Customer Experience: Not only can artificial intelligence be applied to provide faster and superior customer service using bots, but its deep learning capability provides insurers the ability to explore and launch new products, in an altogether new geographical area with newer customer segments based on trends, patterns and offer recommendations leading to the expansion of product lines and revenue. Some use cases include:

  - Using a video analytics platform to reduce driving accidents by sending alerts to drivers through real-time monitoring of the weather and road conditions.
  - Using voice biometrics and natural language processing to analyze the behavioral patterns of a customer's voice when they call the customer center to access the account and compare it with the stored voiceprint. This saves the hassle of providing multiple identifications and remembering the answers to the security questions, thus enhancing the customer experience.

- Using cognitive bots to work as sales agents for making calls to customers, gathering their requirements, answering all the questions, and issuing the policy on the spot without being pushy like human agents.
- Using artificial intelligence and deep learning tools to help investment managers analyze unstructured financial data from sources such as news articles and analyst reports, and provide valuable insights and recommendations to customers so that they can make good investment decisions.

Manufacturing Industry

Companies in the industrial sector are utilizing AI for operational efficiency in the warehouse and factory to improve workforce productivity, increase operational efficiency, and do accurate planning. Some of the areas and use cases where AI can be applied in the manufacturing industry are described below:

- Warehouse and Plant: AI with intelligent machines has the power to create a smart factory where the robots will replace human workers, leading to optimization and efficiency in manufacturing. Some use cases include:
  - Utilizing intelligent robots in the daily operations on a manufacturing assembly line to execute tasks such as placing inventory at the correct location, inspecting, packaging, palletizing, and precision assembly.
  - Using bots to perform the repetitive tasks at the manufacturing plant to increase throughput and save labor costs.
  - Enabling robots to deliver efficient instructions to workers based on the analyses of a large amount of data and the past routine and habits of the workers to improve work efficiency.
- Field Operations: AI is disrupting the way businesses are traditionally run for large-scale operations such as mass production of products, managing heavy machinery and equipment, and worker safety, leading to operational excellence. Some use cases include:
  - Utilizing artificial intelligence in road construction equipment so that it is intelligent and can exert the correct force on the soil to make it dense.
  - Using robots backed by machine learning capabilities in farm fields to make the robots learn the shape and color of the crop and its leaves to determine the need for watering or removal of any species destroying the crop.

- Using visual analytics through the camera to watch the entry gate in case a passenger follows someone else for entry without a ticket. It has the capability to send the image and alert the inspector, who can then decide to stop the passenger and ask them to produce a valid ticket.

- Planning: AI is involved in making real-time decisions by simulating real-life scenarios before actual manufacturing to identify problems in the simulated environment and take corrective action, leading to significant cost savings and efficiency. Some use cases include:
  - Using AI to schedule and produce weekly and quarterly plans for all the engineering-related tasks to maximize resource utilization, improve maintenance efficiency, and realize significant cost and time savings.
  - Using big data and artificial intelligence to analyze data related to ocean shipping and economic affairs and forecast the shipping market and bunker prices with greater accuracy.

AI Opportunities by Functional Area

An enterprise can deploy the artificial intelligence solution as part of the transformation journey in various business areas such as finance, planning, supply chain, procurement, sales and distribution, customer service, and HR. Some of the AI capabilities involved to derive the benefits include machine learning, predictive analytics, virtual agents, intelligent automation, and natural language processing. Some of the use cases and benefits of AI by functional area within the enterprise have been listed below for reference.

Record to Report

AI can be deployed in the finance function for the following processes:

- General Ledger Accounting:
  - Prepare, classify, and post journal entries to the correct chart of accounts and legal entity within the global enterprise.
  - Reconcile the subledger to the general ledger such as banks or assets to general ledger.
  - Audit the preparation of expense reports.
  - Accelerate the month-end closing process by increasing the accuracy of ledger posting and reducing any late adjustments posting.
  - Reduce manual inputs leading to human errors and fraud.

- Decrease the number of unreconciled intercompany transactions.
- Adhere to accounting controls; comply with enterprise data standards, and maintain stringent security access.
- Maintain and sync master data in various systems.

■ Accounts Receivable:

- Identify, match, and clear cash transactions.
- Generate and send reminder e-mails and late notices to the customers.
- Improve revenue and cash flow by reducing the number of disputed invoices.
- Monitor customer credit.
- Improve customer satisfaction by reducing the number of days with deductions outstanding, decreasing the number of credit holds, and lowering the cycle time to resolve disputes.
- Improve collections, and reduce customer risk and bad debt exposure.
- Streamline the billing processes.

■ Accounts Payable:

- Identify, match, and clear cash transactions.
- Utilize efficient self-service requisitions and e-invoicing.
- Utilize automated invoice processing with reduced manual process steps during invoice verification.
- Validate the pricing and terms before the payment due date and reduce manual errors.
- Improve working capital by reducing the payment leakage and optimizing the days payable outstanding.
- Maximize savings by utilizing the early payment discount.

■ Financial Planning and Analysis:

- Speed to insight and analysis of complex data.
- Use of predictive analytics to improve the accuracy in forecasting and planning, and provide business insights.

Procure to Pay

AI can be deployed in the supply chain function for the following processes:

■ Supplier Strategy and Planning:

- Provide 24/7 virtual assistance to handle any vendor inquiries.
- Eliminate manual processes related to vendor invoicing.
- Automate dynamic discounting solutions.
- Automate demand forecasting using real-time data and baseline forecasts to create a more efficient production process and eliminate waste.

- Gather, analyze, and input data on materials and labor to recommend the optimum level of output.
- Sourcing:
  - Automate price benchmarking and predictive pricing and costing.
  - Analyze information on potential suppliers and provide a recommendation based on the requirements of the enterprise.
  - Gather real-time data on all suppliers and manage vendor claims using virtual agents.
- Supplier Engagement:
  - Analyze the product portfolio of the enterprise to discover patterns in the market and identify the products that are the best sellers.
  - Identify new product opportunities by gathering buyers' requirements and demand for the product that does not exist in the market.
  - Analyze competitors, current pricing trends in the market, and supplier profiles to recommend negotiation strategy and target pricing.
- Performance Management:
  - Identify patterns causing vendor performance issues.
  - Analyze data in performance reports and recommend changes to be implemented in supplier operations.
- Procurement:
  - Monitor compliance with the contract.
  - Extract requisite data from the contract.
- Invoice Processing:
  - Scanning of invoices and routing to the right department.
  - Approval and routing for payment.

Order to Cash

AI can be deployed in the sales and customer service function for the following processes:

- Customer Service:
  - Route customer applications to the person responsible for review.
  - Automate approval for customer applications meeting guidelines.
  - Route approval to the approver responsible for customer applications outside of guidelines.
  - Notify requestor after application approval.
  - Utilize virtual agents to support customer requests.
  - Support the customer with a diversion to either human or virtual agents based on the complexity of the request.

- Provide intelligent insight for customer recommendations on products and services.
- Route service requests to most suitable agent based on agent availability, nature of the request, customer attributes, and other factors.
- Automatically assess real-time customer satisfaction through sentiment and tone analysis.
- Augment the automated customer support capability in phases by continuously training the model with the data sets.

- Product Strategy and Promotion:
  - Analyze product data to uncover patterns in the market and identify which marketing campaigns have provided the best results.
  - Leverage predictive analytics to deep-dive the user rating data or preference for products on the market.
  - Recommend additional capabilities to increase product profitability.

- Product Promotion:
  - Apply machine learning to analyze historical success with delivery channels and recommend the most effective channel for product promotion and campaign.
  - Apply computer vision techniques to detect patterns and effectiveness of promotional material and recommend specific promotional material including color, content, images, etc.

Human Resources

AI can be deployed in the HR and talent management function for the following processes:

- HR Policies and Practices:
  - Use a combination of both human and virtual agents to intelligently manage employee inquiries and route to human HR personnel and virtual agents based on the type of request. For example, a virtual agent would support benefits inquiry and policy questions, while a human representative would support employee complaints.
  - Discover what employees and prospective new hires need from HR while working or at the time of hiring at the enterprise.
  - Automatically evaluate real-time employee satisfaction using sentiment and tone analysis.
  - Increase the automated support capabilities by training the virtual bots continuously.

- Workforce Hiring Strategy:
  - The enterprise can assess the existing skill set within the organization and identify gaps in expertise by combining human input and machine learning recommendations on the hiring strategy.
  - Improve workforce utilization by assessing the demand, skill set, and employee availability in real time and assigning projects and tasks to the employees as deemed fit.
  - Minimize relocation and transfer cost of the geographical spread-out workforce by matching skill sets and demand and assigning work within the closest proximity to the home office of the employee.
- Workforce Scheduling:
  - Scan existing employee or potential hire resumes matching project roles that align with experience and skill set and recommend the best fit.
  - Analyze the strengths and weaknesses of each employee and recommend teams that will most efficiently and productively work together.
  - Analyze employee performance and skill set and recommend opportunities to align with their career trajectory.

Use Cases

Artificial intelligence use cases are certain scenarios where the goals and objectives of an enterprise are addressed to automate certain business processes to save costs and make the operations more efficient. Let's study some scenarios along with real-life case studies to see how the journey to robotic process automation is facilitated to result in an intelligent enterprise.

1. Case Study: Utilizing a Digital Agent (Bot) to Perform Online Banking Operations and Enrich the Customer Experience
   - Scenario
     - A large bank with a long-term vision to transform its internet banking division wanted to create a brand name for itself by providing digital banking services that provided its customers access to the bank from anywhere in the world.
   - Approach
     - A digital assistant was created to provide banking customers with digital banking operations via social media such as opening a new account, checking balances, and transferring money.

- Results
  - The bank was able to get customer engagement and retention by running new types of social media campaigns.
  - New revenue streams were introduced such as micropayment operations, where the banking customers can perform simple transactions such as mobile charge, bank transfers, etc.
  - The bank was able to enrich the data by integrating the customer profile with their social media data such as taste, preferences, channels, etc., and providing more personalized service.
  - Customer service was enhanced by providing accurate answers to the requests of the banking customers.
  - The bots answered a lot of customer queries, resulting in a reduction of calls at the call center, which finally resulted in call center cost savings.

2. Case Study: Vendors Interacting with the Virtual Agent for Help Desk Assistance Related to Accounts Payable
   - Scenario
     - One of the world's largest oil and gas companies generates products and services to analyze, drill, evaluate, complete, and produce oil and gas reserves and then transport and refine the hydrocarbons.
     - The enterprise wanted to deploy the vendor invoice inquiry service.
   - Approach
     - The accounts payable solution was deployed and configured on the enterprise's self-service portal.
     - It enabled the vendors to interact with the chatbot for assistance related to invoices and payments.
   - Results
     - Vendors were able to interact with the digital assistant chatbot and receive the status of their invoices.
     - The services provided by the chatbot included checking invoice status, searching for invoices in back-end systems, uploading invoices, and creating troubleshooting service tickets.
     - Significant cost savings were achieved over five years due to eliminated human interactions and more efficient processing.

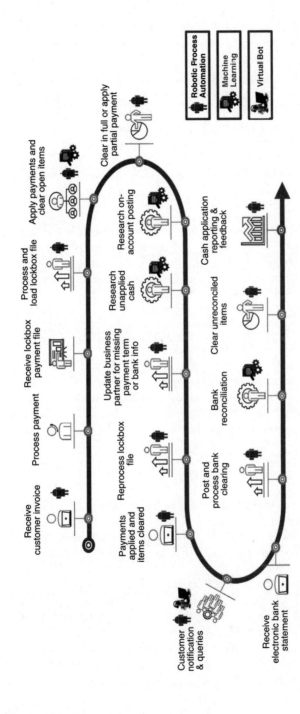

Figure 7.2 Cash application in accounts receivable.

177

3. Case Study: Auto-Cash Application to Clear Open Accounts Receivable Invoices

- Scenario
  - The auto-cash application tools on the market including the ERPs can only clear 40–70% of the open invoices due to their inability to handle unstructured data and complex exceptions on how the customers make the payments.
  - A/R accountants and the collections team need to spend significant time to research and reconcile payments with invoices rather than focusing on analyzing and monitoring the collections activity.
- Approach
  - The accounts receivable process needs to be decomposed into the various activities, and the application of AI techniques such as cognitive automation, machine learning, or virtual bots need to be determined for each of the processes where the enterprise can get the value, as shown in Figure 7.2.
- Results
  - Machine learning and smart matching capabilities help in increasing auto-match rates.
  - Enhanced visibility of cash improves cash flow forecasting and working capital management.
  - Improvement in outstanding receivables at the invoice level helps the collection team drive more focused and informed communication with the customers.

Conclusion

The emergence of digital technologies has reformed customer service and satisfaction levels in the last several years. In the coming years, the world is going to face even more profound changes as artificial intelligence creates more advanced cognitive assistants to help enterprises interact with customers and exceed their expectations.

AI is the foundation of how businesses will be run in the future, as it drives enterprise growth, sustainability, profitability, and high performance. The AI-enabled intelligent enterprise strategy drives efficient and effective processes with cognitive RPA and machine learning capabilities embedded in it, and intelligent products that can sense, think, act, and adapt based on environmental conditions and leverage the capability to extract unstructured complex data and get insights.

CHAPTER 8

Machine Learning

T his chapter provides an understanding of machine learning technology, the mechanics and challenges, and the rationale for enterprises to move towards it. It also discusses the key steps that should be taken to build a machine learning model, the implementation methodology, and some of the typical industry solutions and use cases for deploying machine learning to predict future outcomes and make the enterprise intelligent.

Machine Learning Overview

Machine learning is the pattern recognition technology that allows machines and computer programs to automatically improve their performance through experience by learning, analyzing, and making predictions based on historical data. It performs data analysis by using algorithms that iteratively learn from that data and present insights. It provides consistent, repeatable decisions and results by learning from prior computations. Machine learning empowers the computer system to imitate the working of the human brain.

Understanding Machine Learning

Some of the characteristics of machine learning are described below:

- Machine learning is a subset of artificial intelligence, while deep learning is a subset of machine learning.
- Data science is a combination of machine learning, computer science, and visualization.
- Big data and data mining support machine learning, which, in turn, supports natural language processing, speech recognition patterns, computer vision, and simulated modeling.
- In a traditional programming mode, a set of rules are defined to convert the input data to the desired output. In machine learning, based on the combination of a large amount of input data and output examples, the rules or algorithms are derived.

- Machine learning models are built based on observations.
- Machine learning learns the rules and recognizes patterns to make optimum decisions or predictions.

Why Are Enterprises Moving Towards Machine Learning?

Some of the key reasons machine learning has gained popularity within the enterprise are mentioned below:

- Machine learning can be used in various computing tasks where designing and programming explicit algorithms is not a feasible option by the enterprise.
- Machine learning requires a huge amount of historical data for learning, and in the current scenario, enormous amounts of data are produced on a daily basis. Thus, there is no shortage of data points.
- The storage of such a huge amount of data is much more affordable now compared to some years back.
- The cost of computational power to process the data has significantly decreased.
- Machine learning can deliver faster and more accurate results, as it can leverage the big data capability of analyzing bigger and more complex data, drawing valuable insights from the data, reducing risks, automating processes, and improving customer satisfaction.
- Machine learning can spot differences and similarities not visible to the human eye between each data point and make sensible groupings based on these characteristics, which the enterprise can leverage to offer personalized services and product offerings catering to each group's requirements.
- Machine learning can create high-performing predictive models from the data without requiring explicit programming or coding instructions.

Mechanics of Machine Learning

Machine learning works on the following mechanism as described below.

- Collecting Data: This activity requires gathering historical data to learn from the trends and patterns.
- Preparing Data: This activity requires selecting the correct data from the collected data.

- Training the Model: This activity requires selecting the appropriate algorithm as required to train the model from the data.
- Evaluating the Model: This activity requires testing the accuracy of the model built during the training exercise.
- Improving Performance: This activity requires choosing another model for enhanced performance.
- Executing the Model: This activity requires running the model for predictive analytics and data insights.

Challenges Faced by Machine Learning

Some of the key machine learning challenges that enterprises need to overcome to reap the full benefits of the technology are described below.

- Data: In most enterprises, the data quality is quite poor and is inaccessible, as it is stored in silos on multiple legacy systems. The integration of data from all the sources onto a cloud platform is key to a successful machine learning solution.
- Customer Preference: Some of the older generations and less tech-savvy customers still prefer interacting with humans rather than communicating with robots. The enterprise needs to educate and showcase the benefits to these customers to on-board them with current trends.
- Regulation: Some self-learning models cannot be traditionally validated and therefore may be deemed insufficient by the regulatory authorities in certain industries. The enterprise needs to conduct thorough research into the legal and statutory requirements prior to implementing the solution.
- Skill Set: The introduction of machine learning solutions to a business requires a shift in skill set and talent requirements from operational management to analytics and data science. The enterprise needs to build and train its employees to cope with the new trends and needs to hire the right coders to enhance and manage the solution.
- Culture: Traditionally, businesses have the mind-set of keeping the data within themselves. With machine learning, there has to be a shift in the enterprise culture, with users being provided with incentives and encouraged to share data between business divisions so that proper insights can be extracted.
- Tools: As the machine learning technology is still evolving, there are various tools and products that are on the market supporting

the digital transformation. The enterprise needs to do a thorough review of the tools and products before making the purchases for the implementation.

Machine Learning Algorithms

Machine learning algorithms can be broadly classified into the following three types as listed below.

- Supervised: In this model, the computer is presented with the inputs in the form of past data and outputs in the form of labels, and the objective is to create an algorithm and rules that map the inputs to the outputs. The algorithm learns the mapping function from input to output. The algorithm is based on both the input and the output data where the prelabeled data trains the new data to predict outcomes. The model is deployed if the output is satisfactory. Some of the common algorithms in this class include the following:
  - Classification: This includes categorizing new data against a predefined set such as classifying e-mail into the spam folder, predicting employee turnover, etc.
  - Regression: This includes predicting a target value based on a set of learned data such as predicting real estate sales or the stock market based on historical data patterns, predicting a student test score based on his test scores in prior examinations, etc.
- Unsupervised: In this model, the algorithm needs to find a structure from the input data, as no labels or output is provided. The algorithm is based on the input data where the nonlabeled data self-organizes to identify patterns. The model is deployed if the algorithm is satisfactory. Some of the common algorithms in this class include the following:
  - Clustering: This includes grouping the data into categories based on their similarity to each other such as customer segmentation, grouping similar products for analysis, etc.
  - Dimension Reduction: This includes reducing the number of dimensions that are represented in a data set while minimizing loss of any critical information such as different features in a garment, attributes of a customer, etc.
- Reinforcement: In this model, the computer program has an objective to achieve the desired outcome by interacting with the dynamic environment. The algorithm is based on the input data where the model

learns from interacting with the environment. Examples include driving a car, real-time decision making while playing a game against an opponent, etc. The model is always in the production state and needs to learn from the real data to present actionable outcomes.

Enterprise Machine Learning Model

The life cycle of a machine learning model involves multiple iterations of preparing the data set, selecting the model, testing the model, and occasionally revisiting objectives when there are barriers from data and algorithms. Machine learning requires a laborious process of acquiring and cleansing large amounts of data and modifying the algorithm before the model can be deployed for use.

The enterprise should take into consideration the following key steps for building a machine learning model:

- Generating the Hypothesis:
  - The enterprise needs to define the problem that it needs to resolve.
  - The objectives for the modeling exercise need to be clearly stated.
  - The approach needs to be laid out for applying the machine learning model.
- Preparing the Data:
  - Collect and gather the relevant data sets to be used to train and evaluate a model.
  - Variables need to be included as part of inputs into the model.
  - Labels need to be classified to identify the expected outcomes.
- Setting Up the Experiment:
  - Prepare data and structure experiments that will be used to test the hypothesis.
  - Divide the data sets into testing, training, and validation buckets.
  - Define how the performance of the model will be assessed against the defined problem.
- Selecting the Model:
  - Multiple models might have to be built with data sets and variation in algorithms.
  - The enterprise needs to select the model or suite of models that is a close match to address the problem.
  - The enterprise might also need to define the architecture and select the features for the model.

- Training the Model:
  - Training the model with multiple data sets using the designated training examples is key to building a successful model.
  - Teach the model how to self-correct in the future.
  - The results of training the model need to be compared against the testing data set.
  - The model needs to be redesigned if the performance from training is below expectations.
- Evaluating the Model:
  - Apply the test and validation data sets to the model.
  - Measure the performance of the model against the stated objective of the enterprise.
  - Compare the results of the model with the defined acceptance criteria.
  - Make the decision about whether the solution as per the built model is feasible for the issue.
- Deploying the Model:
  - Deploy the model for use within the enterprise production environment.
  - Continuously monitor the model performance based on historical data against feedback from the actual real-world data.
  - The enterprise needs to put in effort to retrain the models as needed or when new examples become available that need to be captured in the functioning of the model.

Machine Learning Implementation Methodology

Similar to artificial intelligence, the effort to drive the implementation of machine learning requires the collection and storage of rich data repository within the enterprise which can be utilized along with untapped data to learn and discover hidden insights and make the enterprise intelligent. Machine learning delivers high quality forecasting and real-time intelligent predictive solution by improving the performance through experience.

The methodology for machine learning implementation is driven by an iterative discovery and exploration approach using an agile methodology sprints cycle to support improvement and selection of the algorithms. The enterprise should consider the following phases when implementing a machine learning solution:

Project Preparation

The enterprise should conduct the following activities during the project preparation and environment setting phase:

- Analyze and prioritize use cases and scenarios.
- Assess and confirm machine learning algorithms.
- Identify data sources, formats, volumes, and processing needs.
- Confirm the data loading strategy.
- Confirm development and runtime platform specification, including hosting, network, tooling, security, access, etc.
- Validate all the assumptions with the business.

Data Review

The enterprise should conduct the following activities during the data review and scope validation setting phase:

- Identify the current processes for each scenario that are within the scope.
- Define machine learning to- be process and output.
- Confirm evaluation criteria for machine learning algorithms in each given scenario.
- Access and profile source data.
- Collect and load data into the environment.
- Assess, clean, condition, and transform data sets.
- Provide development environments and runtime platform.
- Identify all the technical and business resources that would be required for the implementation.

Algorithm Development

The enterprise should conduct the following activities during the development of the machine learning algorithms phase:

- Schedule sprints related to develop, test, train, and evaluate.
- Prioritize algorithms and scenarios for subsequent sprints.
- Review the results for each scenario included in sprints.
- Design and develop new machine learning algorithms to get the desired outcome.
- Adjust the algorithms for speed and accuracy.

Test and Train

The enterprise should conduct the following activities during the testing and training of the model phase:

- Train and test algorithms.
- Present results of algorithms including any plots, graphs, tables, and observations.
- Cleanse and transform data sets for new test scenario.
- Generate any required artificial data set.
- Prepare training and testing data sets.
- Run the end-to-end journey and identify any gaps.
- Resolve gaps and identify any workarounds.

Evaluate and Monitor

The enterprise should conduct the following activities during the evaluating, monitoring, and reporting of the results of the model phase:

- The enterprise needs to aggregate the final outcome for each of the scenarios and algorithms tested to make the analysis.
- Evaluate the outcome against the objectives and criteria defined earlier, including accuracy and algorithms.
- Determine the feasibility of the machine learning approach based on the criteria and identify other scenarios that could potentially be used for the machine learning solution.
- Document environment and data sets used for each of the scenarios executed for future reference.
- Document any technical findings from the platform and tools perspective that the enterprise should consider in the next wave of implementation.

Machine Learning Solutions by Industry

Machine learning provides solutions to some of the most critical challenges faced by enterprises in various industries. Let's analyze some of the industry-specific business areas and use cases where an enterprise can utilize a machine learning solution to resolve problems.

Banking Industry

Some of the areas and use cases where machine learning can be applied in the banking industry are described below:

- Machine learning helps in detecting fraud, anti-money-laundering activities, and credit risk exposure.
- Machine learning helps in generating automated reports for compliance and solutions for stress testing, and conducting a behavioral analysis of e-mails to determine suspicious employee behavior.
- Banks can segment their customers and offer a personalized, targeted product offering using unsupervised learning algorithms and techniques.
- Machine learning offers banks the speed and agility they need to compete with other banking and financial firms and to make use of big data.
- Machine learning provides the opportunity to automate many back-office risks, finance, and regulatory reporting processes in conjunction with robotics.
- Digital and machine learning skills are in very high demand these days. The algorithms can be used to evaluate resumes of successful employees and search for and identify candidates with the required traits and experience for new hire.
- Machine learning accurately predicts the credit default likelihood based on both quantitative and qualitative data.
- It makes real-time credit decisions for self-service credit applications by removing the need for any manual checks, approvals, and workflows.

Use Cases

Machine learning use cases are the scenarios where the enterprise objectives are addressed to make predictions from historical or new data. Listed below are some real-life case studies to understand how the journey to machine learning can be facilitated to result in an intelligent enterprise:

1. Case Study: Detecting Credit Card Fraudulent Activities
   - Scenario
     - A global credit card provider wanted to invest in the machine learning algorithms to analyze historical transaction data for each customer and understand their individual spending patterns

where any anomaly would indicate fraud at a very early stage, thus reducing their exposure to risk.

- Approach
  - The credit card provider implemented the machine learning algorithms that had the ability to learn from the new scenarios and data and quickly adapt to new means of fraud. This would help the enterprise stay ahead of people involved in fraudulent activities.
  - The technology was deployed to automatically review transactions in real time with huge amounts of data for millions of customers from multiple sources. This would have not been possible with human intervention.
- Results
  - The credit card provider was able to lower losses from fraud.
  - They were able to lower operational costs with significantly less manual analysis.
  - They were able to improve customer service.
  - They were able to improve their enterprise reputation by reducing the number of frauds.
  - They were able to reduce regulatory risk arising from the theft of credit card information.

2. Case Study: Detecting Quality Issues Using a Combination of the Internet of Things and Machine Learning Algorithms
- Scenario
  - A leading mining company installed sensors to take readings every five seconds throughout the manufacturing process but the data was not used effectively.
  - The enterprise wanted to use sensor data to predict quality issues in advance in order to take corrective action.
- Approach
  - The enterprise used machine learning techniques to predict quality issues.
  - Quality issues were predicted multiple hours before the occurrence of the event.
  - The algorithms maintained the balance of accurately predicting poor quality and the risk of false alerts when the quality was good.
- Results
  - The solution accurately predicted the quality problems in more than 90% of the scenarios.

- The false alerts were less than 5%.
- The enterprise was able to identify the three most important drivers of quality problems.
- The enterprise was able to reduce the number of sensors and their associated data to optimize the quality of prediction.

3. Case Study: Analytics for a New Product Launch

- Scenario
  - One of the largest footwear companies has many seasonal products with short life cycles and low demand accuracy. The retailers ordered and returned the unsold products, which resulted in high retailer returns and huge revenue losses.
  - The enterprise wanted to leverage machine learning and optimization techniques to create a new, accurate way of predicting new product sales and allocating capacity accordingly.

- Approach
  - The enterprise collected the historical data on product launches and used machine learning algorithms to determine the size and shape of their demand profiles.
  - The new products were mapped to prior launches using advanced methods and multiple attributes such as retailer account, price, customer age group, etc.
  - The production and allocation were now based on demand profiles.

- Results
  - The enterprise was able to predict demand for new products a year in advance of the launch of the product in the market.
  - All the production and allocation activity was managed by machine learning algorithms.
  - The accuracy of the forecast improved by more than 20%, which resulted in a significant reduction in lost sales.

Conclusion

Machine learning is one of the most advanced data analytics tools that is available to predict future outcomes. It is changing the analytics landscape and ecosystem from the traditional product-centric to customer-centric data analysis, batch processing to real-time information, individual data models to relationship-based data models, structured data to insights from any data, and static models to self-learning models.

The primary goal of an enterprise in using machine learning technology is to build new algorithms or use the existing ones and train the model to learn from the enterprise-specific data to provide accurate predictions or find a pattern for the unseen similar data in order to have a competitive advantage.

CHAPTER 9

Blockchain

*T*his chapter provides an overview of blockchain as a distributed ledger technology along with its benefits to the enterprise and a detailed understanding of the architecture supporting it. It also discusses the implementation methodology and some of the typical applications and use cases for deploying blockchain to securely transfer information with trust and make the enterprise intelligent.

Blockchain Overview

Blockchain is in its nascent stage; it is a complex technology capable of disrupting many businesses and operating models of enterprises in the long run. Blockchain is generally associated with bitcoin, but that is not correct. While blockchain is the technology, bitcoin is just one of its applications for which it has been proven to date that the technology works.

Blockchain is considered to be one of the most transformative innovations since the inception of the internet. As it poses threat to the existing businesses, it also encompasses new opportunities and business models for the enterprise to adopt. This is one of the paths for an enterprise to become intelligent and get ahead in the race from its competitors.

What Is Blockchain?

Without going deep into the technical aspects, let's understand the fundamentals of what blockchain is, how the technology works, and most important, how it can be leveraged in various use cases both within the organization and to customers.

Blockchain is the list of data that is shared among the users or participants such that the integrity of the data is maintained and all users access the same set of data, the data is secure and cannot be altered by the users, and the data is not maintained at a single location and, hence, it cannot be altered by someone with power at the centralized location.

Blockchain comprises a series of blocks, with each block made up of several transactions, and each transaction storing a value. Thus, blockchain is the technology which keeps the shared ledger of transactional data secure, indisputable, and decentralized. This technology was invented with the use of bitcoin as a digital currency which uses the ledger to record, store, and maintain the integrity of all transactions between accounts, similar to how banks maintain various bank accounts with a set of all records transacted through the accounts.

In the blockchain, the participants are recognized as a distributed network of computers where they execute transactions and exchange information with trust and no involvement of any third-party validation. The participants could be individual users, organizations, or devices.

Need is the mother of all invention. Blockchain technology meets the following needs:

- Multiple users need to view the same data.
- Multiple users need to record transactions and update data.
- Multiple users need to trust and authenticate the transactions.
- Need to simplify the ecosystem by reducing intermediaries and reduce cost.
- Need to have secure and unalterable data while maintaining transparency among the users and integrity of the data records.

Salient Features of Blockchain

As a globally distributed database which allows secure transactions with no need for centralized control, blockchain has the following key features (Figure 9.1):

- Distributed Database: All the transactions are recorded in a globally distributed database of independent computers. Thus, no centralized version of the data is available for someone to corrupt.
- Peer-to-peer Network: Blockchain uses a peer-to-peer network, where all users have access to the same data.
- Data Replication: The transactional data is replicated to all the systems in the network on an almost real-time basis.
- Transparency: All users can add blocks and have access to the complete set of records and transaction history.
- Single Source of Truth: All users have access to the most recent version of the data, which ensures all the peers have a single source of truth without the need to reconcile the data from multiple sources.
- Open Source: The technology is available for anyone to use at no cost.

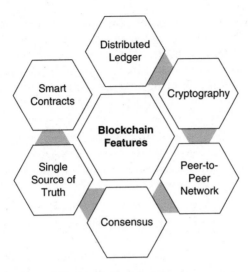

Figure 9.1   Key blockchain features.

- Trust: Allows individuals and enterprises to transfer value and information through an identified address that is secure and can be trusted.
- Safekeeping: Manages the entire life cycle of the asset, contract, and data ownership without having physical possession.
- Decentralization: Blockchain operates in a way where all the users in the network have the same access, with no central authority in control.
- Consensus: Any transaction posted in the blockchain is validated by achieving a majority consensus among the users within the network.
- Cryptography: Blockchain uses cryptography and digital signatures to authenticate the users, validate the transactions, and maintain security.
- Smart Contracts: Blockchain has the ability to automate rule-based agreements and run additional business logic that requires limited human intervention.

Benefit to the Enterprise

Having gone through the features of blockchain, the question arises as to what benefit it brings to the enterprise and how the enterprise can take full benefit of blockchain technology.

- The distributed ledger makes the data available to all the users in near real time. Thus, it can save substantial employee hours that they would have spent on reconciliation of data from multiple sources and databases.

- Blockchain uses the cryptographic function for security that prevents an unauthorized user from altering a transaction in the network. It saves the enterprise from spending a huge amount on security, as it is built into the design and architecture of blockchain technology. As a data breach is one of the topmost priorities and concerns for any enterprise, this eliminates the possibility for any user to alter the data without authorization from the majority within the network.

- The consensus feature ensures the validity and integrity of the data on the chain, as the users can form a consensus and authenticate the transaction. It helps the enterprise automate the validation process without any paper approval or workflow.

- The shared contracts facilitate the enterprise in automating the agreements with business rules and eliminate the reliance on intermediaries and their fees.

- The settlement and clearing time of financial assets is significantly reduced due to the inherent automation design of blockchain, resulting in lower governance and reconciliation costs.

- Assets can be transferred across the world to any person or machine in seconds or minutes.

- Blockchain enables the tracking of the entire history of an asset and all its associated transactions as it travels in the physical or virtual world.

Evaluation to Implement Blockchain

The enterprise needs to conduct a case study on whether blockchain is the correct solution for its organization or business. The following criteria need to be evaluated to make the judgment:

- Is there a need for multiple users to view and share a common set of data?

- Is there a need for multiple users to simultaneously update and change the data?

- Is there mistrust between the various users viewing or interacting with the data?

- Is there a sufficient number of network participants to reach consensus on the validity of transactions?

- Is there a need for multiple users to verify the transactions that are recorded?

- Is there a need to track and trace real-time information to locate shipments?

- Is there a possibility to reduce cost and complexity by removing intermediaries without impacting the functionality or business process?
- Is there a possibility to reap business benefits by reducing the
  end-to-end time taken for the business process to execute?

Market Pulse

The market for blockchain technology is rapidly growing and is expected to
cross $2.5 billion by 2021. Blockchain is making a paradigm shift in how we
access the internet for gathering and communicating information and how we
can exchange assets using a trusted mechanism. To date, we have been relying
on government or banks as intermediaries to trust and verify information. The
blockchain is the next-gen revolution, where you can eliminate the need for
any intermediary, as the chain is a trusted source of truth. This will help the
enterprise save on intermediary fees and eliminate the bottleneck and time it
takes to retrieve information from such sources.

The concept of blockchain started with bitcoin as a digital currency in
cash-related applications such as currency transfer, remittance, digital payments, etc. The next phase of the revolution is deploying blockchain in the
formation and maintenance of contracts, particularly in the financial services
sector such as bonds, stocks, loans, mortgages, titles, smart property, etc.

Enterprises are researching how blockchain can be utilized in broader
industry applications such as global payments, private records such as
passports and transcripts, government, transportation, utilities, health, cloud
storage, etc., to transform the organization and make it intelligent with
automation, business logic, and algorithms.

Some of the industries and businesses that are prone to disruption
from the blockchain technology include security and commodity exchanges,
financial services, real estate, banking, supply chain, insurance, and brokerage
services.

How Blockchain Works

The working model of blockchain is constructed in a way which allows users
to securely write and update information to the distributed ledger while maintaining a consistent history of transactions and interactions. Figure 9.2 depicts
a simple model of how a transaction is added to the distributed ledger.

- There are four participants in the distributed network of computers as
  shown in Figure 9.2.
- The participants are represented as Nodes marked as 1, 2, 3, and 4.

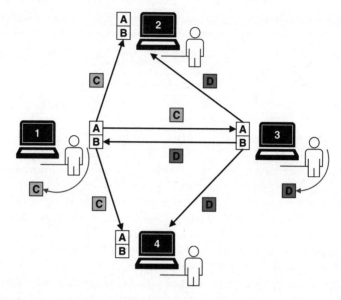

Figure 9.2   Adding a transaction to the blockchain.

- Blocks A and B are part of the distributed ledger shared across the nodes.
- Node 1 adds a transaction C and Node 3 adds a transaction D.
- Corresponding Blocks C and D are created, representing the transactions requested by Nodes 1 and 3.
- Blocks C and D are shared with all other nodes within the network.
- Nodes validate the transaction, and once the consensus from the majority nodes are obtained, the transaction is considered authentic.
- Once validated, the blocks are added to the existing ledger in the blockchain. The new block added is permanent and cannot be altered.
- Each node will now consist of four blocks in the ledger, namely, A, B, C, and D. A and B already existed, while C and D got added to the blockchain.
- This completes the life cycle of a transaction in blockchain.

Some of the functionality of the blockchain technology includes:

- The blockchain consists of **nodes,** which are represented by a computer and its underlying program.
- The blockchain **shares** transactions that represent the exchange of information between two or more nodes within the network.

- The blockchain **validates** the transaction through the automated process carried out by the program at the nodes to achieve necessary consensus based on the models and rules. Each node is responsible for authenticating the validity of the new transactions being added and letting other nodes know whether they agree or disagree with the group's version of history.

- The blockchain is **indisputable** and its design ensures the ledger will always provide an accurate history of transactions. Cryptography is used to ensure that all copies of the ledger at each node are identical, with no duplication of transactions.

- The blockchain is decentralized, which allows all the participants within the distributed network to interact with one another without having to rely on intermediaries or any central authority.

- The blockchain is **transparent,** with each node comprising an identical copy of the ledger with a complete record of the transactions in the system.

- The blockchain can be implemented within the enterprise towards the goal of making it intelligent or it can also be implemented in a public network to be used by the customers of the enterprise as a new business or revenue **model.**

Understanding Blockchain Architecture

Blockchain architecture is based on the principles that all the enterprise applications and data components are designed and operated to ensure business continuity, the architecture components should be adaptable and flexible to support a multitude of infrastructure platforms, the architecture should ensure data integrity and support data privacy norms, and it should enable the new IT infrastructure. The following are the details of how the blockchain architecture is constructed:

Set Up the Distributed Network Architecture

The most commonly used client-server architecture is one where a central server is remotely connected to various computers or nodes.

The blockchain architecture works on the distributed, or peer-to-peer, network as shown in Figure 9.3, where each computer or node has the same capability and responsibility, with no central monitoring. In this decentralized network, all peers are equal, serving as both client and server, and share the same resources.

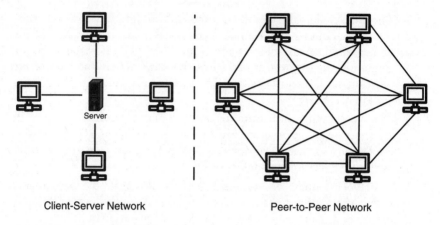

Figure 9.3   Peer-to-peer network.

The Transactions Are Represented as Blocks

In the blockchain architecture, all the nodes share the same copy of the ledger, which contains a chain of blocks where the transactions are written, as shown in Figure 9.4.

In the blockchain data structure, the transactions are organized and stored as blocks in the form of a chain. The block has a header record which includes the technical information of that block, a reference to the previous block in the chain, and a timestamp which serves as pointer and time of reference for transactions. The transactions take up the majority of the data in a block and are passed through the hash function so that the hash of the data is stored.

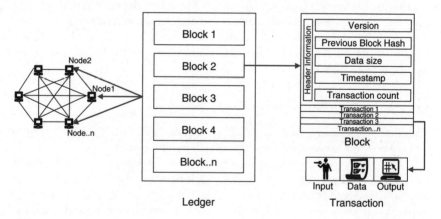

Figure 9.4   Blockchain transactions.

A hash function is used to convert input data of any size to a fixed size output. The hash function uses an advanced mathematical formula where the input of any byte is passed to transform it into a fixed byte output string of letters and numbers. The hash algorithm works in such a way that if the input string is similar, it will produce the same hash output. The security is built in such a way that from the hash output, it is nearly impossible for anyone to know the input string. The output is derived from the input or the source information. Thus, even when there is a slight change in the input by any user, the corresponding hash output string will also change. Hash validates the data in the chain of blocks, which ensures that the blockchain is internally consistent. An example of the hash function is illustrated in Figure 9.5.

The user representing a node within the network creates a transaction that needs to be added to the block within the ledger. Before it gets distributed to all the nodes, there are a lot of technical steps involved, such as security, authentication, and validation of the transaction, which requires key and hash function, as discussed in the next section.

The User Creates a Transaction

Historically, cryptography started with the concept of Symmetric-key, where both the sender and receiver share the same key to encrypt and decrypt the message. As this requires a separate key to be shared between each distinct

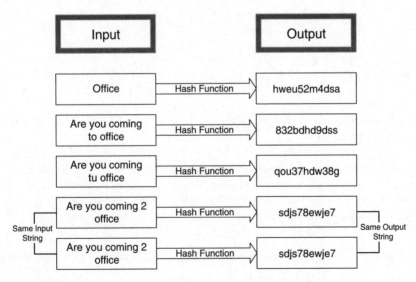

Figure 9.5   Hash function.

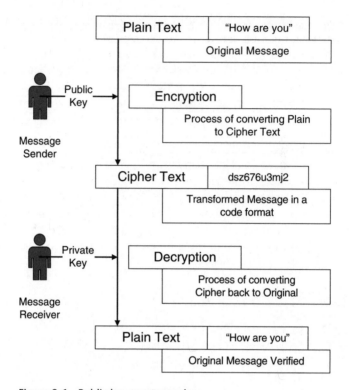

Figure 9.6   Public key cryptography.

pair of users, managing the number of keys became an issue. The public-key concept mathematically generated two distinct but related keys – public and private key, where they both work as an interrelated pair.

Blockchain uses the public key cryptography as a means of user identification, which allows the user to add transactions to the blockchain as depicted in Figure 9.6 above.

The public key as illustrated in Figure 9.6 is freely distributed for the users to encrypt and send messages while its paired private key is kept confidential with the receiver of the message to decrypt the message. The keys are used in this process for encryption and decryption to securely distribute the message. A hash function is used in the blockchain technology to generate keys.

The Transaction Is Shared with All the Nodes Within the Network

The digital signature uses the public-key cryptography and the signature is associated with the original signed document so that it cannot be copied or

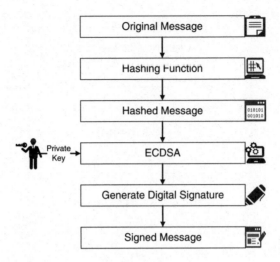

Figure 9.7 Digital signature.

moved to another document without getting detected. The private key is used to process the message or the hash of the message, generate the digital signature, and then send the signed message, while the corresponding public key along with the signed message (Figure 9.7) is used within the network to verify the authenticity of the signature.

When a user wants to add or send information to the blockchain, the system needs to certify who wrote the data to the blockchain. This is done by signing the data that authenticates the user who submitted the information to the ledger. As the information can be in various forms and sizes, it is passed through the hash function so that the hashed message is a standardized fixed-length output.

The private key of the user sending the message and a hash of the original data are fed through the algorithm called the elliptic curve digital signature algorithm (ECDSA), which creates the signed message. This signed message is then used in verifying that the message was sent to the blockchain by the proper user.

The Nodes Validate and Approve the Transaction

When a user within the network adds information to the ledger, all other users represented as nodes need to verify that the information is correct and the user from where it is coming is genuine. Unless the majority of the nodes agree and form a consensus, the information is not added to the blockchain. This ensures

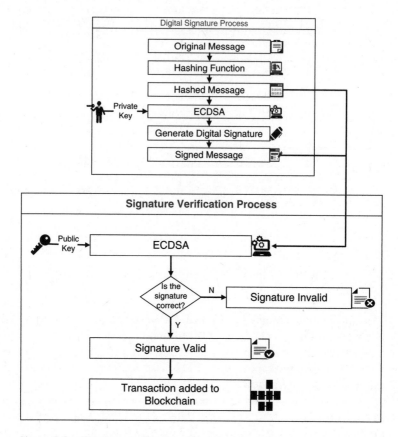

Figure 9.8 Signature verification through consensus.

each node has the same ledger and all transactions are verified before they are added to the ledger.

In the verification process as illustrated in Figure 9.8, the node receiving the message needs to verify that the transactions received are signed using the private key associated with the sender of the message. The security protocol works in such a way that the receiver of the message doesn't require access to the private key of the signer. To check the validity of the signature, the receiver node needs the following information:

- The hash of the original message from the sender node
- The public key that has been derived from the private key of the sender
- The signed message generated during the digital signature by the sender

These three items are passed through the ECDSA verification algorithm, which will specify whether the signature has been correctly signed (valid) or incorrectly signed (invalid). If the signature is valid, the transaction will be added to the list of transactions or it will be added to the next block and the chain of block continues.

Blockchain provides a lot of options for the verification process. When designing the architecture, it should be taken into consideration whether all the data should be made available to the public and anyone can verify the transactions or whether it should be restricted to only a few users.

The Transaction Is Added to a New Block of Data in the Ledger

Once the transaction is verified by the majority of the nodes with consensus, the transaction is added as a new block to the existing blockchain. Blockchain being a transactional data structure, it keeps a record of all the transactions related to the account before deriving the account balance.

Distribution of Ledger

Each node is replicated, with the most recent version of the ledger with validated transactions as added by the user and verified by the nodes. Thus, full transparency and data integrity are maintained at all the nodes, eliminating the need to reconcile the data from multiple sources.

Storing the Data in the Ledger

In traditional data storage, a value can be changed and overwritten in the table as many times as necessary and there is no additional storage required to change the existing value. In blockchain, which uses the transactional database concept, any changes to the existing record require a new transaction to be added to the block. This means, with time, a lot of storage capacity will be required to record all the transactions in the ledger.

As shown in Figure 9.9, the traditional or relational database only changes that segment of the data where the change is requested, while the transactional database adds any new changes to the transactions and stores the record so that its trail can be used at any point of time.

In Figure 9.9, the balance amount of User A is computed by analyzing every transaction in the chain that is relevant to User A and adding the amount of "to A" transactions while subtracting the "from A" transactions.

The Transaction Is Marked as Complete

Finally, the life cycle of the transaction processing is deemed as complete in the blockchain.

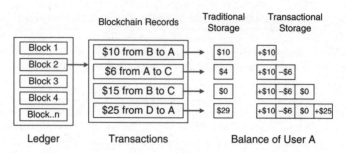

Figure 9.9   Storing blockchain transactions.

Smart Contracts in Blockchain

Smart contracts are programs that use business logic and algorithms to facilitate, verify, administer, and automate the execution of contracts between multiple parties on a distributed ledger, thus eliminating human intervention. A smart contract protects the assets in that ledger. It works with the following sequence of activities:

- Define the Contract: The users define the terms, specification, and event trigger rules related to the contract and the parameters between the parties involved in the contract.

- Generate an Event: The program checks if a predefined condition has been met and then triggers an event based on the business rules.

- Verify the Contract: The parties are interconnected through the blockchain network, and once they verify the contract information, they provide their consensus.

- Execute the Contract: Once the consensus is achieved in the network, the contract is executed as per the terms and integrated with any third-party APIs for additional services.

- Settle the Contract: Finally, the accounts of all the parties involved are settled and the information is transmitted throughout the network.

Enabling this concept with blockchain greatly reduces the dependency on third-party validation and automates the contract execution functionality, leading to process efficiencies, error elimination, time savings, and cost reduction.

Blockchain Execution Roadmap

To build a use case and implement blockchain technology, an enterprise needs to first execute a proof of concept. Once the proof of concept is successful, the enterprise needs to prepare and execute the project plan to build the final project. An outline of an agile development process for implementing a blockchain project is described below:

Identify Opportunity Areas

The enterprise should conduct the following activities during this phase:

- Define enterprise goals and objectives for the project.
- Confirm use case(s) for proof of concept (PoC).
- Identify the product or customer segment that would offer the highest value and benefits to support the PoC.
- Understand the market and solve the challenge that the enterprise is facing currently.

Identify Potential System Integrator

The enterprise should conduct the following activities during this phase:

- Identify system integration partners for this pilot innovation.
- Evaluate blockchain technology and platform vendors and capabilities that meet the vision and requirements of the enterprise.
- Finalize the blockchain vendor partnership agreements.

Execute Proof of Concept

The enterprise should conduct the following activities during this phase:

- Execute iterative design in a sandbox environment.
- Identify and prioritize use cases.
- Develop value drivers for the use cases.

Build a Pilot

The enterprise should conduct the following activities during this phase:

- Collaborate with selected technology partners on specific data sets required for simulation and testing.

- Finalize the contract with the system integrator.
- Execute the blockchain technology with a focus on the select use case.
- Incorporate learnings from the PoC phase into the pilot.

Configure, Build, and Test the Pilot

The enterprise should conduct the following activities during this phase:

- Configure and build business logic and rules based on the use case(s).
- Initiate simulations and user acceptance testing.
- Make adjustments to configuration and logic and refine data sets as necessary during the sprint session.
- Provide for continuous learning of the enterprise on the blockchain technology.
- Complete high-level assessment and the roadmap to transition.

Gather Pilot Metrics

The enterprise should conduct the following activities during this phase:

- Gather transaction metrics.
- Assess key learnings.
- Confirm the business case and key performance indicators for expansion.

Prepare a Project Plan

The enterprise should conduct the following activities during this phase:

- Finalize the use case as part of the blockchain implementation project.
- Prepare a project plan with the timeline, cost, and resource details.
- Get stakeholders' approval and funding to move ahead with the expansion.

Launch the Product

The enterprise should conduct the following activities during this phase:

- Implement a plan for all project phases – prepare, design, build, test, and deliver.
- Track performance and variance for all phases and activities.
- Launch the new product or system involving the end-to-end blockchain solution.
- Train the users and ensure seamless integration into the existing ecosystem of the enterprise.

Expand and Sustain

The enterprise should conduct the following activities during this phase:

- Expand the platform to additional business units and products.
- Deploy ongoing improvements and learnings.

Blockchain Security

The use of a distributed ledger in the blockchain technology allows the data to be shared between all parties on the network, which presents potential data security risks and confidentiality concerns. The enterprise needs to assess the entire technology architecture of the blockchain initiative to identify, understand, and address any security challenges.

The critical success factor in the blockchain adoption by the enterprise is to find the right balance between security and transparency that the technology offers. Some of the potential security challenges are listed below.

Shared Data

The enterprise has the responsibility to conduct a thorough evaluation of the data (both hashed and otherwise) that must be shared with business partners and others in the network to achieve the desired level of transparency which is required for successful adoption and execution of the process.

Data in Transit

The enterprise must leverage encrypted connections such as HTTPS, SSL, TLS, FTPS, etc., to protect the content of data in transit, including the APIs that are used to communicate with the data stores.

Persisted Data Outside Blockchain

The enterprise needs to implement appropriate encryption standards to protect sensitive data and meet the compliance standards to ensure only authorized individuals are able to decrypt and view sensitive information.

Smart Contracts

Smart contracts are programs run on a blockchain involving people, processes, and technology which may cause errors and faults in code. The enterprise must take proper measures throughout the smart contract's life cycle to prevent gaps in the design, development, deployment, upgrade, or maintenance of the distributed application.

Cryptography

Private keys are used to authorize activities within an account, and if the key is compromised, it can allow unauthorized users to access data, wallets, and assets. In public blockchains, there is no means to track the attempts made to decrypt private keys generated from the ledger.

Thus, the enterprise is faced with the security challenges that exist around the usage and storage of keys. The enterprise needs to review the hashing algorithms being used and set up the recovery mechanism for lost keys.

Consensus

In a public blockchain network, the majority consensus is used in the validation process. Taking control of a significant portion of the blocks could allow an adversary to take control of the network or lead to corruption of the transaction validation process. As part of the ongoing security operations, the enterprise needs to constantly review the logs and monitor if any node within the network has increased processing power and is executing more than an average number of transactions.

Identity and Access Management

The enterprise should have proper security policies around identifying the users and objects on the blockchain network along with the access management controls.

Governance

The codes and algorithms related to rules around the governance of blockchain ledgers must be addressed to allow for the efficient and secure use of blockchain networks. The blockchain security policies and consensus mechanism must be aligned with the enterprise objectives along with the regulations around disaster recovery and the process of deploying code updates.

Challenges of Blockchain-enabled Transformation

Blockchain technology is relatively new from an applications standpoint and is on a very fast growth trajectory, but it also comes with its own set of challenges, some of which are listed below:

- As blockchain is in its nascent stage, a lot of corporations and customers want to get in when the technology has matured, with success in its use cases.
- The ability to gain the trust of all the participants that their transactions are secure. It took some time before the internet payment gateway kicked off among the masses.
- The readiness of the users to share the information to participate in the network.
- Budget constraints to implementing new technology and waiting for the payback period.
- Lack of any global regulatory authority to set the standards and rules for the transactions posted in the blockchain network.
- The integration and compatibility of blockchain technology with the existing landscape of the enterprise.
- Finding the solution and use cases to support sufficient volume for that particular process.
- Change of mind-set, where the verification process is performed in real time to monitor and authenticate the transactions from other users.

Applications of Blockchain

The enterprise can leverage some of the applications and use cases that are described below for reference purposes:

- Payments
  - Commercial and corporate payments
  - Cross-border money transfers
  - Smart device payments
  - Public or private cryptocurrency
  - FX exchange
  - Direct e-commerce payments

- Capital Markets
  - Optimized clearing and settlement
  - Syndicated loans
  - Corporate bonds
  - Custodial management
  - Retail brokerage
- Trade Finance
  - Digital letter of credit
  - Letter of credit settlement
  - Automated bill of lading validation
  - Sensor trigger smart contracts
  - Custom duties
  - Embedded insurance
- Insurance
  - Instant claims disbursements
  - Reinsurance
  - Industry fraud utility
  - Warranty registration and validation
- Public Services
  - Smart elections
  - Global criminal records
  - Public records
  - Licenses
  - Census and population data
  - Digital notary service
  - Asset titles
  - Refugee tracking
- Healthcare
  - Healthcare provider credentials
  - Provider network
  - Health care records
  - Driving better patient outcomes
- Customer Data
  - Employee benefits and insurance
  - Global credit reporting
  - Travel documents and records
  - Credit bureau
  - Passports and visa tracking
  - Criminal records
  - Diplomas and certifications tracking

- Identity Management
  - Digital identity
  - Global ID
  - Smart device identification
  - Birth records
- Transaction Processing
  - Smart contracts
  - Smart payroll
  - SLA agreement performance
  - Smart accounts receivable
  - Enterprise software license
  - Content management
  - Ride sharing
  - Retail payments
  - Secure messaging
- Fixed-Asset Management
  - Property ownership tracking
  - Content distribution and access
  - Inventory management
  - Loyalty
- Utilities
  - Retail switching enablement
  - Energy market settlement
  - Wholesale market settlement
  - Appliance-level disaggregation
- Security
  - Data integrity
  - Reduce exposure from data hacks
- Supply Chain
  - Product track and trace
  - Anti-counterfeit and ability to confirm the source of products
  - Tracking cause of product defect for recalls

Use Cases of Blockchain

Though bitcoin and blockchain are sometimes used in the same context, bitcoin was the first major application of blockchain in the form of cryptocurrency as an alternative currency. Let's analyze some of the industrial applications and use cases where blockchain can create a hallmark going forward.

Cross-border Payments

Currently, cross-border payments go through multiple intermediaries; hence, the settlement of the fund takes several days and incurs higher costs to the customers sending funds.

Blockchain can provide real-time cross-border payments to customers across the globe. The funds transfer is executed directly between the sending and the receiving banks with full visibility without going through any intermediaries. It can be used both for corporate remittances and for retail customer payments. A simple overview is shown in Figure 9.10.

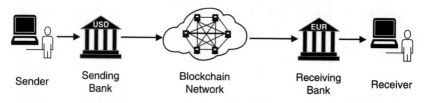

Sender   Sending   Blockchain   Receiving   Receiver
         Bank   Network   Bank

Figure 9.10   Use case – global payments.

The following process takes place with blockchain technology:

- Both the sender and the receiver's bank are on the distributed blockchain network.
- The sender initiates the transfer through its bank.
- The information is exchanged between both banks using encrypted messaging.
- Once the sender approves the transfer with the real-time foreign exchange rate and fee, the payment is made to the receiver in real time.
- Once the fund is transferred to the receiver, both the sender and the receiver are notified.

The technology allows both banks to transact directly, make real-time settlement of funds, trace the funds from the sender to the recipient, eliminate fraudulent transactions, authenticate documents, and reduce the cost and fees charged by multiple intermediaries.

Food Supply Chain

The entire food supply chain from production to consumption is quite complex and involves a lot of exchanges, as shown in Figure 9.11.

The supply chain involves:

- The farmer, who produces the product
- The manufacturer, who processes the product

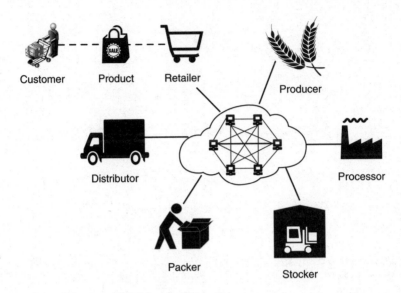

Figure 9.11 Use case – supply chain.

- The warehouse, where the product is stored
- The packer, who packs the product for shipment
- The distributor, who supplies the product to a different location
- The logistics provider, who sends the product to the retailers in trucks
- The retailer, who displays the product in the shelf for the consumers to buy

Currently, if there is any contamination in the product, it is very difficult to trace the entire supply chain back to the original farmer for a root cause analysis. Blockchain can solve such issues where each party in the supply chain provides updates in the product's supply chain. Each party would be allowed to edit any information and thus it would be possible to monitor the product in real time. The customer would have full access to the entire life cycle of the product – the journey from the farm to the retailer.

Settlement of Stocks in the Stock Exchange

When a customer buys stocks, the clearing and settlement process takes multiple days in the stock exchange. This prohibits the buyer from selling the stock until such time and involves higher fees and multiple intermediaries.

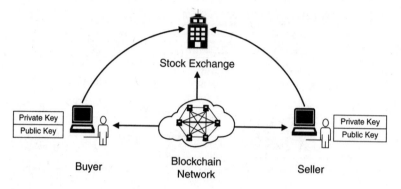

Figure 9.12   Use Case – settlement at stock exchange.

Blockchain technology can utilize smart contracts to enable custodial services and provide automated clearing after the completion of stock trading. It can provide real-time updates on the positions of the underlying security and provide transparency and traceability of the transactions. A simple overview is shown in Figure 9.12.

The following process takes place with blockchain technology:

- The buyer sends a request to the stock exchange for buying XX shares.
- The seller sends a request to the stock exchange for selling XX shares.
- The buyer agrees to buy the shares from the seller and sends the offer to the stock exchange.
- The seller accepts the offer and sends payment details to the buyer.
- The buyer makes the payment.
- The seller receives the payment with traceability through the blockchain network.
- The seller sends the digital asset through the blockchain transaction to the buyer by signing the transaction with his private key.
- The buyer accepts the asset using the public key associated with the seller's private key and his own private key.
- The ownership is then transferred from the seller to the buyer.

Thus, blockchain simplifies the operations while creating a cryptographically verifiable audit trail.

Selection of Energy Provider

Consumers should be able to select their energy provider in their homes with the capability built by a combination of blockchain distributed applications, smart contracts, connected homes using IoT, and bitcoin payments. A simple overview is shown in Figure 9.13.

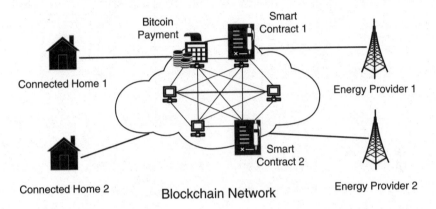

Figure 9.13   Use case – utilities.

The smart contracts are defined with all the terms and conditions of the energy provisioning between the energy provider and the consumer. Connected homes can verify, agree, and subscribe to the smart contracts that are deployed over a blockchain distributed ledger. Each connected home is connected to the bitcoin wallet from which they can make the payments for consuming the energy. The consumers in the connected homes can select the energy provider by simply subscribing to a newly distributed smart contract offered by another energy provider within the network.

Value Chain of an Automobile

An automobile such as a car goes through many processes and activities and changes owners during its life cycle. Blockchain technology can keep the track record and history of its entire journey throughout its value chain from manufacturing, sales, maintenance, to resale. A simple overview is shown in Figure 9.14.

The following process takes place with blockchain technology:

- The manufacturer assigns a unique identifier to the vehicle at the factory upon the completion of production. This vehicle identification number remains unchanged throughout the life cycle of the vehicle.

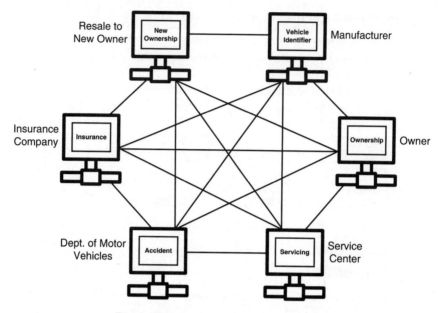

Blockchain Ledger of an Automobile

Figure 9.14   Use case – automobile value chain.

- The vehicle identification number is recorded to the vehicle blockchain ledger, which transmits the information to all ledgers distributed worldwide.
- When the vehicle is shipped from the factory to the distributor and further sold to the owner, the vehicle's change of ownership transaction is recorded in the blockchain ledger.
- All events related to the vehicle such as servicing, repairs, accidents, and insurance records are updated in the distributed ledger of the vehicle throughout its life cycle and usage.
- At the time of re-sell, the new owner can have full transparency by having access to the vehicle history from the point of production with a timeline of all events.

This can reduce the paperwork and any fraudulent activities during the entire value chain.

Track and Trace in Pharma Supply Chain

The pharmaceutical industry is faced with the challenge of fraudulent medical products that are circulated around the world, where millions of people are put at risk of death by consuming ineffective medicines.

Enterprises can come up with an innovative solution using blockchain technology by enforcing end-to-end serialization with the officials controlling the entire physical distribution chain throughout the globe. The serialized tracking of individually recognizable units ensures authenticity and creates transparency for both the patients and pharma enterprises, as shown in Figure 9.15.

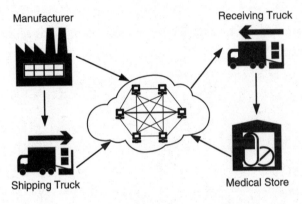

Figure 9.15   Use case – track and trace in pharma supply chain.

The following process takes place with blockchain technology:

- The manufacturer writes to the blockchain that goods have been dispatched from the factory.
- Information such as batch number, destination, and additional requirements such as temperature requirements for the medicine are transmitted to the blockchain ledger.
- The medicine inventory is loaded to the shipping truck, and this transaction is updated to the blockchain.
- The goods are brought into the warehouse, where the receiving truck scans the goods, reads from the blockchain, and confirms the authenticity of the medicines.

- Once the receiving truck delivers to the medical store, the delivery is confirmed, and the status is entered to the blockchain for full transparency by all parties.

The solution created a shared and trusted approach to the end-to-end pharma supply chain process. The medicines can now be tracked by all the parties in real time. It also ensures compliance with the regulatory requirements around pharmaceutical serialization and prevents the risk of counterfeit medical supply to the stores.

Key Players

The key start-up vendors in the blockchain technology for the following functions are listed below:

- Payments
  - Tokenly
  - PayStand
  - Coinapult
  - Colu
  - BitPagos
  - BitPay
  - CoinSnap
- Authentication
  - Blockstack
  - ShoCard
  - Blockscore
- Security
  - Guardtime
  - Stampery
- Record Keeping
  - Factom
  - BlockApps
  - Records Keeper
  - Tierion
- Supply Chain
  - Skuchain
  - Blockverify
  - Gliding Eagle

- Tallysticks
- Modum
- Customer Ownership and Rights
  - Warranteer
  - Mirror
  - Bitproof.io
- Customer Loyalty and Engagement
  - Chronicled
  - Everledger
  - Tokenly
  - Blockpoint
  - Loyyal
  - Colu

Some of the key vendors providing platform services on blockchain technology include the following:

- Microsoft
- Amazon
- IBM
- Ripple
- Multichain
- Hyperledger

Conclusion

While organizations around the world are researching various use cases that can be deployed in industrial applications, blockchain has the potential to disrupt the existing business models because of the following features:

- Distributed and Secure Transactions Ledger: The common data in the transactions ledger is encrypted and shared by all the users in the blockchain distributed network.
- Elimination of Intermediaries: Assets are digitally held in the blockchain ledger associated with their owner's identities rather than institutional custodians. Any exchange of information is validated through consensus within the network without relying on a central authority.
- Regulatory Compliance: All the transactions can be tracked in real time with a traceable audit trail.

- Process Automation: The execution and settlement of the transactions are automated by design and happen in near real time, thus eliminating error handling and manual reconciliation efforts.

- Smart Contracts: The computer programs, business logic, and algorithms facilitate the verification and negotiation of a contract between multiple parties without any manual interference.

- Cost Reduction: Listed below are some areas where blockchain can significantly reduce the cost of operations for both the enterprise and its end customers:
  - Reduction of infrastructure, technology, and operations costs.
  - Reduction of third-party and intermediaries costs, as these are eliminated by design.
  - Reduction of transaction costs associated with the custody of the asset.
  - Reduction of the cost of capital due to near real-time settlement.
  - Reduction of audit, compliance, and risk-management fees, as it simplifies and improves the record-keeping process, keeping the regulatory control and compliance checked with a cryptographically auditable trail of transactions.

Blockchain has a long way ahead. It will have to extend its applications from B2B models to B2C models, directly engaging its customers with potential new business and revenue models. The payment infrastructure along with the reduction of intermediaries need to be stabilized and standardized before it can find usage and adoption among the masses. With new developments, the distributed ledger systems will become standardized, matured, and regulated, which will lead to new operating models in the financial services industry. The smart contracts need to expand their footprint from syndicated loans to real estate and insurance claims.

CHAPTER 10

Drones

*T*his chapter provides an overview of the drones technology, various types of drones, and their ability to capture visual data for further processing. It also discusses the risks imposed by this technology, its application, and some of the typical use cases across business processes and industries, where the drones have the potential and ability to make the enterprise intelligent.

Drones Overview

Drones are flying robots embedded with sensors and GPS that can be operated autonomously on a predefined flight plan or can be controlled remotely by a user.

Drones belong to the unmanned aerial vehicles sector. They come as smaller consumer electronics aircraft equipped with batteries, HD cameras, gimbals, etc., and also as very large aircraft in size, complexity, and functionality.

They are powerful tools that are used in various industries and have transformed the way an enterprise can collect high-quality and relevant data, which further supports a fast and better decision-making process.

Drones have found an industrial use in land survey, media, safety and surveillance, and shipping and logistics. Commercial use has grown drastically with small, inexpensive drones that can be controlled with a mobile device. Drones are widely used in the military sector and continue to see overall positive and increased growth. Currently, the revenue from the drone market is around $11 billion and is growing more than 35% annually.

Salient Features

There has been a growing interest in the drone's capability of collecting and monitoring aerial data. Drones can deliver significant business value to the enterprise in conjunction with deep learning and computer vision technology for data analysis and insights. The commercial use for drone applications will increase significantly in the agriculture, infrastructure, and transportation industries. Some of the salient features that will accelerate the implementation of drones include the following:

- Drones can be operated on a predefined flight plan or can be controlled remotely by humans. Thus, they can easily be used in high-risk areas or where a high level of precision is required.
- Drones contain cameras, sensors, GPS, and other mobile technologies to enable successful flight capabilities and capture requisite data.
- The same technology can be applied at the large-scale military or industry level or at the smaller-scale consumer goods or gaming level.
- A key concern in the application of drones for both the industrial and consumer level remains in the creation and understanding of regulatory measures.

Drone Configuration

From an engineering point of view, drones can be distinguished by their underlying primary configurations, namely tricopters, quadcopters, hexacopters, and octocopters. The nomenclature is derived from the number of rotors that drive the drones. Within that primary differentiation, subconfigurations (I, V, X, Y, IY) allow a more detailed differentiation. The subconfiguration indicates the order of the rotors related to the course.

Drone Properties

The number of rotors influences several drone properties such as stability, maximum payload, and flight time. The configuration of the rotor directly impacts the price and weight of the drones. Some of the drone properties related to their configuration include the following:

Tricopters

The configuration of a tricopter drone has three vertical rotors. It's the least complicated among all four configuration models. The functions are simple, and these types of drones are used by kids as part of their recreation and pleasure. They are cheap and easy to build.

As the materials used to build a tricopter are not of very high quality, they have a limited and run the risk of getting damaged early.

Some of the models in this category include FlyFly Hobby RC, DK CX-33S RC, and Goolsky CX-33.

Quadcopters

The quadcopter is the most popular multirotor configuration that is propelled and lifted by four rotors. In general, quadcopters are fast, highly controllable, economically priced, and have a simple four-propeller design. The main disadvantage of this configuration is the absence of a backup motor, which means the drone will crash if there is an engine failure.

Some of the models in this category include DJI Phantom 3, DJI Mavic Pro, Typhoon Q500, and Parrot Bebop.

Hexacopters

Though the quadcopters are known to fly for a longer period of time, the hexacopter, with six rotors, offers more power, efficiency, elevation, speed control, and capacity for carrying heavier cargo and freight. Due to the increased number of motors, they're very stable in the air and can take spectacular aerial images. The flip side of the higher stability is the higher cost, lower agility, and lower flexibility of the hexacopter.

Some of the models in this category include DJI S900, Aperture, Alta 6, and Walkera H500.

Octocopters

Octocopters are the most powerful, as eight-propeller drones that are efficient, expensive, capable of carrying the heaviest payloads from one place to another, and offering the greatest stability in the air.

They are very fast and can withstand heavy rain and strong winds. This configuration is the most suitable solution for producing high-definition video and image recording from any altitude.

Failure of a single motor won't really affect its flying capabilities, except for efficiency in terms of battery life, and it is very expensive to replace parts. The power consumption is very high, as it needs to power eight motors at the same time.

Some of the models in this category include DJI Agras, DJI Spread Wings S1000, Tarot X8, and Alta 8.

Key Players

The focus of drone manufacturers is shifting towards commercial drone markets, as that is where the maximum growth and profit potential exist.

Some of the emerging players in the commercial drone market include the following:

- Airware: The enterprise is involved in building a software platform for commercial drone applications. It provides the software, user interface, and drone analytics for enterprises to take appropriate and timely action.

- Skycatch: The enterprise is involved in developing drones for job site inspection and monitoring while maintaining compliance and regulations. They are used in multiple constructions, mining, and energy organizations all over the world.

- DJI: The enterprise is involved in the manufacturing of drones and cameras for both commercial and recreational purposes. Some of the industries it supports include agriculture, emergency response, construction, and entertainment.

- Movidius: The enterprise is involved in designing microchips and other components for computer vision that are used in drones.

Drones as Data Collector

Drones have the technology to operate either autonomously on a predefined flight plan or be controlled remotely during operation. GPS signals often serve as a navigation tool to guide the path, which is also achieved through Wi-Fi or infrared signals.

Drones are embedded with sensors which aid in collecting the data and capture aerial photography. They perfectly complement other data sources from satellite imagery and manned aircraft, which are very expensive sources of data. The information captured by drones is used in various fields to support a fast and better decision-making process by extracting data insights and delivering results to a smartphone or other display.

Challenges

Listed below are some of the challenges faced during data collection with drones:

- Once the data collection process is complete, still images are aggregated and uploaded to a database on the cloud. Real-time streaming of data remains a challenge and is only possible if there exists a reliable and secure wide-area wireless broadband signal viable in the area of the collection. However, in some remote and backward regions, there is not even cellular coverage so it is all the more difficult to stream real-time images or videos.

- On-board sensors used in the drones are still in the nascent stage and lot of new developments are taking place in the hardware space. Once the technology matures, it will even become very cost-effective. Various types of signals exist and can be deployed for drones. Both visible and multispectral, such as infrared, imagery needs to be captured and collected for data insights. Even the laser sensor modules of the drone for 3D mapping can be a very expensive solution for mass adoption.

- Drones have not matured enough to replace other data collection methods such as satellites. They still complement these methods and are still in the prototype stage. Thus, the data service providers currently rely on satellite, manned aircraft, and other kinds of imagery as the primary source, while drones act as a secondary source of data.

- The ecosystem of the data service providers is still emerging. To streamline and simplify the data collection and analysis process, service providers not only need to be carry out the aircraft operations and management, but also need to involved in data management, analysis, modeling, and analytical application development.

Risk Considerations

Drones present both mechanical and legal risks, and the enterprise needs to consider these risks to make drones a viable solution that can be used widely. Listed below are some of the risks that drones present during operation:

Mechanical Risks

Mechanical risks can be caused by the following factors:

- Crash: Drones pose a great risk of damage for manned aircraft like helicopters, agricultural aircraft, and aircraft landing or departing from airports, as they can cause midair collisions with these aircrafts.

- Falls from Height: Drones carry a potential risk for factory, warehouse, and project site workers, as the drones might fall from their height and cause safety hazards at the workplace.

- Loss of Control: Drones can lose control while flying due to a system failure.

- Out of Range: Drones might fly beyond the signal range into an area where communication is interrupted, causing significant damage to property and lives.

- Frequency Interference: Drones automated operation can interfere with other frequencies, causing them to miss the designated path.

- Operator Skills: The commercial and military drones require an experienced pilot to take control of drones while in the air to resolve any mechanical issues.

Regulatory Risks

Data and regulatory risks can be caused by the following factors:

- Hacking: Interpreting signals, hacking into the radio or Wi-Fi signal, and sending malicious commands.
- Data Security: Drones pose a threat to data security during the transmission of information to the centralized control station.
- Data Privacy: Drones are prone to cyberattacks where data privacy is breached to obtain gathered and stored data.
- Spying: Drones can be used as an emerging threat, trespassing and spying to target critical infrastructure.
- Terrorism: Drones can be used in an act of terrorism by being filled with explosives and targeting aircraft in flight or planes on the ground.
- Regulation: There are no standard regulations that have been framed for drone safety yet, leading to potential claims against enterprises, data operators, and drone manufacturers.
- Liability: Drones also pose liability and insurance issues, where more clarity is needed in the future to combat the risks.

Drone Applications

There are various types of drones that can be used in private, commercial, or military applications. Drones differ in size, speed, duration of flight, durability, stability, camera resolution, and the integrated sensors based on the field of application and the usage.

Private Applications

In private applications, drones are primarily used for taking images and capturing videos of inaccessible landscapes. They are also used by teenagers as recreational tools to play with. The drones in this category are small, cheap, lightweight, and less stable compared to the commercial and military counterparts.

Commercial Applications

Drones have multiple applications in the commercial area. They can be used for the surveillance of a large event or area and also in the context of property surveying. The most common application is in the logistics space, where Amazon and other logistics providers are trying to improve their supply chain performance. One of the most upcoming beneficiaries is the agriculture industry, where drones can conduct the surveillance of fields and crops. The sensors and high-resolution cameras equipped in the drones detect any pest invasion, inadequate watering, and other anomalies at an early stage so that the crops can be protected from getting damaged.

Military Applications

One of the most common applications of drones is in the military, where the drones can be classified as micro drones, tactical drones, and strategic drones.

Micro drones have the capability to provide intelligence, surveillance, target acquisition, and reconnaissance services.

Tactical drones are heavier and sturdier than micro drones and are used in situational analysis to offer protection and conduct surveillance.

Strategic drones are very large in size and are used to determine the exact location of the enemy and compile a list of targets.

Opportunities by Industry

Drones, as an emerging technology, have created new business, revenue, and operating models for many enterprises across industries. Drones, in combination with computer vision, have the potential to significantly impact the future growth opportunities of many industries.

Each industry is unique and requires a different type of drone in terms of features that can provide the right service and functionality to the enterprise. Drone services, though in their nascent stage, can be flexible and customizable to serve the use case for a particular industry. The biggest opportunities and applications for drones are found in the transportation, infrastructure, and agriculture industries.

Transportation

There has been an enormous amount of spending to automate the processes in the logistics and delivery of goods. Robots have been used lately to deliver and assemble parts in a workshop. Drones can now be utilized to complement the standard ground-based delivery systems within the warehouse and help with the supply of parts through the air.

Some of the potential and real-life use cases for drones include the following:

• **Warehouse Delivery.**   A potential use case for the automotive industry consists of a fast delivery service for small items such as reorders and emergency orders. Since the ground-based traffic via forklifts has limitations that lead to longer replacement times, the traffic volume with drones can be increased through the air. This can automate the transportation of smaller parts in the workshops.

Though drones can follow the direct route for express calls through the air, a limitation exists in terms of the cargo weight and the size of components to be transported, as the technology is still maturing.

• **Inventory Maintenance.**   Drones can easily take over tasks such as stockpiling and inventory audit at warehouses located at dangerous sites or at places where the toxic levels are very high, endangering human lives.

Some of the camera-based applications such as inspections, surveillance, and monitoring of machines, stock, maintenance of equipment, and safety of workers can easily be accomplished through the use of drones.

Agriculture

Implementation of digital technology and revolutionary strategies have been growing at a faster pace in the agriculture industry. Increasing productivity of farmland for grains is one of the key drivers of the adoption of high-tech gadgets. Drones can definitely play a vital role in a smart farming transformation.

Some of the potential and real-life use cases for drones include the following:

• **Crop Analysis and Field Monitoring.**   Seed planting patterns were planned using precise 3D maps of the fields, soil drainage, and surface erosion. The statistical analysis of the data that was gathered generated analytical reports and insights about the expected harvest. Soil drought and crop diseases were determined early through the use of hyperspectral sensors. Some of the other benefits included prevention of crop wastage, assessment of endangered areas within the fields, and monitoring of animal activity, which can prevent any crop damage.

- **Risk Prevention.** Drones can help prevent risks arising from the structure of the land by improving the irrigation plans using aerial images and 3D models.

- **Planting and Maintenance.** Drones were able to plant accurately using distance-measuring equipment and scanning the topography of the land. The technology also helped in adapting to geography and environmental variations and sprayed the right amount of water and pesticide by modulating the height from the ground. This kept the plants healthy without any human intervention.

Infrastructure

The infrastructure development of the transportation and energy industries is a crucial factor in the growth of any modern society. Drones can be used in transport infrastructure maintenance for precise inspections of infrastructure, construction sites, the general environment, high-voltage power lines, wind turbines, etc.

Some of the potential and real-life use cases for drones include the following:

- **Remote Inspection.** The monitoring of the project is challenging when the construction or infrastructure sites are scattered over a large area. For line infrastructure with separate construction sites spread all over the country, drones can be replaced with in-person surveillance, which accelerates the process and helps mitigate risks.

Drones can provide full HD images, full views, and also real-time progress monitoring. The systematic gathering of information about the sites, the condition of the infrastructure, machinery, used materials, and number of working employees is a valuable advantage because it triggers timely corrective actions and significant cost reduction.

The same holds for applications in the security sector and for insurance purposes since the same capabilities of surveillance, monitoring, and analysis of visual data provided by drones are leveraged.

A geospatial app can be developed to leverage the visual data generated from the drones for monitoring and maintenance of railways.

Retail

The global retail industry is worth around $30 trillion and is faced with challenges such as regulatory pressures, cross-border trade wars, and changes in consumer behavior. Investment and spending in retail technology have been on a growth trajectory for many years and will continue the same trend to keep pace with consumer demands and maintain a competitive edge.

Some of the potential and real-life use cases for drones include the following:

• **Warehouse Inventory.**   Stock taking in warehouses was automated with the use of drones in conjunction with computer vision algorithms. The proto-type carried out for automated tracking and monitoring of inventory with mini drones was a successful initiative tested at many retailers across the United States.

Drones helped in the reconciliation of shelf content to inventory and min-imized mismatches. Employees at retail stores took much less time to find a particular item, which reduced the costs both in the number of employees and in inventory storage.

• **Inventory Movement.**   The drone technology was leveraged for an indoor flight where small drones flew around safely and read the RFID tags on the stock from a distance. This enabled employees to work, manage, and move materials at the same time.

• **On-time Delivery.**   In crowded areas, drones can be very useful for taking over the last mile through the air to achieve on-time delivery.

Media and Telecommunications

Drones have found an immense use in media coverage, entertainment, and the telecommunications industry. Traditionally, only large media and new com-panies had the deep pockets necessary to afford a helicopter for taking aerial shots, but in today's world, even local journalists and small-scale media enter-prises can easily capture aerial footage for news coverage through the use of drones. In addition, drones have the flexibility to get into smaller areas, lower to the ground than a helicopter can travel.

The recording of real-time visual materials has been greatly simplified with the embedded HD cameras in the state-of-the-art drones that are avail-able on in the market today.

Some of the potential and real-life use cases for drones include the fol-lowing:

• **Rescue and Emergency.**   Drones have proven to be a valuable discovery for rescue and recovery operations. Let's consider telecom infrastructure in remote or destroyed areas where there is no connectivity. Since drones do not necessarily rely on wireless connectivity, they can serve as cell-sites on wings, operating in damaged regions in order to provide temporary fixes until permanent telecom replacements can be established.

Drones provide many other commercial opportunities to the telecom providers, as they can be used to extend the networks and cellular coverage to remote places such as islands and can be used as additional devices at events where the demand for data coverage is high.

Energy

The monitoring and maintenance of long-distance circuits and transmission lines that reach millions of customers has always been a challenge in the energy and power transmission sector, which provides a great opportunity and use case for drones. The maintenance process can be automated and expedited with the use of image data analytics.

Some of the potential and real-life use cases for drones include the following:

- **Cable Connections.** Drones can be used in the supervision of on-ground pipelines and maintenance of power lines and cables by capturing real-time images and videos.

- **Construction Projects.** Drones can be used in monitoring the day-to-day construction of projects, gathering and processing of data, and any technical support as required in the project.

- **Power Plants.** Drones can be utilized in the inspection of emitters and cooling towers and in the supervision of fuel capacity for predictive maintenance, prevention of potential breakdown, and cost reduction.

- **Green Energy.** Drones can be used in the inspection of the wind turbine and blades on wind farms and technical inspection on solar farms where it is difficult for humans to reach.

- **Topographical Data.** Drones can map solar farms. By gathering real-time data and using these accurate topographical maps, drones help in expediting land surveys. The design cycles can become far more efficient using this innovative approach, which allows for competitiveness in the fast-paced solar-energy industry.

Use Cases

Use cases for drones are scenarios where drone technology was used to provide multiple benefits such as inspection, cargo delivery, rescue operations, etc. Listed below are some scenarios along with real-life case studies to show how the drone adoption journey can be facilitated to result in an intelligent enterprise.

1. Case Study: Monitoring of Crops
   - Scenario
     - A global agriculture enterprise needs to assess soil drainage, monitor surface erosion, conduct statistical analysis of the fields and crops, produce analytical reports concerning current and expected harvests, and plan the seed sowing.
   - Approach
     - The enterprise used drone technology and detected the soil drought and crop diseases with the help of embedded hyper-spectral sensors.
   - Results
     - The enterprise was able to identify specific endangered areas within the crop fields.
     - It inspected and prevented crop wastage and damage caused by diseases, pests, and animal activities.

2. Case Study: Capital Project Monitoring
   - Scenario
     - An infrastructure enterprise planned to build more than 1,000 miles of linear infrastructure throughout the country. There would be more than 60 separate construction sites spread all over the country. The enterprise wanted a reliable progress reporting monitoring process so that it could update the institutions that financed the project.
   - Approach
     - The enterprise replaced in-person surveillance with drones that supported all the geographic locations.
     - The drones captured HD-quality images of the construction sites.
   - Results
     - The enterprise was able to get the complete view of the construction site with real-time monitoring of the progress.
     - The enterprise was able to monitor the progress with the project plan to check any time, budget, or quality issues.

- A proper control was put in place on a number of working employees, machinery, and materials used.

3. Case Study: Maintenance of Transmission Lines
   - Scenario
     - The power transmission enterprise wanted to automate the management of more than 20,000 circuit miles of transmission lines that supported more than 1.5 million customers.
   - Approach
     - The enterprise enhanced and automated the maintenance processes by implementing image and data analytics process on the information captured by the drones.
     - The enterprise changed its strategy from the data acquisition methods and analysis approach to implementing a predictive maintenance approach.
   - Results
     - The enterprise was able to prevent breakdowns causing power failure at the customer's premises.
     - The enterprise was able to assess the vegetation collisions with power lines by planning the work schedule with the forestry department.

4. Case Study: Delivery of Medicines
   - Scenario
     - A not-for-profit enterprise wanted to deliver vaccines and medicines to remote and rural areas.
   - Approach
     - The enterprise used drones to deliver medical supplies and blood packages to remote areas, where it was a very time-consuming process for humans to reach.
   - Results
     - The drones provided a mechanism for delivery of essential medicines, vaccines, and emergency blood supplies that saved hours and days and potentially many lives in countries where roads were either not maintained or did not exist.

Conclusion

The rapid development in drone technology will augment the capability and functionality of drones, which will further lead to broader applicability and usage of drones in transportation, logistics, agriculture, retail, and other industries.

The embedded sensors in the drones will enable capturing of visual data during industrial inspections and enable it to be available on a real-time basis. The immediate access to information and insights will further boost the implementation of drone technologies for mass adoption. Improved computer algorithms will enhance the quality of the data and the subsequent data analysis.

CHAPTER 11
Virtual Reality

*T*his chapter provides an overview of the virtual and augmented reality technology and its ability to create a computer-generated immersive experience for a user or augment new layers of information to the real world. It also discusses the architecture and technology components required, commonly used platforms, and some of the typical processes across industries that are potential candidates for AR/VR use cases to make the enterprise intelligent.

Augmented and Virtual Reality Overview

Virtual reality (VR) and augmented reality (AR) are two closely linked technologies that combine an array of sensors, speakers, and visual display elements to create and perpetuate the illusion of a virtual or augmented world. While virtual reality is able to transport the user to a completely new place within the virtual environment, augmented reality does not move the user to a new world, it just augments the current state of existence.

Oculus Rift, Samsung Gear VR, and Google Cardboard are some of the examples of VR that provide a fully immersive experience. Monitorless AR glasses provide a real-world experience with computer-generated overlays which provide an improvement over the location where the user is currently present.

In both VR and AR, digital content is presented to the user that informs and interacts with the senses that depicts a new experience of that place to achieve an immersive experience. Thus, these technologies are also referred to as immersive technologies.

Choosing the Right Reality

While augmented and virtual reality are the two most frequently used technologies, mixed reality (MR) is also entering into the array of conversations. While each of these technologies was introduced to provide a specific and unique experience, the distinguishing factors among these are sometimes unclear, create confusion, and are intermixed during conversations.

AR and VR can be considered as the same domain, with normal, everyday physical reality on one end to the left and fully immersive, completely digitized virtual reality on the other to the right. Mixed reality falls somewhere in the middle, moving to the right on the spectrum by introducing more elements of the virtual world and moving to the left by replacing more of the virtual world with physical elements. Thus, the technologies that fall to the left of the spectrum are known as augmented reality, while those that fall more towards the right are known as virtual reality, and the technologies that fall somewhere in the middle are known as mixed reality.

Capabilities of Augmented Reality

AR superimposes the digital content generated by the computer on a user's view of the real world in order to provide contextual information.

AR allows the user to remain connected with the physical world in order to move around and interact with various objects. It also enables social interaction, as multiple users can interact with the same digital content while still seeing each other. AR is more relevant for users on the go while shopping or as support for physical tasks such as repair or surgery. The most common use cases are modeling, design, and medicine.

Some of the benefits provided by augmented reality include real-time delivery of relevant information to workers regardless of time or location, greater flexibility, mobility of operations, and increased efficiency.

Capabilities of Virtual Reality

VR covers the whole view that blocks the real world and isolates users from their surroundings to create an immersive visual of a new world and immerse the user in a new digital experience.

VR is useful when a user needs to be transported to an altogether new world as in gaming or advanced military training. Users' lack of awareness of their physical surroundings often limits their mobility or requires dedicated space.

Some of the benefits provided by virtual reality include faster prototyping, design, and training, cost-effective solutions compared to real-world applications, no safety concerns, and increased flexibility of work and location.

Capabilities of Mixed Reality

MR superimposes computer-generated objects on a user's view of the real world such that the virtual objects can interact directly with the physical objects to provide a new kind of experience to the user.

MR allows the user to remain oriented in the physical world in order to move around or interact with digitally generated virtual objects. It enables social interaction, as multiple users can interact with the same digital content while still seeing each other. MR is more relevant when it is necessary to add elements to an experience. A great example is placing furniture in a room to determine fit and look, or seeing a part exploded out in 3D next to the real-world object.

AR and VR in the Current Ecosystem

The smart mobile phone is the most widely used device in the ecosystem today. A VR experience can be created on a mobile phone for a user sitting at home by using Google Cardboard, which has the necessary display and sensor technology. Similarly, Apple's ARKit makes it possible to create an AR experience and share it with family and friends. As smartphones continue to improve with high-resolution cameras and effective motion tracking enablement, there might be some final elements required to enable widescale user adoption of this technology.

In the gaming industry, there has been a shift from 2D to 3D graphics. As 3D games gained popularity and became the industry standard, enterprises began to license the established 3D engines instead of every company making investments to build their own. This became the new revenue model for a lot of enterprises and laid the groundwork for creating 3D experiences using the AR/VR technology.

One of the key barriers to the growth of this industry is the creation and distribution of quality 3D content. As the 3D modeling tools become cheaper and new technologies such as 3D scanners and 360° cameras become more commoditized, a boost is provided to the supporting infrastructure for AV/VR technology to mature.

Understanding AR/VR Architecture

The AR/VR architecture outlines all the technical components required to create and deliver an AR/VR experience to a user.

First are the tools required to create 3D content. Then comes the infrastructure and apps to develop and package the content with the logic. Finally, a display platform is required to distribute the content in one of the AR/VR devices for the users to get the experience. In order to determine the optimal architecture for any specific use case, all possible options and decision points need to be defined and evaluated.

3D Content Creation

Some of the tools that aid in the creation of 3D content are listed below:

3D Scanners

3D scanning is the process of capturing the data of a real-world object and transforming it into a three-dimensional digital model. This model often includes the shape of the object in the form of a geometric mesh and the associated colors and patterns as textures. 3D scanners involve three basic techniques:

- **Digital Photogrammetry.** Photogrammetry is the process of taking multiple photos of an object, person, or environment from different angles and matching the overlapping patterns to build a 3D object by loading all the photos in 3D creation software. It produces both the geometric mesh and the associated textures, though the algorithms necessary are intensive and need to be run in postprocessing mode. The best practice is to take a minimum of 20 photos to get a good 3D output. The image can then be printed using a 3D printer.

The technique can be used in both indoor and outdoor applications provided there is enough light on the object. The type of object scanned has a great influence on the picture constructed. Objects with smooth, featureless surfaces such as plastics may not provide enough unique patterns and curves to match, while shiny or transparent surfaces such as metals or glass will not work, as the refraction patterns would change with the observation angle during the scanning process.

- **Laser Pulsar (Lidar).** Lidar stands for Light Detection and Ranging. 3D Lidar scanners use sensing technology that sweeps a pulsating laser across an object or scene to measure ranges. Each pulse emits light, which is then reflected off the scene and collected by a sensor. The time of travel for the beam reveals the surface's relative distance. This is used to generate a large data set composed of 3D point data of the environment, which can then be converted to a geometric mesh. Texture data can be captured through other means and mapped to the geometric mesh as required.

Lidar is highly accurate for both indoor and outdoor scanning but requires very precise instrumentation, which makes it very expensive. It does not perform well for transparent or dark surfaces, which don't reflect light effectively.

- **Structured Light (Infrared).** Structured light scanners work by projecting a known pattern of light onto a three-dimensional object. This pattern appears distorted from any perspective other than that of the projector, and that distortion can be used to reconstruct the 3D shape of the object.

The system only works indoors, as sunlight would wash out the projected pattern and is often employed in the infrared spectrum in order to make it invisible to the eye. The technology is deployed in many commercial handheld 3D scanners and is also used for spatial mapping systems such as Microsoft's Kinect, which was originally developed as a gaming accessory for Xbox.

3D Modeling Tools

Unity is the world's largest platform for game developers and creators, which provides some basic features for 3D model design. The developers use specialized tools to create complex virtual content, which is then imported into the game engine such as Unity to provide the virtual experience. Some of the 3D modeling tools that can be considered are listed below:

- **Parametric Modeling.** The parametric approach focuses on precise specifications, feature relationships, and design history and is typically used by engineers and architects. It can be used to define constraints on a model's design or simulate physical or thermal strains. In virtual reality, these type of models are useful when a model is expected to react and move naturally to forces acting upon it. Some of the examples include Solidworks, Autocad, etc.

- **Direct Modeling.** The direct approach is quite flexible to use and is typically used by artists and industrial designers. Direct modeling allows changes to be made on the fly, and small changes are not necessarily related to any other defined point of the geometry. This is best for more static content that can be created and modified quickly. Some of the examples include Maya, Blender, etc.

- **VR Modeling.** The VR modeling tools utilize the VR hardware itself to design 3D content with the reimagined user experience. This is the most agile and intuitive method, as designers can experience their creations exactly as users would. The limitation of these systems is precision, as they mostly rely on the intuitive imagination of the designer. Some of the examples include Gravity Sketch, etc.

360° Video

While virtual reality is making the gaming experience more immersive, 360° video is doing the same for the cinematic experience. Users can view a video from any direction just by moving their heads as if the screen wrapped completely around them. Some of the considerations are mentioned below:

- **Right Story.**   360° video puts the audience in the story. This can act as a powerful tool where a journalist wants to convey the feeling of a place or where a movie producer wants to produce a sensitive emotional response during a horror movie scene. This tool requires new storytelling techniques, as directors no longer have tight control over the object of attention but must instead use various audio and visual cues to guide the audience. Scene transitions must also be carefully planned to create a smooth visual transition and center the audience into a new scene. 360° images have also been used by car dealers and real estate agents to allow potential customers to experience the product before visiting the car shop or home.

- **Right Technology.**   Specialized cameras such as the Ricoh Theta, which combines input from two opposing lenses, each with a wide field of view, is used to capture 360° video or images. For a higher-resolution panoramic video, six or more cameras are mounted in a specialized rig and stitched together to get the resulting feeds. This can produce a much sharper image, though the stitching process can be laborious even with specialized software such as VideoStitch Studio. The capture system should be mounted on a tripod or drone at about eye level to get the most natural perspective of the surroundings.

3D Content Marketplace

The creation of a quality AR/VR experience starts with high-quality content. Below are some of the marketplaces available online that provide quality 3D models, photos, videos, sounds, and textures:

- 3D Warehouse
- Cgtrader
- Flickr
- Textures
- Archive3D
- SketchFab
- Freesound
- Voxelus
- Clara
- Turbosquid

Application Development

Some of the tools that aid in the development and deployment of the application are listed below:

Infrastructure

For the virtual reality technology to be adopted by the masses in their day-to-day life, it needs to offer a virtual world for the users that is worth going to, a world that is expansive, interactive, and where actions have consequences that persist through time and space. This presents a huge challenge in computation capability and storage space availability.

The current online games model works as a single server per game, where the number of possible players and simulated entities is limited by the capacity of that server. To support large numbers of simultaneous players, the developer needs to run multiple versions of the game, each on a separate server, with players divided up between them. This diverges the virtual world and limits its scope.

Additionally, the memory limitations constrain developers to only model the parts of the world that are currently being played by the user. This inhibits true object persistence and limits the possible experiences to predefined scripts and localized events.

New gaming platforms such as Improbable's SpatialOS overcomes these challenges by offering a distributed operating system that can run an expansive virtual world which persists whether a player is there to experience it or not. For example, a character in a game from a battle high on a mountain can float down a river and reach players in a distant town days after the original event. This is achieved by creating a virtualized layer that allocates server resources in real time and by separating the graphics from the simulation while the simulation continues even when players are not around.

This architecture also enables a game developer to run multiple clients that interact with the same world such as players on PC, console, VR, and mobile, where all can play together. The ability to simulate complex systems across a distributed computing architecture has applications in gaming, city management, defense, healthcare, and economics.

Game Engines

The development of an AR/VR application that is engaging for the users requires a combination of high-quality 3D content, a set of rules that govern how that content interacts with the player and environment, and hardware-specific drivers that provide access to the sensors and user I/O channels. The game engine is the tool that combines all of these elements to bring a coherent experience. There are two game engines that are very popular and dominate the market:

- **Unity.** Unity is a gaming engine with both 2D and 3D capability that was launched in 2005 and has rapidly gained market share with more than 60% of VR developers using Unity as the gaming engine.

It is known for its intuitive user interface, extensive documentation that helps developers, active community to discuss any issues or share any learnings, and low learning curve, with familiarity with the language used for development. Unity is best for both novice developers and those making lighter applications for mobile.

- **Unreal Engine.**   Unreal Engine was one of the first game engines that led the market and was widely available for development with a focus on high-end console games.

It is best known for its advanced rendering engine, high performance, and low-level system controls. Unreal Engine is best suited for professional developers who are working on large projects intended for console or PC.

VR Ecosystem

The ecosystem surrounding virtual reality closely resembles the mobile application model with dedicated devices, app stores, and native development. As the number of devices and VR apps grows, VR needs to be made more interoperable so that any app can work on any device. Some of the projects are listed below:

- **Open Source VR.**   OSVR is an open source initiative with two independent components, namely hardware and software. The open hardware platform consists of a virtual reality headset called the Hacker Development Kit. The open software platform provides a Software Development Kit for virtual reality developers to detect, configure, and operate virtual reality devices across a wide range of operating systems in order to deliver a high-quality immersive experience. Some of the enterprises or games using OSVR include Sensics, Razer, etc.

- **OpenVR.**   OpenVR is a Software Development Kit that allows a VR application to run on any supported VR headset without relying on specific hardware. The API creates a consistent experience across devices by providing app developers with a set of libraries for capturing the rotation and location settings from the headset and controllers. Some of the enterprises or games using OpenVR include Valve, etc.

- **WebVR.**   WebVR is an experimental Javascript API that integrates virtual reality into the web browsing experience. It allows web content to be rendered for VR headsets and supports various input devices. Because it's implemented through the browser, it retains many of the features that make the web a great platform for the creation and distribution of content. This includes easy access using URL addresses with no downloads or installs required and navigation between sites. Some of the examples include Mozilla, Google, etc.

Application Marketplace

Each of the major hardware platforms has a supporting application marketplace for distribution and discovery. These marketplaces are often available through the web and also within the AR/VR environment. Applications can be exported directly from the chosen game engine using the plugins. Some of the products available in the marketplace include:

- **Oculus Rift.**   Oculus launched the experiences marketplace which features 100+ apps and growing for the Rift and Gear VR.

- **Microsoft HoloLens.**   HoloLens is still primarily a developer platform and features multiple applications designed to showcase its functionality.

- **HTC Vive.**   HTC's Viveport offers a subscription model where a user can choose the specified number of titles per month from their curated list.

User Interface

The display platform provides the window into the virtual world and is the most recognizable part of the AR/VR ecosystem. These devices incorporate a number of sensors, display technologies, and unique user interface paradigms, which together create the desired illusion. Listed below is an overview of the components and how they are combined to support different AR/VR use cases:

Form Factor

Different levels of immersion, social interaction, and user controls are enabled by various form factors in terms of size, configuration, and computational power of the device. They also target different customer segments, markets, and price points. Developers need to carefully consider how much immersion their target user is willing to pay for. Some of the examples include the following:

- **Phone.**   For the casual user, phone or tablet displays are ideal for everyday activity and require no additional hardware purchase. Users can use the touchscreens for interaction and can also easily see each other and share in social applications.

- **Head-Mounted Phone.** A head-mounted phone or tablet such as Google Cardboard combines the cost efficiency of using existing hardware with the hands-free immersion of a head-mounted display. The lack of dedicated hardware does not provide a rich and superior experience in terms of comfort and graphics.

- **Head-Mounted Display.** For the serious user, dedicated head-mounted displays such as HoloLens or Oculus Rift provide the most comfort and graphics processing power. They also free up a user's hands for interactions using gestures or controllers. This is the most common form factor for gaming.

Processing and Storage

The inherent trade-off here is between mobility and processing horsepower. As most AR applications commonly incorporate the environment around the user, they tend to be stand-alone. VR applications have to render more virtual content at every moment and so tend to be tethered. Some of the examples include the following:

- **Tethered.** Tethered devices such as Oculus Rift are able to offload power, computing, and storage onto a nearby computer, which provides much more horsepower for the display at a much smaller form factor. This creates a superior viewing experience, with the obvious drawback that the user is bound to the computer with a cable.

- **Stand-alone.** Stand-alone devices such as HoloLens need to contain all the necessary components within the headset itself, which places constraints on the battery, computing, and storage. Weight distribution must be carefully planned in order to provide a stable and comfortable experience. The benefit of stand-alone devices is that a user can move freely through the environment.

Optics

While standard mobile and tablet displays are used for handheld applications, truly immersive AR/VR relies on displays with wearables very near to the eye. These dual displays are mounted just a few centimeters from each eye and deliver two slightly adjusted views of the content to create the illusion of depth. There are two types of these depending on the preferred experience, as mentioned below:

- **Opaque Displays.** An OLED is the most common display for VR applications, with the current industry standards being 2160 x 1200 resolution, 110° field of view, and 90Hz refresh rate. This type of display can also be used for

AR applications if digital content is combined with a live stream of the user's surroundings. Examples include Oculus, Vive, etc.

- **Transparent Displays.**   AR headsets are able to layer digital content on top of a semitransparent lens using a technology called planar waveguides. Light is directed along the surface of the lens and then redirected into the eye using the same principles that govern fiber optics. It allows the user to view digital content within the context of the real world, though the effect still suffers from a limited field of view and a fluorescent color palette, since the display can only brighten but never darken. Examples include HoloLens, etc.

Digital Content

While all types of AR use information about the real world to trigger digital content, the different types of experiences and degrees of immersion created vary based on the type of sensors and information used. Below are the three primary types of AR:

- **Location-based AR.**   Location-based AR apps such as Pokémon Go provide contextual data based upon the location and orientations of a device. These apps are most often used for outdoor applications such as help with directions in a particular city, locating a vehicle in a parking lot, or understanding constellation patterns in the night sky. Digital content often feels as if it is floating in front of the user, but it does not exist in relation to any of the physical objects in the vicinity.

- **Marker-based AR.**   Marker-based AR apps such as coloring books trigger digital content based on the identification of a particular object or marker and can manipulate the digital content in relation to that marker in real time. These apps are most often used for close-range applications and have the benefit that digital content moves with the physical markers they are bound to. The dependence of a physical component does limit the possible use cases.

- **Markerless AR.**   Markerless apps such as Roboraid on HoloLens accurately detect and create three-dimensional representations of the real-world environment around a user. Walls, tables, and other objects are mapped and allow virtual objects to interact with these objects. These apps provide the most immersive experience in that virtual objects and real-world objects seem to occupy the same three-dimensional space.

User Controls

Any AR/VR system needs to provide a way for the user to issue commands and manipulate the virtual world. Touchscreens remain the obvious paradigm for handheld applications, while head-mounted platforms are still very new and lack common interface standards that users are familiar with. A combination of any of the below can be used across various platforms.

- **Gaze.**   The most basic interface involves placing a set of crosshairs directly in front of a user's gaze and allowing them to linger on an object in order to select it. This is quite limited but has the benefit that it doesn't require any additional sensors or hardware to implement.

- **Gesture.**   Head-mounted depth cameras can track a user's hand movements. While broad gestures mapped to commands are fairly simple to implement, fine-grained manipulation of virtual objects is still a challenge, as the lack of tangible feedback makes it difficult to sense where the hand is in relation to those objects.

- **Voice.**   Voice commands are a natural choice for a hands-free interface, at least in quiet environments. Directional microphones in the headset can amplify a user's voice against background noise, and over the ear bone conduction can be used to issue responses. This interface can be useful for higher-level commands but can get tedious for repetitive actions.

- **Controller.**   Handheld controllers provide the most robust control options with multiple assignable controls and fine motor control. They are also a natural extension from the gaming industry. The downside is the need for additional hardware, which must be tracked just like the headset.

Tracking

In order to adopt digital content in accordance with a user's movement, AR/VR devices use a combination of the sensors to orient the device in space. The ultimate goal is to track all six degrees of freedom experienced by a rigid body in space. The three translations include up/down, forward/back, and right/left, and the three rotations include pitch, yaw, and roll. Some of the examples of position tracking include the following:

- **Orientation Tracking.**   An Inertial Measurement Unit (IMU) is a tiny sensor bundle that includes a magnetometer, accelerometer, and gyroscope. These sensors are now standard in mobile and tablet devices and work together to capture precise rotations across the three axes: pitch, yaw, and roll. These sensors alone are unable to capture linear translations through space.

- **"Outside In" Position Tracking.** "Outside in" position tracking uses one or more infrared transmitters placed outside and around the device along with the internal IMU in order to capture both rotations and translations through space. This allows the device such as Vive or Oculus to track all six degrees of freedom with high accuracy, though it limits a user's movements to a designated area free from obstacles, as the AR sensors require a direct line of sight to the device.

- **"Inside Out" Position Tracking.** "Inside out" position tracking uses a combination of the IMU and various onboard depth and RGB cameras to capture both rotations and translations. This system achieves all six degrees of freedom without the need for external infrared devices, granting users complete freedom to move around their environment. Accuracy and responsiveness are still slightly worse than "outside in" systems but optimizations in computer vision algorithms will solve this problem.

Emerging Technologies

First-generation headsets have really focused on maturing head tracking and display technology in order to ensure high-resolution smooth images. While these capabilities are the foundation for any AR/VR experience, the next-generation devices are expected to expand their capabilities across two broad domains:

- Increase the degree of immersion by incorporating more sensor channels and more accurately re-creating the sensory signals of the real world.
  - 3D audio is a technique that emulates audio coming from a precise point in a 3D virtual environment, simulating sound in the natural way we hear it, and providing depth and immersion beyond traditional stereo sound. There are two techniques for achieving this: object-based, which uses sound objects placed within a scene, and ambisonics, which determines the sound field produced at the position of the listener.
  - Haptics describes technologies that mimic the real-world stimulation of our cutaneous (skin) and kinesthetic (muscles/joints) sensory systems. Cutaneous haptics produces sensations of touch, vibration, and temperature, while kinesthetic haptics produces the sensations of force on the bones and muscles. The entire field is still nascent, with multiple areas of research still being conducted.
- Capture the real-time emotional and attentive state of the user in order to automatically optimize the virtual experiences and gather valuable data on individual and aggregate preferences.

- Facial tracking has been used in the movie industry to map the expressions of real-world actors onto virtual characters. In the AR/VR domain, it is likely the key to unlocking social VR, the ability for users to have natural interactions in the virtual world. The effect requires tracking the movement of the mouth, often through a 3D camera on a short boom, and the movement of the eyes and eyebrows, either with an inward-facing camera or strain gauges added to the foam padding along the headset.
- Eye tracking tracks the direction of a user's gaze through their eye movements. The primary technique, called pupil center corneal reflection, directs an infrared beam into the pupil of the eye and measures the reflection in the cornea. This technology was first introduced to track how a customer consumes and turns the attention to products and products in a retail setting. Within the VR ecosystem, eye tracking technology has the potential to enhance the user experience and even the performance of VR applications.

Platform

Listed below are some of the popular platforms used in the development of AR/VR applications:

Apple's ARKit

Apple's ARKit is able to achieve high-precision motion tracking without any additional hardware or specialized cameras. It achieves this by combining reading from the camera (Visual Inertial Odometry) and the IMU (Dead Reckoning) and continuously using one to adjust for the errors in the other.

This successfully negates the "drift" that occurs in similar systems through tight integration and precise calibration across the hardware and software stack. Some of the iPhone components include the following:

- Monocular camera
- IMU orientation tracking
- Video see-through AR display
- Touchscreen controls
- Motion tracking SDK

Microsoft HoloLens

The HoloLens is an experimental AR headset primarily focused on enterprise applications. The whole system is self-contained, with onboard computing,

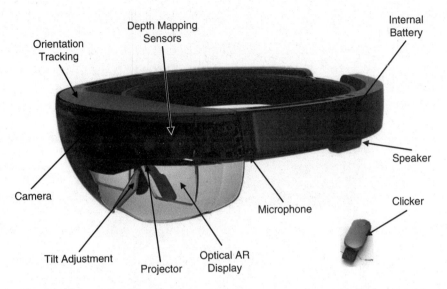

Figure 11.1   Microsoft HoloLens.

storage, and power. Digital content is displayed on two semitransparent planar waveguide lenses.

HoloLens utilizes "inside out" position tracking to map its surroundings without external sensors. While this design does free users from a designated area, it also limits the use of controllers, as there is no external system to capture their position. In place of a controller, HoloLens uses a combination of gaze, gesture, voice commands, and an included "clicker." The components of a HoloLens are depicted in Figure 11.1.

HTC Vive

The HTC Vive is primarily a VR gaming headset. The headset tethers to a nearby computer and uses two IR "lighthouses," for project blinking and sweeping infrared light. This light is registered by the array of IR sensors on the headset and controllers, which, together with an internal IMU, compute their relative position and orientation.

The system achieves fine-tuned tracking of the headset and the controllers but requires the setup of the lighthouses and a dedicated space without obstruction. The components of a Vive are depicted in Figure 11.2.

Security and Privacy

The mass adoption of AR/VR presents security and privacy challenges. It manages to combine the data protection risks of the cloud, the user privacy

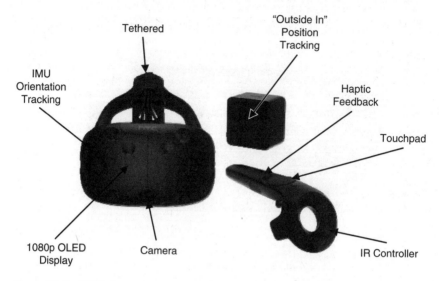

Figure 11.2   HTC Vive.

concerns of social media, and the hardware security risks associated with IoT, all rolled into one. Some of the concerns include the following:

User Privacy

The social media model of providing the service and monetizing on the data will likely continue with social VR; it will be much more detailed with targeted data sets. Preserving the user's moment-by-moment emotional responses and other sensitive data and privacy is key to the success of this technology.

Data Security

As AR/VR becomes more widely accepted, it will inevitably mature beyond entertainment to service the boardroom and beyond. Fully immersive virtual meetings are one of the use cases. As business users start to conduct sensitive business in VR, careful consideration needs to be given to the implications of data locality, security, and encryption. The challenge is to present financial projections or technical specs to an intended audience but keep that information encrypted to all other observers.

Hardware Security

The connected IoT devices such as baby monitors and security cameras are easy targets for hackers to steal data and sensitive information from, and the same risks apply to AR/VR headsets. Hackers could tap into the sensors on the device such as the camera or microphone to spy on the physical environment or tap into the video feed to see what the user is seeing. They may even be able to modify the virtual environment with harmful or misleading content. Proper security around the hardware is key to the success of this technology for mass adoption.

Opportunities by Industry

Both VR and AR provide ample opportunities and new challenges in gathering, analyzing, and acting on data from the environment. Some of the industry-specific business processes where virtual and augmented reality have been used to provide an enhanced and immersive customer experience and have the potential to grow further are described below.

Retail

The global retail industry is worth around $30 trillion and is faced with a myriad of challenges, such as volatile exchange rates, regulatory pressures, trade wars, and shifts in consumer behavior. Investment in retail technology is on the rise year after year to keep pace with consumer demands and have a competitive edge.

Some of the potential use cases for AR/VR include the following:

- **The Virtual Shopping Center.** The concept of stores is changing. In some cases, foot traffic is on the decline and retailers have begun to look at profit per square foot; whereas for other brands physical stores are used more as engaging experiences to build a different type of relationship with their customers. Physical stores are essentially now another "screen," and they are coming under pressure to be more innovative in how they show their product lines.

Virtual shopping combines the convenience of online shopping with the immersiveness of physical shopping. Some elements of virtual shopping include sensory feedback, which is achieved either through clunky solutions or prototypes that are not yet widely available, but the technology will eventually find its way to consumers. This would allow consumers to feel the texture of fabrics and the weight of electronics, and even enable virtual interactions with objects.

From a business perspective, there is no rent on virtual stores. They can be as large or as small as needed. The key variable cost will be the servers and infrastructure that sit behind them, and this cost will increase only with activity.

The real strength of the virtual store becomes apparent once it is combined with artificial intelligence. With an AI solution that tracks what users are looking at and how long they are spending in various sections, it can quickly draw conclusions or trends about individual consumer preferences. Once it has logged these, the store becomes a malleable place which is constantly adapting to the changing preferences. It would be different for every consumer every time they reentered the space, as it's a constantly changing environment.

- **Enhanced Customer Experience.**   Some enterprises such as IKEA and Dulux are using VR/AR technologies to augment the shopping experience. IKEA's VR app enables users to customize a kitchen by changing colors with the touch of a button and offering interaction with the cupboards and the hob. Dulux's mobile app allows people to paint their room to see what it would look like before they even purchase the paint.

In the future, enhanced versions of these applications will be used more widely as mixed reality gains ground. The rise of mixed reality will allow applications to understand the dimensions and structure of rooms, making any visualizations more realistic and useful to the consumer.

- **The Virtual Trial.**   In the near future, consumers could be accurately represented in the virtual world by a character of their choice or close resemblance based on a 3D scan of their body. This would allow them to try on clothes and accessories, eliminating one of the key issues of shopping for clothes online and getting the right size and fit.

A similar concept can be tried for customers who want to try hundreds of different makeover looks by using the Makeup Camera app on their smartphones as a magic mirror before making a purchase.

Healthcare

Expenditure for global health care is around $9 trillion, and there are multiple use cases for VR/AR in the healthcare industry. These will likely continue to grow as this technology is explored further. From medical training to actual treatments, VR/AR technology has great potential to impact all players in the healthcare industry: patients, doctors, hospitals, pharmacies, etc.

Some of the potential use cases for AR/VR include the following:

- **Training and Surgery.**   Growing demand from doctors, pharmaceutical companies, and the increasing number of medical programs in the world have created a shortage of corpses. These are used by medical students and doctors as an important learning tool, but their limited numbers are further pressured by suitability criteria and opposing cultural beliefs.

VR/AR technology can be used in place of physical corpses to provide an effective simulation of the human body. Additionally, any number of conditions can be applied to help teach doctors and students about niche medical cases and operations.

Further use cases for the technology include performing diagnostics without invasive procedures and combining VR with robotics to enable telesurgery where the surgery is performed remotely.

- **Medical Treatment.**   VR has also been used in conjunction with other technologies to create actual treatments for a number of mental illnesses and physical disabilities.

Virtual reality is also being used in combination with noninvasive brain-machine interfaces to help those who have paralysis. This was to see if touch sensations and voluntary control of muscles in legs could be regained.

The experiment was conducted with eight patients, all of them suffering from a spinal cord injury. By the end of the research, all eight patients saw improvements in their ability to feel sensations on their skin including cold and warm sensations as well as touch, pressure, and pain.

Other examples include using virtual reality to help retrain the brain to combat vertigo, treat phantom limb pain, treat PTSD, and help regain movement poststroke. These are all current real-life examples which indicate a strong potential for VR to become a mainstream method or tool for treatment in the future.

Automotive

The global automotive industry is a significant force in the world, with revenues of more than $9 trillion. It faces disruption from a number of technologies and cultural changes including the rise of the sharing economy, autonomous vehicles, and electric cars. The automotive industry has been positive about embracing the use of VR and AR for exterior car design. It has moved on from pencil and paper to computer-aided design, which is created and viewed on a 2D screen and is now at the stage where VR/AR technology is being used to better visualize the vehicles in a more realistic way that is measured to scale.

Some of the potential use cases for AR/VR include the following:

- **Exterior Design.**   Throughout the exterior design process, clay modeling has been a staple technique for almost a century, and it is still used today in combination with VR/AR. This will likely become less prevalent in the final stages of design as VR/AR gets wider adoption.

While VR/AR now plays an important part in the exterior design process, it has great potential to impact the human-machine interface design of cars. When considering the dashboard and control system of vehicles, it is important to get an accurate scale and understanding of where the controls fit and how easy they are to access from an ergonomics and safety perspective. This is difficult to achieve using traditional methods when there is input from multiple teams that often conflicts, requiring continuous iterations to be made and tested.

- **Autonomous Vehicles.**   A number of car manufacturers have developed prototype AR head-up displays (HUDs) to bring relevant information to the driver's line of sight at the right time, improving safety and creating a more streamlined experience for the driver.

  AR technology is also important as a stepping-stone to fully autonomous vehicles, as a lack of information and trust is one of the main obstacles to the public's accepting semiautonomous features such as cruise control and lane departure warnings. AR tackles this by conveying visually to the driver how it is forming judgments, such as highlighting the car in front when considering cruise control speeds.

  There are a number of business and technical challenges left to solve with AR HUD technology including its high cost to manufacture and overcoming speckle, an optical phenomenon in which the light appears granular on its projected surface.

- **Online Buying Experience.**   From a marketing and sales perspective, consumers are becoming more confident in purchasing products online across a number of different industries. People are more confident in buying a car online and unseen compared to a couple of years ago.

  This sentiment will be reinforced by VR technology as virtual car showrooms become more popular, offering consumers a more immersive way to experience, customize, and even test drive a vehicle from the comfort of their own home. It also present dealerships with a scalable way of deploying a showroom with a car manufacturer's entire range at short notice and with little space required. As more sales are conducted online and in smaller showrooms, this could, in turn, reduce the staff requirement for sales representatives, creating cost savings for the industry.

- **Driver Safety.**   Augmented reality can be used on vehicle windshields to provide interactive GPS instructions as well as other useful information on the dashboard, which helps from the safety standpoint, as drivers are kept informed, with their eyes still on the road.

Education

The value of the global education market is around $6 trillion. University courses face competition with massive online open courses (MOOCs), many of them free, which have exploded in popularity. This, combined with the ever-rising cost of traditional education, means that many students now seek courses that are best for value.

VR/AR in education is full of possibilities to break down geographical barriers and augment and expand the way students experience and build knowledge. Ultimately, technology presents students with a unique and stimulating way of learning that can complement traditional methods. Textbook reading is unlikely to be replaced, but students will be able to literally step through history, build empathy with others, and test ideas. It is clear that in order to attract and retain the best students, educational institutes will have to disrupt themselves to find a more compelling offering.

Some of the potential use cases for AR/VR include the following:

- **No Geographical Barrier.**   One incredible strength of virtual reality in education is the idea of using it to democratize education. Schools and labs are expensive to build in reality, while in virtual reality they are far cheaper and, once built, can be accessed from anywhere in the world through a headset.

- **Effective Retention.**   Numerous sources point to virtual reality as being effective in increasing the retention of information in those undertaking training. This trend should continue and bring similar results in the classroom.

Entertainment and Media

The global revenue of the entertainment and media industry is around $2.5 trillion, with around a 4.5% compound annual growth rate. There are interesting trends that underpin the changes in the industry such as shifts of power to countries with high youth population, local content being key, growth being driven by emerging economies, and smaller nimbler players disrupting the media giants.

Some of the potential use cases for AR/VR include the following:

- **New Experience.**   The industry is broad, consisting of segments including publishing, film, digital advertising, music, radio, TV, and video games. The related applications to video games are clear and can be seen currently. What makes VR, in particular, so disruptive to entertainment and media is that it is a step-change in the medium for the public to experience. In the same way that TV offered a new way to experience media visually, VR offers a new way with an immersive experience.

- **Live Events.**   Live events are particularly ripe for disruption, as they suffer from a lack of scalable supply, and it is difficult to increase the number of seats for a concert in accordance with demand, as venues have physical space limitations.

If a small portion of this space was invested in a setup that supported VR live streaming, this would allow consumers from all over the world to experience the event in a more immersive way than simply watching it on a screen.

This is disruptive for business, as it opens up an entirely new revenue stream. Due to the potential scale of VR live streaming, where user numbers are limited only by the strength of the backend systems to support such numbers, the price point is likely to be accessible for consumers, creating a win-win situation for both sides.

When combined with the trend of social VR and multiuser VR environments, VR streamed events become an even more powerful proposition, enabling users to share experiences.

VR live streaming will never be a perfect substitute for attending a real-life event, but it may get close enough to offer significant value to consumers over current solutions and enable consumers to feel they are part of an event where it would otherwise be impossible or inaccessible.

Engineering and Construction

Construction is not necessarily the first industry that springs to mind when thinking about emerging technologies and innovation. It is also one of the least digitized industries, with less than 1% of revenues spent on research and development compared to 4–5% in some other industries.

Some of the potential use cases for AR/VR include the following:

- **Cost Optimization.**   VR/AR presents a lot of opportunity for disruption, along with emerging technologies such as drones and 3D printing, as it has the potential to provide cost reduction and optimization benefits across the industry.

A prototype is being built to enable engineers to visualize building information models in full scale at their offices or to superimpose information on an on-site structure. This application could improve the workflow efficiency of building inspectors, who can use a device like Microsoft HoloLens to walk through a site and see a superimposition of the finished building on top of the real-world model. They can, therefore, assess in a timely manner the progress that is being made and assess what work is outstanding.

- **Remote Inspection.**   From a health and safety perspective, critical infrastructure such as bridges can be inspected from anywhere in the world without inspectors having to physically visit the site, reducing safety risks and creating cost and time savings.

Virtual reality can also be used to create a solution for consumers to explore buildings that haven't yet been constructed or an interior design recommendation that has yet to be implemented.

Use Cases

Virtual reality use cases are scenarios where the VR technology was used to provide an immersive experience to a user. Let's study some scenarios along with real-life case studies to see how the journey to VR can be facilitated to result in an intelligent enterprise.

1. Case Study: Virtual Tourism
   - Scenario
     - A global travel company wanted to increase user experience for someone planning to visit a place for a vacation.
   - Approach
     - The virtual reality provided an elevated experience to a user for any place of their choice.
     - The potential traveler was able to navigate and visit several nearby sightseeing locations using 360° videos and get data points and necessary information before making a decision to visit the place.
   - Results
     - The enterprise was able to provide a condensed environment to acquaint the user with what the place has to offer using 360° video content.

2. Case Study: Auto Showroom
   - Scenario
     - An auto manufacturer wanted to display its cars to the potential buyers in a new, sophisticated manner.
   - Approach
     - The virtual reality experience brought the buyer into a virtual auto showroom, where they were able to select various features and models for the car that they were looking for.
     - The users were also given the facility to visit the latest auto show and see what new models were presented.

- Results
  - The enterprise was able to provide a classy environment to familiarize the user with all the possible options and interact with the car using 360° video content.
  - It was a very new car buying experience that the user had never experienced before.

3. Case Study: Planning Retirement
   - Scenario
     - A financial services company wanted to create a visual effect before making a retirement decision.
   - Approach
     - The virtual reality experience helped the users plan how they would like to live their life postretirement.
     - The users were provided with multiple options based on their criteria, and based on the VR technology, they could choose an ideal location of where they could retire and live comfortably.
   - Results
     - The enterprise was able to provide an environment to familiarize the user with all the possible options and interact with the location of their retirement using 360° video content.

Conclusion

Virtual reality, augmented reality, and mixed reality are all emerging technologies in the development stage and need a lot of prototyping and testing before being accepted by the enterprises as a solution to their business process or revenue model. Some of the key concerns that persist include:

- Connectivity interruption due to power outage or poor internet connection that might impact the availability of real-time data, resulting in inaccurate actions by users and poor experience.
- Content creation and hardware development have a long way to go before virtual reality products are commercialized for mass usage.
- Though the virtual and augmented reality industry is still in the nascent stage, there is a school of thought that the users may lose touch and real-time interactions with the real world.
- There is a lack of standards pertaining to AR/VR technology in terms of information, data, support, integration, and algorithms.
- Privacy-related concerns still remain on the type of information that should be augmented on top of the real world without breaching any privacy laws.

CHAPTER 12

3D Printing

*T*his chapter provides an overview of 3D printing technology, the steps required to execute the printing process, some of the benefits and challenges around the technology, and the application areas. It also discusses the methodology for adoption and some of the typical use cases across industries to make the enterprise intelligent.

3D Printing Overview

3D Printing is the additive manufacturing technology that is used to create a three-dimensional object from a digital model by adding material layer by layer. It allows designers and manufacturers to build complex parts such as tools, toys, spare parts, etc., at a fraction of the cost compared to what it takes to buy the actual product and saves the time involved in the copying, molding, and shaping processes.

Plastic polymers are the most commonly used material used in the 3D printers, but with the advancement of technology, the printing process uses various other materials such as metal, ceramic, sand, wax, cast iron, and inks. Recently, glass and wood have also been used with the 3D printers.

In the past, the cost of 3D printing was high, and the technology was only used by large enterprises, but the development of consumer-friendly desktop 3D printers has made the technology more accessible to small and midsized businesses and home users.

3D printing is one of the emerging disruptive technologies that has been on a rapid growth trajectory with a global market forecast of more than $21 billion. It has the potential to disrupt the traditional manufacturing process in factories and logistics, with printers being set up in close proximity to the consumers.

Printing Process

The following are the basic steps that need to be followed in a 3D printing process:

1. Plan for the object that needs to be printed.
2. Create the complete design and blueprint of the object that needs to be printed.
3. Modeling software such as Inventor, Blender, Cinema 4D, Shapeways, or AutoCAD can be used to create a new 3D model, or an existing model from the software can also be used.
4. Finalize the design and save the 3D design file.
5. The finished design file is sent to the printer.
6. Most printers have the provision to hold the raw material, usually plastic, used for printing the object in a three-dimensional space.
7. When the printer receives the design file, it pulls the material from the device, starts the printing process, melts the material during the process, deposits it into the plate in layers, and then instantly cools it.
8. The outcome is a completely printed 3D object that has been created through layering, where the printer will add one layer of the object at a time until the fully formed structure is printed completely.

Benefits

Some of the key benefits of using 3D printing are listed below:

- Allows fast turnaround on prototyping.
- Promotes innovation and creativity.
- Helps the enterprise achieve speed to market due to a reduction in lead time and shorter transit times.
- Enterprises involved in research and development can greatly benefit from innovative designs.
- Introduces a culture of innovation and research within enterprises.
- Helps in streamlining the supply chain process.
- In certain industries such as high-tech, the technology overcomes the design limitation for extremely complex parts.
- On-demand printing of spare parts and obsolete inventory and parts contributes towards the profitability of the enterprise.
- Substantial reduction in cost due to savings in labor, raw materials, inventory storage, and transportation by printing near the customer location.

- Reduced investments by the enterprise in tooling and other production-related costs.
- Improvement in service levels by promising faster supply of spare parts.
- Increase in customer satisfaction by providing a catalog with a wide range of available spare parts and accessories and also catering to changing customer demands.

Challenges

Some of the key challenges of using 3D printing are listed below:

- The cost of 3D printing is still high, as the 3D printers have not been commoditized yet.
- It allows users more options, which causes more change requests.
- The printers consume energy, which needs to be factored into the cost of production.
- A few of the complex 3D designs cannot be measured to scale using the modeling software.
- 3D printing can lead to legal risks concerning who would be responsible in case of any accidents – the original design and model creator or the printer manufacturer.
- There are still some limitations on the types of material that can be used in 3D printing.
- Scalability of the technology to large-scale manufacturing is also a big challenge.
- Lack of in-house 3D technology expertise hinders the growth.

Application Areas

Some of the key application areas of using 3D printing are listed below:

- Assembly parts
- Tooling patterns
- Presentation models
- Research and development
- Healthcare and smart medical devices
- Prototyping
- Supply chain optimization

- Bridge manufacturing
- Metal casting patterns
- Visual aids
- Customized products
- Production at a remote location

Opportunity by Industry

Some of the key industries that have either benefited or have the potential to derive the benefits by using 3D printing technology are listed below:

- Aerospace
- Automotive
- Industrial tools
- Pharmaceuticals
- Hospital
- Consumer goods
- Education
- Fashion

Methodology

The 3D printing methodology provides an all-in-one solution to scan, analyze, assess, and digitize 3D printing at scale so that it increases the adoption rate within the enterprise facilitated by the ease of use, automation, and proven methodology. The key elements of the methodology are described below:

Scan

The product that needs to be printed undergoes a dimensional check and the output from the scanned image is then analyzed.

Data Collection

The physical data and other information of the part are collected for further analysis.

Analyze

From the overall product portfolio, the parts that can be printed are recommended based on the technical feasibility of the 3D printer.

Cost Driver

The costs incurred through traditional manufacturing of various parts are gathered.

Assessment

The cost-benefit assessment is conducted by comparing the cost components between additive and traditional manufacturing. Based on the assessment, the parts that are suitable for 3D printing with potential cost savings are finalized and a business case is prepared for stakeholders' approval. The assessment also involves finalization of the operating model with a decision on in-house or outsourced printing.

Design

The 3D design of the object is prepared using 3D modeling software. The digital blueprint is integrated into the system for optimizing the material and design of the product.

Execution

The enterprise needs to ensure that 3D printing is securely executed based on the finalized version of the design. Blockchain technology can be used to share the 3D design file that can then be uploaded to the 3D printer for its execution.

Use Cases

3D printing use cases are scenarios where the technology was used to provide cost reduction, innovation, and rapid prototyping. Let's study some scenarios along with real-life case studies to see how the journey to 3D printing can be facilitated to result in an intelligent enterprise.

1. Case Study: Business Case Assessment of 3D Printing in the Spare Part Supply Chain for a Ship Manufacturer

- Scenario
  - A global ship manufacturer had a total spare part portfolio of more than 1 million SKUs.
  - 20% of the spare parts cost was attributed to transportation while 60% of the spare parts had a lead time of more than six weeks.
- Approach
  - The enterprise prepared and assessed the business case of 3D printing in the overall spare part supply chain by analyzing all the cost components and compared it with the cost of 3D printing.
  - Various scenarios were created and analyzed such as a direct printing facility at each of the manufacturing locations and creating major 3D printing hubs to supply the spare parts with least supply chain bottleneck.
- Results
  - The current spare part portfolio was mapped on the current 3D print technology maturity.
  - A supply chain cost model was built with different implementation scenarios for 3D printing.

2. Case Study: Rapid Prototyping by the Automotive Parts Manufacturer
   - Scenario
     - A global automotive parts manufacturer specialized in automotive interior components for passenger, commercial, and heavy construction vehicles.
     - Their customers, who are the auto manufacturers, demanded shorter R&D and product delivery times with an increase in quality standards.
   - Approach
     - The enterprise changed their model to 3D printing that manufactured the parts quickly.
     - The digitization of the design helped them check dimensions, fit, ease of assembly and the practicality of the design, which exceeded the quality standards.
   - Results
     - The enterprise saved a substantial amount in the expenses related to prototyping.
     - It shortened its product development cycles.
     - Some of the intangible benefits included discovering problems early, producing new product faster, and exceeding the customer's quality requirements.

3. Case Study: Enhancing Product Development
- Scenario
  - A global pump manufacturer designs a wide range of pumps and heating systems that include plastic and rubber parts for consumer and industrial applications around the world.
- Approach
  - The enterprise switched over to 3D printing after careful consideration and business case preparation.
- Results
  - Traditional prototype development used to take more than a month, which was reduced to a day by changing the model to 3D printing, resulting in huge savings.
  - The prototype development cost with 3D printing was reduced by 90%.
  - This shortened the enterprise's R&D process.

Conclusion

3D printing has been gaining momentum and mainstream acceptance over time. The usage is not just limited to spare parts and manufacturing but has now expanded to the fashion industry in the manufacture of personalized and perfectly fitted garments, in the jewelry industry for prototyping ornaments, and in the footwear industry to offer customized pairs of shoes to customers.

Some of the challenges related to scalability and safety still prevail and needs to be resolved through governance and policies around 3D printing. Once the 3D printers become a commodity for mass scale usage, the cost of printing would significantly decrease, which would facilitate economies of scale.

CHAPTER 13

Big Data

*T*his chapter provides an overview of big data technology, and its ability to enable agile business decisions based on information visibility and analytics capabilities. It also discusses the technology components and the architecture involved along with the use cases and opportunities across industries to make the enterprise intelligent with data-driven insight.

Big Data Overview

With the growth of digital media and content creation, the amount of available storage capacity in any form of a disk is becoming redundant. Based on the estimated 44 zettabytes, which is equivalent to 44 trillion gigabytes, of data that we have created, less than 15% can be stored in any form of storage media.

Big data refers to very large and complex data sets that cannot be stored or processed by traditional data analytics tools and methods. Big data technology has emerged as an improvement to the existing infrastructure for the enterprise to store, access, and harness the value of data for better insights and decision making to drive innovation.

The economics of data is based on the idea that value can be extracted through analytics. Big data is changing the way analytics were commonly viewed—it is about extracting valuable insight from data, not about transforming data into information through dashboards and reports.

Data Explosion

With the amount of unstructured data getting doubled every couple of months, below are some facts about how the data is exploding every second:

- Around 1.7 megabytes of new information for every human being is generated per second.
- More than 1.5 trillion search queries are executed every year.
- With the introduction of the Internet of Things, the data volume exploded exponentially in recent years.

- More than $450 billion per day in business transactions are executed through the internet including business-to-business and business-to-consumer (B2B and B2C).
- Around 6 billion people use smartphones all over the world.
- More than 50 billion connected devices exist all over the world to collect, transmit, analyze, and share data.
- More than 500 hours of video is uploaded to YouTube every minute and more than 400 million photos are uploaded online every day.
- With more than one-third of all enterprise data being stored in the cloud, the data passes through all the connected networks.

Features of Big Data

More than 85% of the data that is generated from e-mails, blogs, video, logs, and social media is unstructured. It requires a framework and architecture to increase the computational power for faster and easier data modeling and data research. The five key attributes that differentiate big data from traditional data are denoted by 5 V's:

- Volume: Volume is the total amount of data generated from increasing data sources such as IOT sensors, social media messages, smartphones, connected cars, network traffic data, credit card transactions, web page clicks, video, photo upload, etc., that is so large that it cannot be stored or analyzed using the traditional database technology. Collecting such large amounts of data and analyzing it to make intelligent decisions is one of the characteristics of big data.
- Velocity: Velocity measures how fast data is produced, collected, and modified and the speed with which it needs to be processed to generate meaningful insights for the business. An increased number of data sources, instantaneous transmission with high-frequency internet connectivity, and the enhanced power of data-generating devices drive velocity. Financial trading, retail transactions, telecom, geographical location, and medical or fire hazard information from sensors all require real-time data feed with low latency. Analyzing a large amount of data while it is generated without storing in the database is one of the characteristics of big data.
- Variety: Variety defines various types of data coming from different sources, within the enterprise and from the outside environment, thus requiring integration, management, and governance. Primarily, there are three types of data:

- Structured data is organized in tables with rows and columns of data values. The intersection of a specific row and a column has a unique value. This type of database is referred to as a relational database, as there is a direct relationship between the row and the column. Examples of structured data would be a customer service enterprise that stores their sales data with customer name, product, amount, and quantity on an Excel spreadsheet or CSV file or in the ERP database.
- Semistructured data is also organized without the table structure so the data can be more easily read and manipulated. An example of semistructured data would be an XML file or RSS feed for a webpage.
- Unstructured data is the most common category which is not organized and is found everywhere including text messages, e-mails, videos, sensor data, and social media updates. Unstructured data does not have an organizational structure, and big data is used to add structure to this type of data.

Adding a structure to the unstructured data and allowing the simultaneous use and analysis of both structured and unstructured data is one of the characteristics of big data, which provides an integrated solution for different varieties of data.

- Veracity: Veracity refers to the quality, accuracy, and reliability of the data. Most of the social media posts on Facebook or Twitter have no authenticity of the data, as anyone can post on these social media platforms. Being able to use the correct data for any decision-making process is priceless, and big data helps in identifying patterns and predicting behavior with high volume, velocity, and a variety of data. Integrating the data from both authorized and unauthorized sources which can be used with authenticity is one of the characteristics of big data.
- Value: Value refers to the worth of the data being extracted by the enterprise for generating value and its return on investment. The enterprise needs to conduct the cost-benefit analysis of collecting and analyzing the data so that the data that is generated can be monetized before undertaking a big data project initiative. Cost-effective mobilization of massive-scale data is one of the characteristics of big data.

Sources of Big Data

Most of the data is generated from the internet, social media, business transactions, and the Internet of Things. The data is in the form of structured, semistructured, unstructured, or any combination of these varieties from these sources. Most of the data that is generated as an outcome of the business activity is recorded as structured or semistructured data type, while electronic documents, videos, and pdf files are considered as part of the unstructured data types.

Some of the major sources of big data are listed below:

- Social Media
  - Social networking such as LinkedIn, Facebook, Twitter, etc.
  - Uploading photos at Instagram, Picasa, etc.
  - Uploading videos at YouTube
  - Internet search
  - E-mails
  - Blogs
  - Personal documents
  - Mobile text messages
- Examples
  - 250 billion plus e-mails sent out each day
  - 50 million plus tweets are posted each day
  - Forecasting the stock market index with great accuracy through Twitter feeds
  - Mobile apps messages such as WhatsApp, BOTIM, Letgo, etc.
- Business Activity
  - Banking records
  - Insurance purchase
  - E-commerce trade
  - Credit card transactions
  - Medical records
- Examples
  - Identifying unhappy customers while in conversation with bots or representatives through speech analytics methods
  - Predicting the store's customer inflow by counting the cars in a parking lot
- Internet of Things
  - Sensors providing traffic, weather, location data
  - Security and surveillance videos and images
  - Satellite images
  - Connected vehicles

- Examples
  - Flights or trains providing real-time arrival and departure information
  - GPS tracker providing the exact location of a mobile phone device
  - Identifying risk and providing real-time alerts from the analysis of video data

Challenges of Implementing Big Data

The enterprise's infrastructure, technology, and data management practices need to be transformed and changed to accommodate the rapid shift in gathering data. The number of devices generating and transmitting data such as sensors, tablets, and smartphones continues to increase at a very fast pace, and such information-sharing options represent a tremendous challenge to enterprises that want to reap the benefits of harnessing the data by using traditional data processing methods. Some of the challenges in implementing big data include the following:

The existing relational database approach does not work best when dealing with unstructured data that needs to be processed faster at scale. But the cost of implementing big data might be outside the budget for many enterprises.

A lot of enterprises remain conservative in adopting big data, as the laws related to data privacy issues and compliance are not yet firmly established. Big data implementation can only be successfully and widely accepted once the intellectual property rights governing the data, ownership title, consequences, and liability due to data inaccuracy are all clearly specified and established.

Data visualization and analytics resources are not able to present the data and its insights in a format so that it is simple and efficient for the users to realize value from big data.

The existing information governance and management practices cannot cope with the new features of big data; thus, change management is required to adopt big data, such as moving to the cloud, new security measures, etc.

Getting the right analytics skills and talent to manage and maintain big data and produce actionable insights remains the biggest challenge for the enterprise.

Many enterprises do not have the IT infrastructure to implement big data, which requires capital investment. The maturity of the enterprise to deploy new technologies to support big data infrastructure plays an important role in the success of the big data project.

Why Are Enterprises Moving to Big Data?

As more and more data is being generated, it poses an opportunity for the enterprise to leverage big data technology and become a data-centric organization. The value for the enterprise is to tap the unstructured data from the environment and combine it with other data to generate insights such as customer experience, future trends, product preferences, and supply chain operations. Big data provides significant potential to enhance the operational efficiency and infuse innovation within an enterprise at a time of economic constraints, digital transformation, and steep competition. Below are listed some of the reasons why enterprises are planning to adopt big data as part of the ongoing operations:

- Consolidation
  - Ability to integrate data from all sources and types at one consolidated place.
  - Faster and seamless integration of data from the outside world with the data from the enterprise ecosystem.
  - Combine the external data from social media with the internal enterprise data to understand the customer dynamics and have personalized interactions.
  - Storing the data together with the same meaning but in various formats and structures.

- Data-driven Insights
  - Ability to provide insights combining both structured and unstructured data.
  - Data maintained at the granular level helps the enterprise with valuable insights that are not possible with summary-level data.
  - No need to maintain a separate data storage and multiple business warehouse within the same enterprise and then spend millions to integrate and get meaningful insights.

- Analytical Workforce
  - More staff can be utilized for analyzing the data rather than just collecting and gathering the data.

- Visualization
  - Big data transforms raw data into meaningful insights and presents it in a visually interactive, appealing, and iterative manner so that it is easier for the users to make the analysis.

- Operational Efficiency
  - Big data helps to process high-volume data with low latency so that the users can conduct real-time analysis and decision making for operational efficiency and growth.

- Automated algorithms are replaced by human decision making, thus making it a cost-effective and operational efficient solution.
- Enhanced Productivity
  - Increases employee productivity due to efficient data integration and management.
  - Enables transparency in data sharing.
  - Offers real-time or near real-time response to customer queries.
- Cost Reduction
  - Uses open source and cloud technology for data processing and sharing.
  - Big data technologies provide platforms for cost-effective data management and data governance solutions.
  - Eliminates traditional infrastructure involving hardware, software, storage space, personnel for manual maintenance, and duplication of data.
- Competitive Advantage
  - Enterprise wants to move into the big data solution, as it is perceived as one of the major transformations in the way the business will be done in the next decade.

Big Data Technology

Big data requires new technologies to quickly and efficiently process large quantities of data. A number of new technologies have emerged in recent years to harness and address big data requirements and challenges. Some of the capabilities that big data technologies address are described below along with key products and players supporting the technology:

Data Storage and Distributed Processing

Big data needs to support the storage and processing of large volumes of data. Hadoop is a software framework that uses algorithms and models for distributed processing of large volumes of multistructured data types.

Some of the features supporting this capability include:

- The technology should have a distributed fault-tolerant file system with enormous data processing capability across cluster computers or servers.
- It should be able to process the data in batches for better throughput.
- The new technology framework should be able to process data in real time to deliver immediate response and output.

Some of the benefits to the enterprise include:

- Stores data at a very low cost and prevent data loss.
- Saves licensing costs for storing and processing large volumes of data.
- Can be used as a cost-effective data warehouse compared to an expensive ERP solution.
- Can be used as preprocessing for raw data before execution in the data warehouse.

Some of the products supporting this capability include:

- Some of the key products include Hadoop, Spark, YARN, Cassandra, and NoSQL.
- Some of the key vendors include IBM BigInsights, Hortonworks, Cloudera, DataStax, and Databricks.
- Some of the cloud platforms include Amazon Web Services, Microsoft Azure, and Google Cloud Platform.

Nonrelational Database Structure

The traditional relation-based database does not have the technology to handle the large volume of data without the structures. Big data supports a flexible nonrelational database structure that has the ability to access the data for faster processing.

Some of the features supporting this capability include:

- Supports data structures such as queries, strings, lists, hashes, logs, bitmaps, and indexes.
- Nonrelational or NoSQL database.
- It has a flexible data model, is scalable, and supports horizontal scaling.
- The rigid features in a relational database management system such as atomicity, consistency, isolation, and durability are flexible in big data.
- Nonrelational databases are also programmable and used for commodity storage.
- Distributed and designed for large-scale data storage and parallel data processing across a large number of servers.

Some of the benefits to the enterprise include:

- Dynamic, semistructured data can be used for low-latency applications.

- Provides real-time updates, retrieval, or user-facing web applications.
- Relational databases are predefined, transactional, expensive to scale, and have high storage costs, while the nonrelational database does not have this limitation.

Some of the products supporting this capability include:

- The following are the types of nonrelational databases:
  - Key-value database
    - Based on Amazon Dynamo approach.
    - Simple key-value pairs.
    - Examples include Dynomite, Voldemort, and Tokyo.
  - Column-oriented database
    - Big table clones.
    - Columns are grouped by related data.
    - Based on Google BigTable approach.
    - Examples include Cassandra and HBase.
  - Document-based database
    - Based on Lotus Notes approach.
    - Involves the collection of documents or data objects.
    - Examples include CouchDB and MongoDB.
  - Graph-based database
    - Based on graph theory approach.
    - Data is structured in graphs and not in tables.
    - Examples include Neo4j and AllegroGraph.
- Some of the key vendors include Amazon Dynamo DB, Microsoft Azure Cosmos DB, Redis, Memcached, Accumulo, and MongoDB.

Real-time Streaming

Big data is primarily used for streaming real-time and event-based data such as stock market quotes, news stories, weather info, social media posts, and game scores. The objective of processing data for a live event is to identify, monitor, and analyze the data and then respond to changing environments in real time.
Some of the features supporting this capability include:

- In the traditional approach, data was stored and then analyzed, while in big data, streaming data is analyzed in real time.
- Supports large volume of continuously streaming data.
- Processes data for complex events.

- Maintains ACID (atomicity, consistency, isolation, durability) compliance for real-time transactions.
- Ability to conduct real-time queries and search.

Some of the benefits to the enterprise include:

- Opportunity for additional revenue through real-time ads and promotions on various web portals.
- Responds in real time to events and changing requirements for customer satisfaction.
- Continuous data analysis and quick adaptation to changing data types.
- Ability to handle unpredictable changes caused by the external environment.
- Consolidates real-time events and distributes data to a large number of customers.

Some of the products supporting this capability include:

- Some of the key products include IBM InfoStreams, GemFire, Espertech, Sensage, Zoie, uCIRRUS, and SenseiDB.
- Some of the key vendors include Spark Streaming, Apache Flume, Splunk, Kafka, STORM, and Sumo Logic.

Specialty Data Processing

Big data has the capability to process specialty data that is large, highly complex, closely connected, and semistructured in nature. Managing these types of data requires unique solutions including three-dimensional data processing models developed specifically for this purpose.

Some of the features supporting this capability include:

- Utilizes graph databases, which are specialized solutions for the huge volume of transactions at low latency.
- Simplifies complex queries with a graph query language such as Gremlin.

Some of the benefits to the enterprise include:

- Provides real-time querying and analysis of complex relations.
- Helps in path optimization.
- Supports complex social or hierarchical relationship management.
- Ability to handle complex graphs and queries.

Some of the products supporting this capability include:

- Some of the key products include AllegroGraph, MarkLogic, Neo4j, and FlockDB.

In-memory Computing

The in-memory computing technology is such that the databases reside in the computer's memory rather than on the traditional hard drive. This significantly increases the speed of data processing because the retrieval of data from the hard drive is an inefficient and time-consuming process and will help meet the diverse information and analytics requirements of the enterprise faster than before.

Some of the features supporting this capability include:

- No traditional system bottlenecks of disk reads/writes.
- Leverages lots of memory, sometimes distributed across a cluster.
- The speed of processing data at a large scale.

Some of the benefits to the enterprise include:

- Real-time data feed and analysis.
- Real-time high-volume trading systems.
- Captures sensor data for real-time analytics and insights.

Some of the products supporting this capability include:

- Some of the key products include VoltDB, QlikView, SAP HANA, SolidDB, STORM, Membase, Spark, Flink, DRUID, and Kinesis.

Advanced Analytics

Big data provides a database platform for advanced analytics which consists of an integrated set of servers, storage, operating systems, database management systems, and software installed and optimized for data warehousing.

Some of the features supporting this capability include:

- Scalable databases running complex queries.
- Columnar database structures with high data compression.
- Packaged hardware/software optimized for data processing.

Some of the benefits to the enterprise include:

- Cost-benefit to the enterprise, as it's a low-cost solution for analyzing huge amounts of data.

- Efficiently analyzes a large volume of data.
- Builds complex and advanced analytical applications for structured data.
- Massive parallel processing architecture and data warehousing solution with more structured data.

Some of the products supporting this capability include:

- Some of the key products include Teradata Aster, Greenplum, and Kognitio.
- Some of the key vendors include IBM Insights, Cloudera, Hortonworks, Netezza, and Vertica.

Understanding Big Data Architecture

While the big data clusters act as a single data mart for the entire enterprise, they provides the following architectural challenges:

- Security: It is difficult to enforce the role-based access to the data when all the data is consolidated in one cluster. The basic access method, masking, and encryption are the techniques used to protect data.
- Master Data Management: As consolidated data stores and big data tools hold a very large amount of enterprise data, master data management plays a crucial role in providing access to the data from the cluster.
- Extract, Transform, and Load: The big data process involves extraction, transformation, and loading of data, as the data needs to be transformed into columnar data structures.

Cluster Architecture

Cluster architectures are becoming quite popular in designing the framework for big data analysis, as they present economies of scale on the cloud, extensibility, and agility while maintaining the performance and speed.

In this architecture, several nodes or computers are connected to each other through the network connectivity while one of the nodes is connected to the outside world through the internet. The computational activities are evenly distributed across the nodes while sharing common database storage for accessing the files.

In traditional architectures, the hardware components are not cleanly uncoupled, allowing for expansion, retirement, or upgrading without an impact. Though the hardware is robust and not expected to fail, all the hardware needs to be replaced, which drives up the cost, in case of any failure.

Traditional architectures are designed for computing-intensive applications that require a lot of processing cycles but typically use only a small subset of the data. Big data, on the other hand, needs to analyze and sort through petabytes of data each day, which is not possible by humans or traditional database structures.

Sorting is one of the fundamental requirements of big data analysis. Many functions are performed on the sorted data. Cluster architectures carry out the functionality with economies of scale, speed, and agility while managing the larger volume of data at the same time.

Cluster architectures are highly modular. They can easily be scaled by adding extra hardware components. With data locality, processing of massive amounts of data occurs in parallel, which means that the same amount of in and out operations occur at the same hardware cost as traditional architectures.

Understanding Hadoop

Hadoop has been derived from research that was carried out at Google. It is an open source project with the Apache Software Foundation. It is a data platform that has two primary components:

- HDFS: Hadoop Distributed File System, which acts as distributed storage
- MapReduce: Carries out all the computational capabilities

Hadoop Distributed File System

HDFS is a master–slave architecture that spreads the data, as a file, across a cluster of server nodes using one NameNode and a number of DataNodes. It is written in Java, runs on native file systems, and is highly portable. HDFS works like any file system and internally splits a file into one or more blocks that are sprayed across the servers as shown in Figure 13.1.

A NameNode is the master that manages the file system metadata and controls access to files. It determines where the blocks are stored and understands which blocks are needed to make a complete file. A NameNode is typically run on a separate machine.

NameNode hardware needs to be very reliable because if it crashes, the data in the cluster becomes inaccessible. A NameNode keeps the metadata in memory as well as on the disk so that data is not lost in case of a crash. A separate process called Secondary NameNode helps with housekeeping the metadata by compacting NameNode logs as checkpoints. It is not a backup for the NameNode and cannot take over as a NameNode in the event of a NameNode failure. However, NameNodes can be manually started by using a copy of the latest metadata retrieved from the Secondary NameNode. For

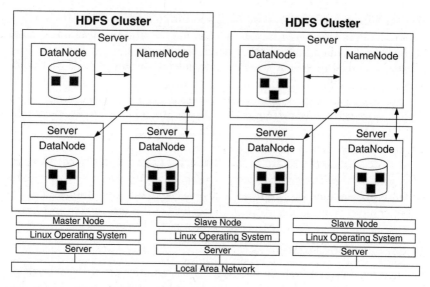

Figure 13.1   Hadoop distributed file system.

reasons of scalability and durability, the Secondary NameNode should be run on a separate server.

DataNodes are where the data blocks are stored. They manage the data blocks according to the instructions sent from a NameNode. DataNodes serve the read-and-write requests for the data.

Blocks are replicated by default into three nodes. The replication factor is configurable and can also be configured at the level of a file and also by file type. Any client application accessing a file first gets the location of its blocks from the NameNode and then directly reads the blocks from DataNodes.

HDFS is a fault-tolerant distributed file system designed to run on a cluster of commodity servers. Its design objectives include:

- Enabling applications to move computation closer to data by moving data across nodes and running computations on the same nodes as data.
- Optimizing for streaming access to very large data sets and very large files instead of random access.
- Modeling process files that are primarily meant for write-once and read many times.
- Emphasizing throughput rather than latency or response time.
- Enabling graceful and automatic recovery from underlying infrastructure faults through quick detection.

MapReduce

MapReduce is a fault-tolerant software framework that processes a very large file or data on a cluster of commodity servers in parallel.

MapReduce happens in two steps, which is easy to remember by its name. The first step is the Map phase, where relevant data is consumed from the input data, transformed, and passed on to the next phase using an intermediate key. The second step is the Reduce phase, where data is aggregated from the intermediate key and summarized to produce the final output.

Developers implement two functions called map and reduce, and the underlying Hadoop libraries take care of distributed storage and computing transparently. Typically, HDFS and MapReduce run on the same cluster. The framework schedules a task on the nodes where data is already present.

How Does Hadoop Work?

A sophisticated system can be developed for storing and processing big data by combining HDFS to store large data and MapReduce to process the data in a parallel environment as shown in Figure 13.2.

A MapReduce job is submitted to a process called JobTracker, which typically runs on the master node and manages the distribution of tasks to Task-Tracker nodes.

A TaskTracker manages the execution of an individual map and reduces tasks on a node in a cluster. A task is a single map or single reduce that works on its own slice of data. Typically, the JobTracker and NameNode are run

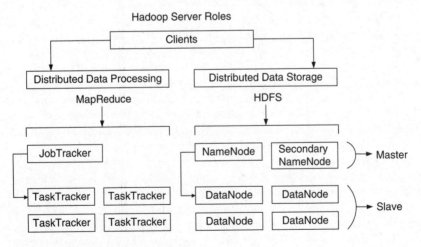

Figure 13.2   Hadoop MapReduce.

on separate machines. The rest of the machines can run both DataNode and TaskTracker. The framework ensures that map tasks will run on nodes that have the required slice of data locally, at least to the extent possible to reduce network traffic.

A limitation with this approach surfaces when a single map task runs slowly, for example, because of a slower CPU or disk controller. This situation has the possibility of slowing down the entire process. The Hadoop framework uses a mechanism called "speculative execution" to detect the slower-running tasks and run them in parallel on other free nodes. It then picks up the results from the fastest finishing tasks and discards the rest of the duplicate tasks.

There are several techniques available from the framework to optimize the transfer of huge amounts of data between the nodes that run the map and reduce tasks. For example, a combined task can be introduced between a map and a reduce task to consolidate data sent out from one map node and thereby reduce network traffic.

Combining HDFS to store a large amount of data in files and using MapReduce to process that data in a parallel environment provides you with a sophisticated foundation for storing and processing big data.

Fault Tolerance and Scalability

Data is replicated across multiple nodes by a replication factor. Policies are applied to get a perfect balance between reliability and performance.

Each data block stored in HDFS is replicated across multiple nodes as configured by a replication factor. The placement of the replicas defines the reliability and performance of an HDFS cluster. When working on a larger cluster, this setup requires a lot of fine-tuning and experience. HDFS replicas are configured in such a way that the NameNode knows which rack a DataNode sits on. Different policies can be applied to how the replicas are placed, which strikes the right balance between reliability and performance.

Placing the replicas on unique racks might improve the reliability, as it guards against an entire rack failure, but it impacts the performance, as the replication has to occur across racks. More commonly, when the replication factor is three, HDFS will put the second replica on a different node of the same rack and the third one on a node on a different rack. This achieves a balance between reliability and performance because there is less chance of a complete rack failure than a node failure.

NameNodes are in constant communication with DataNodes through heartbeats. In the event a DataNode is not available, such as a network failure, server failure, or disk failure, the DataNode will stop sending heartbeats and the NameNode will assume it is dead and all the data on it is lost. Now, because the block reports the NameNode received from that DataNode, the NameNode understands exactly which blocks of a file were lost. NameNode makes a decision to re-replicate those blocks to another DataNode. While re-replicating, NameNode still follows the rule of two copies in one rack and one copy in another rack.

NameNode can also make a decision based on data integrity checks on the data that it receives from a DataNode. NameNode is, in general, considered as the single point of failure in the Hadoop ecosystem. The Hadoop framework implementation needs to take into consideration the possibility of a NameNode failure.

MapReduce ensures high performance in its reads by collating the data on which the processing can occur independently. It is the primary reason for good performance and a significant reduction in usage of network bandwidth and is the core in addressing the big data issue.

Tasks in a MapReduce architecture are not dependent on each other. In case of failure, the MapReduce framework takes charge and spares the programmer from having to think about failures. MapReduce achieves fault tolerance by restarting tasks. A JobTracker and a TaskTracker are in constant communication, and when a TaskTracker fails to respond for a preset interval, the JobTracker will restart the map or reduce a task on a different node. Because the tasks are only aware of their own inputs and outputs, they can be independently restarted, and overall continuity can be achieved.

The architecture can be scaled by adding DataNodes to a cluster. When a DataNode is added, HDFS does not rebalance the existing blocks across this new node automatically. However, it will be considered for storing data blocks of new files. The data can be rebalanced across the full cluster using a tool that is available to the administrators.

NoSQL

NoSQL is a collection of databases that have emerged as an alternative to relational database management systems (RDBMS) due to the massive amounts of data now being created and the need to deal with scaling and performance.

These alternative databases tend to be nonrelational, distributed, open source, and horizontally scalable. When using a distributed system, the CAP theorem states that only two of the three components such as consistency, availability and partition tolerance can be achieved. While it is theoretically impossible to have all three requirements met, in a distributed server system at least two requirements must be met.

Which two requirements are chosen is the deciding factor in determining which NoSQL database is best suited for the given enterprise requirements.

Typically, RDBMS depends on consistency and availability, but compromises on partition tolerance, while NoSQL focuses on availability and partition tolerance and gives up consistency. However, NoSQL solutions like Cassandra are consistent, thereby satisfying all the three conditions by having the user configure consistency preferences. MySQL, SQL Server, and Oracle are examples of a traditional RDBMS.

Consistency

Consistency means that as long as the update to a system is committed, the most updated information will always be retrieved subsequently, even if data is requested right after a committed update. When it comes to how safe the committed data is, any ACID-compliant system can be considered reliable; however, most NoSQL databases do not implement ACID and vary in how durable they are with stored data.

Availability

Availability indicates that the system or the application will always be available for service.

Partition Tolerance

Partition Tolerance tells us the system will continue to operate despite failures in the background. The system knows how to recover from failure and shields the effect of failure from its clients.

NoSQL Databases

There are four primary types of NoSQL data types as described below.

Key-value Store

This refers to an arbitrary value of arbitrary type stored under a key that is typically binary. Stores are also accessed by way of a key. Some of the examples include Memcache DB, Amazon Dynamo, and Redis.

Column-oriented Stores

These are gigantic tables in which each row contains multiple columns. Some of the examples include BigTable, HBase, and Cassandra.

Document Database

This refers to a key associated with a document, typically JSON. This type includes methods of working, such as a query with the content. Some of the examples include MongoDB, CouchDB, and JSON stores.

Graph Databases

These have nodes, and the relationships between them are combined with powerful queries. This makes things easy that are very hard to do in RDBMS, but typically at the cost of scalability. An example includes Neo4j.

Big Data Opportunities by Industry

Big data has significant applications across industries. Let's analyze some of the industry-specific big data applications and requirements as described below.

Utilities

In the energy and utility industry, sensors play a vital role in the integration during production, transition, and consumption of data. The sensor data is collected and used in a large amount to make informed decisions and provide guidance for current state and predictive maintenance.

Healthcare

Patient data comes from various sources and is in the form of both structured and unstructured data types. Healthcare is becoming more streamlined and integrated such that patients are treated with the utmost care and are provided with timely access to data.

Financial Services

Financial services are utilizing big data implementation by compiling internal data and external threat information and converting this into predictive models as part of risk modeling and fraud analysis.

Telecommunication

Enterprises in the telecom industries are collecting more data from smartphones and cable TV boxes and processing this data to get a better understanding of the customer needs and also to monetize the customer behavior from multiple sources. Telecom enterprises also work with car manufacturers and insurance providers to develop telematics as B2B and B2C services.

Use Cases

Big Data Use Cases are certain scenarios where the goals and objectives of an enterprise are addressed to harness the data for better insights and decision making. Let's study some scenarios along with real-life case studies to see how the adoption of Big Data facilitated the enterprise to become intelligent.

1. Case Study: Social Media Monitoring for a Large Wealth Management Bank
   - Scenario
     - The bank wanted to improve the current monitoring capabilities for traditional media such as newspapers and television by adapting reputation risk management to the digital media sphere, with particular emphasis on social media.
     - Reduce efforts for managing a multitude of different vendors providing media monitoring services.
     - Overcome lack of standardization as well as fragmentation of monitoring output and access to media intelligence information across different geographies.
   - Approach
     - The enterprise developed a strategy as well as functional methods for social media monitoring based on industry insights.
     - Designed a multilayer operating model including people, process, structure, and technology components as a comprehensive and fully functional social media capability.
   - Results
     - Global harmonization of monitoring products ensuring a standard approach and consistent output.
     - Integration of monitoring products through a media portal granting fast and easy access to all relevant information.
     - Reduction of complexity and costs with a decrease in the number of vendors.
     - Measuring objectiveness by ensuring unbiased measuring of PR, marketing, and branding effectiveness.
2. Case Study: Data Insights for a Large Insurance Company
   - Scenario
     - A major insurance provider wanted to get an insight from social media and online sources.
   - Approach
     - The enterprise defined a social media monitoring service catalog for a broad range of stakeholders across the entire organization.

- Conducted detail design and integration of services into existing process landscape.
- Created specific insights that define correlations between accidents and driving with the customer and social behaviors.

- Results
  - Digital insight generation at scale.
  - Gained insight for engagement in social media and for marketing.
  - Effectively managed risk appearing in social media.
  - Reacted on social media in a timely manner.
  - Integrated diverse sources of data to create a better understanding of customer behavior.

3. Case Study: Big Data Platform for a Major Telecom Company

- Scenario
  - A major telecom provider started looking at the potential to make monetary and business-related value from capturing and mining different data sources they currently generate in-house. The enterprise engaged itself in the design and delivery of the data platform.

- Approach
  - The telecom company started capturing various business cases that were central to the data that was being captured. After the business cases were captured, they started the process of identifying the data sources that were central to these business cases and correlated data sources for creating added value out of the business cases. They also envisioned the creation of an external data platform that would serve as the data science factory for the customers. The external users and partners would be provided with the data format, minus confidential user information and example patterns to mine the data.
  - The telecom company's primary data-collection platform runs on Hadoop and captures data from various sources such as wireless operations data, web online clickstream data, various operational logs, set-top box usage information, and historical data from various other platforms touched by the user and enterprise usage. The data is consumed using a loosely coupled data router into the big data platform. Data is also captured from legacy environments such as EDW-based systems. The overall data is correlated using a metadata store that keeps track of the customer-centric relationship among various forms of data.

- The data that gets into the big data platform is then sanitized and pushed into an external data foundry for data science–based analytics processing and usage.

- Results
  - The telecom provider enabled an external-facing big data platform that captures data that is cleansed from the internal big data platform. The external-facing data is available for internal data analytics and data scientists to generate various data models to simulate and optimize the data outcomes. Once the data science outcomes are captured to a monetary or operational value, the pattern is formalized and provided to external users.
  - Some of the use cases captured for data science offerings include customer location analytics, ad works, consumer insights, churn migration, and consent management.

4. Case Study: Driving Insights for a Major Insurance Provider
   - Scenario
     - A leading insurance company wanted to develop a safe driving policy discount program that could analyze the driving habits by processing massive quantities of mobile and sensor data in real time and then develop a dynamic risk model based on the collected data.
     - The enterprise needed a next-generation platform to support a high-volume telematics-based analytic application for fast processing of data.
     - The processing platform needed to be high performing, scalable, very secure, and highly available, with business continuity assurance.
   - Approach
     - The enterprise deployed an on-premise big data and analytics platform to meet rigorous SLA, security, performance, and high-availability requirements.
     - Multiple technologies were integrated to support real-time data collection and the analysis of huge data volume.
     - The solution incorporated fast disaster recovery, automated monitoring and alerts, and data archiving strategy.
   - Results
     - The solution was deployed as a pilot in key states, which was a great success.
     - The pilot was then expanded to the rest of the country for global reach.

- The exponential growth in the number of drivers or trips with Amazon delivery, Uber Eats, etc., was completely supported by the big data platform.
- The insurance policyholders who signed up with the mobile app were able to register with the solution and save on insurance premiums based on their safe driving behavior.

5. Case Study: Predictive Analytics Using Big Data

   ■ Scenario
   - A large data security firm creates systems and software that help corporations around the world to store, manage, and protect data. The enterprise's CRM system keeps information on its equipment installed at customer locations around the world. It is a critical component of their ability to provide differentiated customer service and stay abreast of their customers' needs. The enterprise's highly evolved system provides data to the product development team on ways to improve future releases of storage software and systems.
   - The company's data volume exceeds 1 PB, increasing by more than 7 TB each month. The amount of stored data was starting to overwhelm the existing storage system based on traditional databases. To complicate matters, approximately 40 percent of the weekly incoming data is transmitted during a single 18-hour period each weekend, creating inevitable I/O bottlenecks.
   - The system struggled to handle the influx of data and the reporting system took an unacceptably long time to complete its analysis and reporting functions. As a result, large portions of the data were not transferred to the database, severely limiting the value and capabilities of the database reporting system.

   ■ Approach
   - The enterprise implemented an approach that combined the company's existing distributed storage system (DSS) with Hadoop. This approach allowed the enterprise to retain its existing DSS interfaces, which simplified the implementation while adding scalability to reporting and to the generation of ad hoc queries, which would be handled by Hadoop going forward.

   ■ Results
   - The new solution enabled the technical support team to perform deeper analytics than before, providing much better monitoring and in-depth troubleshooting of all customer storage systems.

Conclusion

Data is growing at an exponential rate as enterprises explore new avenues of business and take advantage of the digital disrupters caused by technology advancement, not to mention the mobile and social media that are boosting the explosion of data in parallel.

The traditional methods of storing and accessing data are not well suited to handle the large volume, the unstructured data types, and the flexibility required to visualize and present data insights for business users to understand.

Some of the common challenges faced by the enterprise include data management and governance, securing the data against attackers within the boundaries of regulation, and finding or developing the skill set within the enterprise to manage big data setup and issues. Despite the challenges, enterprises are rapidly adopting big data technologies, as the benefit overrides the challenges faced by them.

In summary, big data is an emerging technology with respective components and architecture approaches that are mature enough to implement reliable solutions.

CHAPTER 14

Analytics

*T*his chapter provides an overview of analytics, the various categories such as descriptive and predictive capabilities, and the components that can be leveraged. It also discusses the methodology and various tools and techniques that can be used along with the use cases and opportunities across industries to provide meaningful insights and make the enterprise intelligent.

Analytics Overview

Analytics is the use of statistical models and tools to generate value from the connected ecosystem of data and technology and process the data to produce insights that help solve real business problems and can be applied towards effective decision making. Analytics includes information management, performance management, statistical and quantitative analysis, operations research, predictive modeling, and data management to drive decisions and actions.

Enterprises apply the power of analytics to the combination of internal business data and connected environmental data to interpret, predict, communicate, and improve business performance.

Data Factory

Data factory is a three-step process for how the data is processed, utilized, and consumed by the enterprise as listed below:

Information

The enterprise is overwhelmed with data coming from all the connected devices and assets. The data elements need to be identified and prioritized based on the enterprise requirements and then extracted, integrated, processed, and managed, which takes the form of information. Data is thus converted to information.

Insights

The enterprise needs to utilize the tools and techniques and follow the processes required to analyze data and uncover insights. The insights help the enterprise move up the analytics maturity scale.

Outcomes

The enterprise needs to put a process in place so that the insights from the gathered data are consumed by the business to make smarter decisions and take real-time actions. The outcomes of analytic insights are assessed, and the benefits realized are tracked over time.

Analytics Categories

There are various categories of analytics based on the increasing level of complexity as listed below. Each enterprise is at a different maturity curve and needs to determine what level of data analysis would be the best fit to meet their business requirements.

Descriptive Analytics

Descriptive analytics describes what happened in the past. The data is collected to describe insights of the past without any rationale or explanation. The data can be used just as information with data visualization tools and offers a reactive approach. Some of the examples include weekly sales or customer returns for a retailer, number of products manufactured in a factory in a given month, number of movies released by a production company during a year, etc.

Diagnostic Analytics

Diagnostic analytics benchmarks or measures historical data to diagnose why something happened. The data provides insights into any existing pattern that helps the enterprise solve a particular problem. The data can be used to provide insights with statistical analysis tools and offers a reactive approach. Some of the examples include sales decline of a particular product during the last 5 years, employee attrition rate increase for the last 5 years, increase in patient admissions within the age group of 5 to 12 years in a region during the last 4 years, etc.

Predictive Analytics

Predictive analytics predicts the future by telling what is likely to happen. The enterprise uses this forecasting tool and optimizes it by improving data quality. The data can be used to provide insights with data mining and predictive modeling tools and offers a proactive approach. Some of the examples include the customers that will pay on time based on the historical payment pattern, subscribers who are likely to spend more than $500 per month on grocery purchases through an online portal, etc.

Prescriptive Analytics

Prescriptive analytics prescribes what needs to be undertaken so that the enterprise can leverage the advantage of a future trend. The data can be used to make decisions with the optimization tools, including machine learning algorithms, and offers a proactive approach. Some of the examples include a decision on how to convert the customers for repeat purchase of a product based on historical sales trend, what needs to be done to increase the sale of a newly launched product, etc.

Preemptive Analytics

Preemptive analytics recommends what can be done to prevent someone else from doing what was planned. The data can be used to take actions with what-if scenarios and simulation tools and offers a prospective approach. Some of the examples include what products can be offered to customers based on their past purchasing history, decreasing the output of the manufacturing product as a preemptive measure in response to the slowing economy, etc.

Analytics and Data Modeling Tools

Some of the key tools available in the market from vendors in the analytics, business intelligence, and data modeling space are listed below:

- RapidMiner
- SAP HANA
- Oracle Exalytics
- Teradata Vantage
- Tableau
- Weka
- Impact Analytix
- Greenplum
- IBM SPSS
- IBM Netezza
- SAS Advanced Analytics
- Alteryx
- Knime

Analytics Components

Analytics is one of the components that have the power to transform an enterprise by creating and applying actionable insights from the data either to solve an existing problem or to tackle new challenges caused by any disruption.

Analytics and data primarily comprise the following components:

Manage Data

This involves identifying the source, gathering, consolidating, and refining an increasing amount of data from internal sources and the external environment to make it relevant.

Implement Analytics

This involves the application of one or many intelligent technologies to extract insights from the relevant data gathered. The enterprise uses a combination of descriptive and predictive analytics to become more insightful decision makers, which helps improve business outcomes.

Data Visualization

This involves converting and presenting the raw data and analysis in a comprehensive and user-friendly format with the intuitive user experience for wide adoption and impact. Enterprises use various visualization tools available in the market such as Tableau, QlikView, etc.

Apply Insights

The enterprise transformation happens when the data insights are harnessed for effective decision making that helps the enterprise increase productivity, growth, profitability, and innovation.

Analytics Methodology

The analytics life cycle depicts the overall view of all the steps during the project life cycle that an enterprise needs to execute to implement analytics. Following is the analytics implementation methodology with various phases that has been proven at multiple enterprises for their analytics transformation projects.

Discovery Phase

The enterprise should conduct the following activities during this phase:

- Identify Problem: The analytics transformation project starts with the identification of a business problem that needs to be solved.
- Prepare Data: Determine the data requirements that are needed to solve the problem, identify the multiple sources of data, create data models, and prepare performance benchmarks for evaluation.
- Explore Data: Data is available in abundance, but it needs to be filtered to select and gather the most impactful data required to process and provide insights.

Design Phase

The enterprise should conduct the following activities during this phase:

- Transform Data: Once the sources and data sets are identified, the data needs to be extracted and standardized by applying the enhanced transformation and design principles. This results in optimized data sets.

Build Phase

The enterprise should conduct the following activities during this phase:

- Build Model: Build a data model with variables, which is explored by the enterprise to conduct thorough data analysis.
- Validate Model: Statistical models, business process rules, and machine learning algorithms are applied to validate the integrity of the data model.
- Test Model: The model is tested with dummy test data as well as operational data to check for any defects in the data model.

Deploy Phase

The enterprise should conduct the following activity during this phase:

- Deploy Model: Once the test results have passed, the model is deployed in the production environment, which is run with the operational data to provide real-time insights.

Sustain Phase

The enterprise should conduct the following activity during this phase:

- Evaluate Results: The results and insights obtained from the model are then distributed to the stakeholders using standard or automated tools to make effective decisions. A lot of new patterns and insights can be further discovered from the reports, which can then be interpreted to take actions.

Analytics Techniques

Some of the analytical tools and techniques that are used to collect data and generate insights have been classified under the categories as listed below:

Unstructured Data Collection

This involves collecting, tagging, and storing real-time data from customer service calls and online data from chats, blogs, forums, and e-mail. An example is call monitoring used by a telecommunication company to identify and track the root causes of customer care calls.

Some of the techniques used include the following:

- Call monitoring
- Natural language processing
- Speech-to-text tool
- Web scraping
- Text mining
- Mystery shopping

Data Cleansing

This involves applying analytical techniques to validate the integrity, consistency, and effectiveness of the enterprise data to make it relevant. An example is a quality control report used in an analytics project.

Some of the techniques used include the following:

- Descriptive statistics
- Missing value analysis
- Master data set

- Duplicate analysis
- Plausibility analysis
- Imputations
- Outliers
- Transformations
- Relationship analysis

Data Relationship

This involves discovering relationships and patterns within the data sets using root cause analysis and dependencies. An example is a cosmetics company identifying the behavior pattern among women opting to purchase a high-end makeup kit.

Some of the techniques used include the following:

- Inferential statistics
- Decision trees
- Bayesian inference
- Analysis of cross-tabs
- Influence diagrams
- Linear regression
- Nonlinear regression
- Logistic regression

Data Sampling

This involves reviewing and selecting a representative subset from a large quantity of data to estimate the characteristics of the entire data set. An example is a media company taking a sample of customers to identify their preferences for television shows that they want to watch.

Some of the techniques used include the following:

- Simple random sampling
- Stratified sampling
- Panel sampling
- Cluster sampling
- Quota sampling

Data Segmentation

This involves identifying groups or clusters within a large data set that share common attributes. An example is a company manufacturing games that needs to identify its target age group for marketing, product development, sales, etc.

Some of the techniques used include the following:

- CHAID (chi-square automatic interaction detector)
- RFM (recency, frequency, monetary) analysis
- Cluster analysis
- Principal component analysis
- Factor analysis
- Neural network analysis
- Conjoint analysis
- Supervised and unsupervised learning

Data Forecasting

This involves predicting and forecasting from historical data using statistical techniques and artificial intelligence algorithms for knowledge discovery, pricing, and market-related forecasts. An example include retailers using time series models to optimize order size, reduce inventory, and decrease deliveries.

Some of the techniques used include the following:

- Linear regression
- Decision trees
- Time series analysis
- Logistic regression
- Game theory
- Survival analysis
- Event studies
- Collaborative filtering
- Neural networks
- Econometrics

Preference Analysis

This involves identifying attributes such as interests, attitudes, behaviors, opinions, and preferences using statistical techniques to drive the decision-making process. Some of the examples include determining the pricing strategy for new products, predicting employee responses to changes in employee benefits, understanding critical drivers of customer experience in the hotel industry, etc.

Some of the techniques used include the following:

- Primary research
- Surveys
- ANOVA (ANalysis Of VAriance)
- Conjoint analysis
- DoE (design of experiment)
- In-market tests
- Response modeling
- Sample design

Data Optimization

This involves modifying a system or process such as a supply chain or airline route schedule to make it work efficiently with fewer resources and costs. An example is a global manufacturer of engineering products optimizing the sourcing of raw materials and its sales and distribution channels.

Some of the techniques used include the following:

- Linear programming
- Mixed-integer programming
- Elasticity modeling
- Genetic algorithms

Data Simulation

This involves building a model to replicate the actual system, a process, or an event to understand the relationship between various input and output variables under different external environmental conditions. An example is a car rental company estimating its revenue and profitability in new markets based on the utilization of cars under various scenarios.

Some of the techniques used include the following:

- Monte Carlo simulation
- System dynamics modeling
- Agent-based modeling
- Discrete event simulation

Profitability Analysis

This involves analysis of enterprise business, products, customers, etc., over time based on certain variables and discounting parameters. An example is a retailer trying to evaluate the profitability per store based on the area of the store, demographics, and certain cost drivers.

Some of the techniques used include the following:

- Discounted cash flow
- Historic profitability and value
- Economic value-add analysis
- Strategic options analysis
- Modeled profitability and value
- Channel and customer analysis

Benchmarking

This involves comparing the key performance indicators to external peer groups or internally within business units. An example is a beverage manufacturer trying to understand and analyze one of the carbonated drinks with its competitors to standardize performance metrics.

Some of the techniques used include the following:

- Dashboards
- Analysis of data from benchmark datasets
- Scorecards
- Survey design

Data Visualization

This involves presenting the data and summary information in a user-friendly, visually appealing manner using graphics, animation, 3D displays, and other multimedia tools so that the enterprise can prioritize the problem areas. An example is a pharmaceutical company plotting the geographical area to illustrate and analyze the market demand, current penetration, and growth of its various products to take appropriate action.

Some of the techniques used include the following:

- Dashboards
- Visualization software
- Scorecards
- Heat maps

Data Insights

This involves building a business case, roadmap, and project plan to execute the transformation using analytics and provide business value to the enterprise. An example is a software company using analytics to determine an acquisition in a high-growth emerging technology space where the enterprise lacks in-house expertise and presence.

Some of the techniques used include the following:

- Executive workshops
- Storytelling

Use Cases

Analytics use cases are certain scenarios where the goals and objectives of an enterprise are addressed to extract insights from the data to make intelligent decisions and take appropriate actions. Let's study some scenarios along with real-life case studies to see how the journey to advanced analytics can be facilitated to result in an intelligent enterprise.

1. Case Study: Product Innovation for a Large Telecommunication Company
   - Scenario
     - The company wanted to help the product managers increase revenue by targeting the right services to the right customers.
     - The company wanted to develop a reusable analytics toolkit, starting with the entertainment business as a pilot and then extending the technology to other areas.
   - Approach
     - The enterprise built an analytics data model to address the issue of how to stimulate product usage.
     - The enterprise also used analytics to assess the product and its performance in the market and evaluated the target customer segments and their buying habits.
   - Results
     - The enterprise was able to identify the product enhancement and product bundle opportunities.
     - The product managers were able to identify differentiated customer segments for cross-selling opportunities.

2. Case Study: Fraud Detection for a Global Insurance Company
   - Scenario
     - The company wanted to detect and prevent automobile insurance fraud.
     - The goal of the insurance company was to address how much revenue leakage can be stopped through the identification of noncompliant activities.
   - Approach
     - The enterprise defined an analytics solution based on three years of open and closed claims.
     - The enterprise applied the analytical model to each claim, and the calculated risk scores were used by claims investigators to determine achievable financial benefit.
   - Results
     - The enterprise was able to identify the claims with high risk for review based on the risk score generated by the analytics model, which resulted in significant savings.
3. Case Study: Identify Global Growth Markets for an Engineering Tools Company
   - Scenario
     - The global engineering tools manufacturer wanted to examine its business to identify growth markets and prioritize future marketing efforts.
   - Approach
     - The enterprise analyzed 65 countries and shortlisted 14 countries with low-risk, short-term revenue opportunities and 5 countries with longer-term strategic growth potential.
     - Metrics were created with various dimensions such as country, industry, customers, business laws, etc., with scores assigned to each dimension.
     - Weights were then assigned to each score, dimension, and metric, and aggregated scores were computed.
     - The relationship between scores was analyzed and countries with higher scores were identified.
   - Results
     - The enterprise was able to identify the countries where they wanted to grow their business in the future, resulting in new revenue models with the help of analytics.

Conclusion

Analytics is the technical process of exploring raw data and transforming it to provide meaningful insight. For the past several years, business intelligence and data analytics have been the top-trending priorities for all the CIOs around the globe. Enterprises are moving towards becoming data-driven organizations where data is used to drive the strategic direction of the business.

Analytics is a very powerful tool and embedding it into operational systems enables key stakeholders to make smarter, faster, and real-time decisions, thus creating an intelligent enterprise.

PART IV
Digital Infrastructure

CHAPTER 15

Cloud Computing

This chapter provides an overview of cloud deployment models, cloud computing attributes and benefits, the cloud transformation and migration framework, the enterprise's roadmap and strategy to move to cloud-based applications, and some of the typical use cases that trigger an enterprise to take the transformation journey to the cloud and make the enterprise intelligent.

Cloud Overview

The C-suite executive of an enterprise purchases solutions to a complex problem faced by the organization and not the technology itself. While traditionally organizations have managed all their IT infrastructure internally, cloud computing allows the IT and business users to access data, applications, and services over the internet, where the infrastructure is managed by cloud service providers such as Amazon, Microsoft, Google, etc.

Thus, enterprises can deploy cloud computing as a business model to access a shared pool of IT resources such as networks, servers, storage, applications, etc., by paying for the services they need when they need them without the hassle of acquiring and investing in these fixed assets, as shown in Figure 15.1.

Some of the other applications for moving to cloud include a platform for testing and development, big data and analytics, backup of enterprise-wide data, and a means to disaster recovery.

Historical Background

With any new invention in computing technology comes disruption to the existing businesses and the creation of new business and revenue models. The 1960s was the era of mainframes, the 1970s was the age of minicomputers, in the 1980s came the massive revolution with personal computers and laptops, 2000 gave way to smartphones and tablets, and from 2010 came the digital transformation with IoT devices, sensors, and cloud computing, where the hardware size and cost have decreased and the speed has increased exponentially.

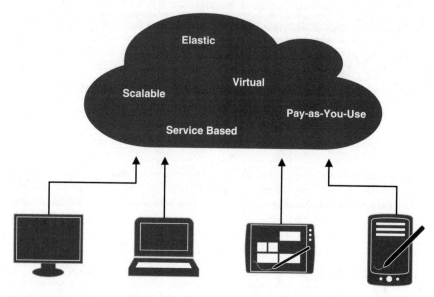

Figure 15.1   Cloud overview.

Cloud technology is the new business model that has matured during the last decade, and it is one of the driving forces for taking the enterprise to the next level of digital maturity. While both the data and application were centralized during the mainframe days, the cloud provides the option for the data to be stored at any location while the applications are being used through any devices.

Why Are Enterprises Moving to the Cloud?

Faster-changing consumer habits, shifts in consumer preferences, uncertainty in economic conditions, and the rapid pace of change in markets and products are forcing CIOs and IT managers to rethink their IT platforms for their enterprises based on new business opportunities and operational models. Executives are starting to explore opportunities to leverage cloud-based solutions across the enterprise to reduce capital expenditure, streamline the IT landscape, provision to scale operations, encourage innovation for new products and services, reduce time to market, and earn customer loyalty and engagement, leading to new sources of revenue. Some of the benefits of moving to the cloud are described below:

- Capex to Opex Model: The traditional IT infrastructure requires huge upfront capital expenditure, primarily in terms of:

- Buying or leasing the physical location for the data center
- Buying the servers, cooling equipment, and backup generators – their installation, maintenance, and support
- Setting up a team of networking engineers to maintain the facility

Moving to the cloud involves a pay-as-you-use cost model whereby the enterprise pays only for the storage and the processing power consumed for a specific period of time.

- **Demand Forecast:** Whether an enterprise wants to launch a new product or a start-up wants to launch a new service, it is extremely difficult to forecast the demand. Thus, the hardware resources consisting of the computation power, the storage capacity, and the bandwidth connectivity become extremely difficult to predict. The cloud helps the enterprise improve the forecasting of IT infrastructure and service requirements for both short-term and long-term demand.

- **Scalability:** In this digital era, consumers have a plethora of options to choose from and their preferences are difficult to predict. While launching an application, the enterprise does not know when and where it will become popular. Thus, the hardware and software resources, including the application, should be scalable to cover the depth and breadth of the market participants if the application becomes viral. Similarly, if the application is unsuccessful, the cloud provides the option to ramp down all the resources immediately without the initial capital cost and any ongoing expenses.

- **Speed to Market:** Times are such that the traditional waterfall method to launch a product or a business idea starting from design, implementation, testing, and deployment does not work, as it takes a much longer time, by which point the technology might have changed or a competitor might have launched a similar idea.

  With the traditional IT infrastructure, it takes a minimum of three to six months just to set up the hardware resources and their networking. With applications on the cloud, an iterative and incremental agile approach can be used that allows for rapid launch, continuous improvement, and the ability to try new features and fix bugs faster while keeping the development aligned with business needs. The entire physical layer is now replaced by cloud companies so that the concept to launch can be simulated and tested very fast.

  Thus, the cloud helps faster deployment of IT infrastructure with shorter application development time, leading to the rapid launch of products and services in the market.

- Lack of Skilled Resources: In the traditional IT setup, a lot of manpower and skill sets are required, such as database administrators, network engineers, software engineers, etc., to set up and maintain an in-house data center. It is difficult to get these skill sets in large numbers to set up the infrastructure, and, moreover, this is not the core business for most enterprises. Only application developers and testers are required when the application is hosted on the cloud, as all the infrastructure is taken care of by the cloud service provider.

- Innovation: Moving the IT infrastructure and services to the cloud helps the enterprise reduce the ongoing IT maintenance activities and focus its resources on business and product innovation using new models. The cloud also brings the agility to deliver new products and services and meet customer expectations with reduced time to market.

- Location: A global company may need to set up its IT infrastructure at multiple locations to cater to all its operating units. Moving to the cloud enables the company to provide seamless IT services to all its geographic locations, as not only do the cloud companies have servers located on all the major continents and in all major countries, it also provides the option of customization based on local demand.

Key Players in the Cloud Infrastructure

- While setting up servers requires huge capital expenditure, the servers on the cloud provide instant access to virtual machines with any specific configuration running at their data centers and the flexibility to scale from one instance to multiple global instances instantly. The maintenance is provided by the cloud service provider. In the physical layer, the following are the key players providing servers for a computational purpose:
  - Amazon Elastic Compute Cloud
  - Microsoft Azure Virtual Server
  - Google Compute Engine
- While it is difficult to predict storage requirements in advance, cloud storage services can scale from 1 byte to 100 terabytes of storage capacity instantly. The following are the key players providing hardware and storage services:
  - Amazon Simple Storage Service
  - Microsoft Azure Blob Storage
  - Google Cloud Storage

- An enterprise can focus on building great applications with no server management and no configuration deployment when they opt for fully managed application platform services from the following key players:
  - Amazon Relational Database Service
  - Microsoft SQL Azure
  - Google App Engine

Key Attributes of Cloud Computing

Automated Self-service: Cloud computing provides self-service access where a user can log in to the service provider's online portal and request resources – both hardware and software. The user is able to request, pay, and use the requisite resources without any human intervention or workflow.

Affordability: Cloud services charge only for the resources consumed, with zero upfront cost and no contractual agreement, using the pay-as-you-use model. When a user consumes 40 machine hours and 1 TB of data, only the consumed machine hours and storage are billed to the user as a service. The maintenance and updates of servers and any other hardware are the responsibility of the cloud service provider.

Elasticity: Cloud computing provides automatic scaling of resources. Suppose a business needs 10 servers during the daytime and only 2 servers during the night to allow optimal traffic on its website. The cloud provides easy provisioning of the resources up or down based on the specific requirements. The charges are also elastic based on the usage per hour/minute, which provides a financial benefit to the enterprise.

Scalability: When an application is launched and acquires millions of customers in no time, the cloud provides the flexibility to scale the resources up or down globally based on the requirements. The process is completely nondisruptive, with no reconfiguration of servers required during expansion.

Multitenant Architecture: Cloud service does not provide access to the actual physical server but the virtual layer above it so that multiple customers can use the same underlying server. This reduces the cost of maintenance, which is then passed on to the users.

Availability: Cloud system access is available 24/7 from anywhere on any device with no IT personnel managing the systems, users, and software updates. As the data centers of all major providers are located at various geographical locations across the globe, a cloud solution can provide localized services within the global IT infrastructure and a framework for the enterprise.

Backup: Cloud service provides backup of the data at another physical location in the same or a different country so that the risk of data corruption from server breakdown or natural calamity is eliminated.

API: Cloud services provide access to the application through the use of APIs (application programming interfaces), where a set of commands, protocols, and tools are used as an interface to use the application. When a user needs to upload or download a file in the cloud application, it can use the user-friendly API interface provided by the cloud service provider without writing a new program.

Cloud Deployment Models

The cloud ecosystem can be operated in one of the following deployment models to serve a particular business need:

Public Cloud

In the public cloud model, the infrastructure and computational resources are provided over a network that is open for public usage. It offers efficiency and affordability, as the cloud service provider uses a multitenant environment where the services are shared with various customers in the same server. The adoption rate for an enterprise moving to public cloud service is higher in cases where their product or service is seasonal, the data is less sensitive, or they have plans to enter into a digital business.

Private Cloud

In the private cloud model, the services are provided for exclusive usage by a single entity on a private network protected by a firewall, delivering utmost security and control. The enterprise can build and manage a private cloud at its own data center or subscribe to one that is hosted by the service provider. The adoption rate for an enterprise moving to private cloud service is higher in case the data that needs to be managed is highly sensitive or the enterprise wants to achieve greater economies of scale while scaling up or down.

A private cloud provides additional capabilities for enterprises that require industry or process-specific functionality and custom configuration capabilities in a dedicated cloud environment. SAP HANA Enterprise Cloud (HEC) is an example of a private cloud.

Hybrid Cloud

In the hybrid cloud model, the services are provided using two or more cloud models such as public, private, or community. It also provides the option for the enterprise to choose which aspects of the business should be deployed in a public or private cloud and which ones should remain on-premise.

Community Cloud

The community cloud model works similarly to a private cloud, but the infrastructure and computational resources are provided to two or more enterprises that have common mission, privacy, security, compliance, and regulatory requirements such as hospitals within the same county area.

Cloud Service Delivery Models

Some of the typical cloud service delivery models include IaaS (Infrastructure as a Service), PaaS (Platform as a Service), SaaS (Software as a Service), and BPaaS (Business Process as a Service). The major differences between these models center around the management responsibility of the enterprise and the cloud service provider. The higher one goes up the stack, as depicted in Figure 15.2, the greater the accountability taken by the service provider.

Let's look at some of the features, benefits, and functionality of the cloud service delivery models that an enterprise can adopt to become intelligent:

Infrastructure as a Service (IaaS)

IaaS provides the base layer where the enterprise can avail itself of the services of computing resources such as servers, virtual machines, networks, storage, load balancers, firewalls, etc., on a pay-per-use model. IaaS providers host the infrastructure at a secure location and manage the entire system maintenance and backup activities so that the enterprise can eliminate the capital expenditure related to hardware, upfront licensing costs, and the ongoing

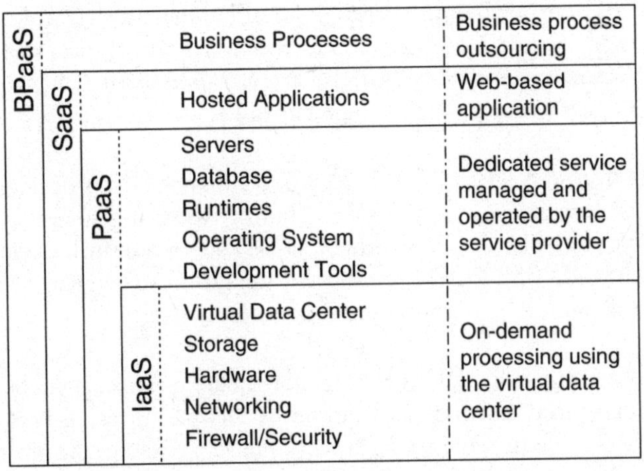

BPaaS		Business Processes	Business process outsourcing
	SaaS	Hosted Applications	Web-based application
		PaaS	Servers Database Runtimes Operating System Development Tools	Dedicated service managed and operated by the service provider
			IaaS	Virtual Data Center Storage Hardware Networking Firewall/Security	On-demand processing using the virtual data center

Figure 15.2   Cloud service delivery models.

cost of hiring in-house experts to manage the infrastructure. A few examples include Amazon Elastic Compute Cloud, Google Compute Engine, Azure Infrastructure Services, Rackspace Open Cloud, and IBM Smart Cloud Enterprise.

The impact of IaaS on an enterprise is as follows:

- **Reduction in IT Resources.**   Once the enterprise decides to use the infrastructure cloud services, the need for servers, network, storage, facilities management, and hardware procurement personnel will be reduced significantly. A few infrastructure personnel will still be needed to manage the virtual resources on the infrastructure cloud. The role of infrastructure architects and designers will change from just managing the infrastructure to more of designing the virtual resources and overseeing cloud providers.

- **Virtual Management Capability.**   Since the infrastructure resources will be all virtually hosted on the cloud, the enterprise needs to develop mature processes and tools to procure, deploy, use, and retire virtual assets. The enterprise will have the flexibility to access the applications from anywhere and on multiple devices.

- **Automated Scaling.**   The cloud will enable the IT resources to be scaled up or down, for which the enterprise will require established processes and tools to support automatic provisioning and optimal capacity of the server, storage, and network resources.

- **Effective Change Management.**   The IT department within the enterprise needs to be capable of managing these virtual resources through the configuration management database (CMDB). This will help to enable an effective change management process within IT.

- **Manage Cloud Security.**   IT needs to develop robust processes to secure all its virtual resources on the cloud, including operating systems, databases, applications, and network. IT will need to be able to monitor all cloud events and automatically link them to necessary operation management tools, and any deviation should be reported for immediate action.

- **Risk Management.**   IT needs to formulate policies which are compatible with shared hosting environments, shared infrastructure, and any location-specific requirements. These policies will help the enterprise to manage operational and legal risks with resources on the cloud.

- **New Service-Level Agreement Based on Application Requirements.** Each of the applications within the enterprise ecosystem will have its own infrastructure requirements which need to be computed to determine the overall enterprise-wide requirements for the infrastructure cloud. The service agreement with the infrastructure cloud provider will consist of operational metrics like system uptime, throughput, etc., and the terms may include penalties if the provider is unable to meet the specifics as laid out in the agreement.

Platform as a Service (PaaS)

PaaS provides a cloud platform and various tools that provide developers with the framework to build and deploy custom applications on the cloud. The PaaS provider delivers the platform over the web that includes operating systems, programming languages, databases, web servers, etc., so there is no need for the enterprise to purchase and maintain the requisite hardware and software. PaaS provides the developers with an option to pick and choose the features they want on a subscription basis. A few examples include SAP Cloud Platform, AWS Elastic Beanstalk, Microsoft Azure, and Google App Engine.

The impact of PaaS on an enterprise is as follows:

- **Reduction in IT Resources.**   Once the enterprise decides to use the platform cloud services, there will be a further reduction in IT staff, as PaaS requires less knowledge and skill to develop and deploy applications. A few of the solution architects and designers will still be required to design a solution that meets the business requirements of the enterprise and also to oversee the cloud provider.

- **New Development Methodology.** Moving from on-premise to platform cloud will require the enterprise to change its existing solution development methodology, operating model, and practices, as the cloud offers new development environments and APIs that the developers need to adapt while developing or prototyping the solution. There are interoperability and portability challenges that an enterprise needs to overcome if APIs are not standardized.

- **Integration Methodology.** Applications developed on the platform cloud need to be integrated with other cloud solutions or with existing services, applications, or solutions. This requires the enterprise to change its service integration methodology.

- **User Rights Management.**   User authentication and rights management need to be configured and set up on the platform cloud so that it's integrated with the enterprise's entire IT ecosystem.

- **Secure Application Development.**   The platform cloud provider is responsible for securing the platform from any outside threats. The enterprise needs to incorporate security best practices to preserve and secure the application development on the cloud.

- **Risk Management.**   IT needs to formulate policies which are compatible with shared hosting environments, shared infrastructure, and any location-specific requirements. These policies will help the enterprise to manage operational and legal risks with resources on the cloud.

- **New Service-Level Agreement Based on Application Requirements.** Each of the applications within the enterprise ecosystem will have its own platform requirements which need to be computed to determine the overall enterprise-wide requirements for the platform cloud. The service agreement with the platform cloud provider will consist of operational metrics like system uptime, throughput, resolution time for any raised ticket, etc., and the terms may include penalties if the provider is unable to meet the specifics as laid out in the agreement.

Software as a Service (SaaS)

SaaS provides applications over the internet so that the users can access those browser-enabled applications with no hardware or software to buy, download, install, maintain, or update. This provides cost savings to the enterprise in terms of software licensing fees and technical staff required to install, maintain, and upgrade the software at regular intervals. The SaaS provider ensures that the user always gets the latest version of the application. A few examples include SAP SuccessFactors, Google Gmail, Dropbox, Salesforce, Concur, Facebook, Microsoft Office 365.

The impact of SaaS on an enterprise is as follows:

- **Reduction in IT Resources.**   Once the enterprise decides to use the software cloud services, there will be a significant reduction in the need for infrastructure design, management personnel, and solution developers in areas where SaaS applications are available. However, a few of the solution architects and designers will still be required to design the solution to meet business requirements, develop integration and customization requirements for the enterprise, and also to oversee the cloud provider.

- **Integration Methodology.** Applications developed on the cloud need to be integrated with other cloud solutions or with existing services, applications, or solutions. This requires the enterprise to change its service integration plan and methodology.

- **User Authentication and Rights Management.** User authentication and rights management need to be configured and set up on the cloud so that it's integrated with the enterprise's entire IT ecosystem comprising both cloud and non-cloud based applications. This might require some process change in the enterprise IT organization.

- **Service Catalog Management.** When the application is hosted by the cloud provider, they have the responsibility to keep the software version updated with all the latest service packs. During the updates, a lot of new functionality might be added that may introduce various services and processes to the users. Thus, a mature level of service catalog management is required to provide the knowledge of the new functionality to the users within the enterprise.

- **Application Portfolio Management Process.** As the market and the demand grow, there will be new application cloud providers providing new services at lower costs. The enterprise needs to have the application portfolio management and vendor management processes to be able to scale appropriately to meet the potential demand.

- **Risk Management.** IT needs to formulate policies and governance that are compatible with shared hosting environments, shared infrastructure, and any location-specific requirements. With applications on the cloud, there are additional risks from the data processed by the applications along with the data privacy requirements. All applications need to comply with both the business goals and the applicable regulations such as HIPAA. These policies will help the enterprise to manage operational, data, and regulatory risks with applications on the cloud.

- **Archiving Policy.** The SaaS providers allow a minimum threshold for the storage and then charge the enterprise once the allocated space limit is exceeded. As the demand grows, so will the amount of data processed by the application. Thus, the enterprise needs to formulate its archiving strategy and policy so that they can plan and optimize their storage requirements and costs.

- **New Service-Level Agreement Based on Business Requirements.** Each of the applications within the enterprise ecosystem will have its own infrastructure, platform, and software requirements which need to be computed to determine whether they meet the overall enterprise-wide business requirements. The service agreement with the software cloud provider will consist of operational metrics like system uptime, throughput, resolution time for any raised ticket, software update timeframe, etc., and the terms may include penalties if the provider is unable to meet the specifics as laid out in the agreement.

Business Process as a Service (BPaaS)

BPaaS provides cloud-based standard horizontal or vertical business process outsourcing opportunities on a consumption or subscription basis to enterprises. It helps enterprises to reduce cost on some of their business processes which can be automated and managed on the cloud. A few examples include ADP, where the payroll of the entire enterprise is processed and managed on a cloud with secured employee data, Google AdSense, and IBM Blueworks Live.

The impact of BPaaS on an enterprise is as follows:

- **Reduced Business and IT Staff.**   Once the enterprise decides to use the business process cloud services, there will be a significant reduction in both the business and the IT resources involved in managing and supporting the business processes, respectively. However, the enterprise would still need business process architects, quality management personnel assigned to each process, internal auditors, and the IT integration team.

- **Knowledge Transfer.**   There is a two-way knowledge transfer that needs to take place when an enterprise decides to move its business process into the cloud. The enterprise needs to transfer its knowledge on business acumen and organizational-specific practices to the cloud provider. The enterprise would leverage the global experience, industry-leading best practices, and standard business processes from the business process cloud provider to adopt and manage the processes going forward. This would involve a good element of change management within the organization.

- **Business Process Integration.**   Moving a business process to cloud involves process reengineering by the enterprise to enable data flow and interfaces with other organizational processes to work seamlessly. It also requires IT integration with the provider's systems to enable information and transaction flows across the ecosystem of the enterprise.

- **Multisourcing Management.**   As the market and the demand for the business process on the cloud grows, there will be new cloud providers providing new functionalities and capabilities at lower costs. An enterprise needs to have vendor management protocols and processes to be able to scale appropriately to meet the potential demand from various vendors.

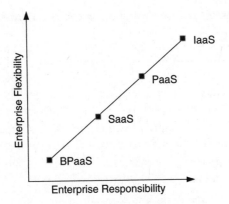

Figure 15.3 Enterprise responsibility vs. flexibility.

- **Risk Management.** IT needs to formulate policies and governance to ensure that the information security and privacy policy of the enterprise is in compliance with that of the provider's hosting environments and also with the regulators such as HIPAA. These policies will help the enterprise to manage business processes across units, data, and regulatory risks on the cloud. The business process cloud provider's internal processes, workforce policies, and cultural traits should also be consistent with the enterprise's own standards and brand value.

As analyzed in the previous section and depicted in Figure 15.3, the enterprise needs to evaluate the option of undertaking more responsibility for managing IT and the flexibility in terms of access to the infrastructure and software development based on the enterprise's business model.

Enterprise Cloud Transformation Methodology

Like every IT project, when an enterprise wants to move to the cloud, it needs to adopt a proven methodology to successfully migrate to the cloud. Following is the methodology with implementation phases that has been proven at multiple enterprises for their cloud transformation projects.

Discover Phase

The enterprise should conduct design workshops to gather and validate their current business requirements, value drivers, planned initiatives, and future requirements. The enterprise should conduct the following activities during this phase:

- Assess the existing governance, risk, and security framework within the enterprise.
- Assess the infrastructure, applications, security, data protection, and compliance standards required for the transformation.
- Assess the changes required and their business impact on the current ecosystem including infrastructure and applications.
- Conduct gap analysis, risk assessment, and mitigation strategies.
- Prepare a business case by identifying benefits and opportunities.
- Finalize the scope of the transformation project.
- Ensure the business is ready for the approach including the change management aspect, training for its business users, and getting the sponsorship.
- Prepare the cloud adoption strategy and long-term application and infrastructure roadmap.

Design Phase

The enterprise should start preparing the roadmap and approach to designing the cloud solution. The enterprise should conduct the following activities during this phase:

- Identify and mobilize the project team for this project.
- Select the cloud technology stack that would be most beneficial to the enterprise.
- Evaluate cloud service providers based on service, cost, and reliability.
- Design cloud security, data protection, and controls.
- Design cloud governance model.
- Design a cloud infrastructure solution that's optimal for the enterprise and also has the flexibility to scale up as needed.
- Develop the cloud architecture design.
- Develop high-level cloud implementation project plan.

Build Phase

The enterprise should start building the cloud solution and infrastructure as per the finalized and approved design. The enterprise should conduct the following activities during this phase:

- Build the cloud environment.
- Build security and controls for the cloud model.
- Build the cloud governance model.
- Build new processes for IT support and service operations based on detailed design.
- Build the change management plan and policies for the organization, structure, and facilities.
- Build the data migration strategy.
- Build technology infrastructure to support the cloud transformation.
- Procure all hardware and software as per the design.
- Re-baseline the scope, staffing requirements, and project plan as discovered during the build phase and communicate to the stakeholders.

Deploy Phase

The enterprise should start deploying the cloud solution and infrastructure as per the implementation plan. The enterprise should conduct the following activities during this phase:

- Prepare and validate the detailed cloud implementation project plan.
- Identify risks and gaps in the implementation plan.
- Develop the interfaces and conversions to support the new infrastructure.
- Complete the configuration of infrastructure components.
- Complete the configuration of security and data protection solutions.
- Validate and perform mock data conversion.
- Perform integrated system testing.
- Perform pilot application migration and production cut-over activities.

Run and Sustain Phase

After the deployment, the enterprise should now be running on the cloud solution in the production environment. The enterprise should conduct the following activities during this phase:

- Rigorously manage the go-live process.
- Conduct training sessions for both the business and IT operations teams.

- Establish a support center and hand over support to the operations team.
- Provide benefits realization and service improvement postimplementation through automation.
- Review and agree on reports with key stakeholders.
- Establish ongoing benefits realization, service improvements, and key performance indicators tracking.

Enterprise Cloud Migration Framework

The enterprise needs to plan and execute application migrations, modernize for cloud or cloud platforms, and prepare applications for deployment to the target cloud platform. The following cloud migration framework and its components can be utilized for execution:

Detailed Discovery

- Application discovery.
- Infrastructure discovery.
- Relationship mapping.
- Service management discovery.
- List target applications.

Application Assessment

- Assessment framework.
- Analyze applications and databases for migration to the cloud.
- Classify applications and databases and mark dispositions.
- Prioritize target applications.
- Identify pilot candidates.
- Develop roadmap.

Target Design

- Develop a target operating model.
- Workload location design.
- Backup and design.

- Policy design.
- Security design.
- Service management design.

Release Planning

- Confirm dependencies and the applications that need to be moved together.
- Confirm infrastructure-to-application mapping.
- Design target state architecture.
- Determine remediation and testing needs.
- Complete release and scheduling.

Remediation and Testing

- Build migration workflow.
- Develop application remediation.
- Develop infrastructure remediation.
- Test transformed application.
- Certify migration workflow.
- Document code and configuration changes.

Deployment Planning

- Refine automated configuration workflow.
- Hour-by-hour scheduling.
- Conduct dry run.
- Develop a rollback plan.
- Conduct go/no-go meeting and decision.
- Migrate configuration and data to the destination.

Deployment Execution

- Set up command center and operational support.
- Build target infrastructure on the cloud.
- Automate migration process.
- Facilitate workload and application migration.
- Provide executive reporting on deployment.

Enterprise Strategy and Roadmap to Cloud

During the journey to the cloud, the enterprise needs to conduct the migration to cloud assessment, define the strategy and plan for the infrastructure required to maximize results, and leverage capabilities provided by the cloud. The end-to-end cloud roadmap helps the leadership team to determine the way their enterprise will operate in the future.

Develop the Cloud Strategy

As a first step, the enterprise needs to define their cloud strategy and develop a strategic roadmap for cloud adoption to maximize business value. The strategy should include both the short-term and long-term vision and objectives of the enterprise and should identify and address key challenges and barriers to success. Some of the key activities would include:

- Assess both the business and IT vision of the business operations.
- Assess the current IT architecture and landscape and how the cloud will fit into the ecosystem.
- Build the future roadmap using the cloud.
- Consider all the organizational and business partner impacts.
- Identify the business drivers supporting the move to the cloud.
- Assess business downtime and implementation risk.
- Assess the cost-benefit analysis and check if it makes financial sense.
- Assess the readiness to execute the cloud strategy based on aspects such as enterprise governance, culture, skill set, IT applications, and maturity.

Some of the strategies that an enterprise should consider depending on maturity and cloud adoption include the following:

- Business Value: Develop a business case to determine and assess how cloud implementation can be realized to deliver greater value to the enterprise's business.
- Application: Examine the readiness of existing applications within the enterprise's ecosystem with respect to the target platform, and create the strategy to achieve the transition where there is value. This would involve identifying and sequencing the application that needs to be migrated to the cloud and creating the requisite interfaces.
- Operating Model: Define the to-be operating model and overall architecture for the enterprise's IT organization to function smoothly after transitioning to the cloud.

- DevOps: Identify the impact on tools, processes, and interaction between development and operations team of the enterprise after the migration to the cloud. Assess the time savings in the deployment of business requirements.

- Security: Evaluate best practices to ensure secure usage of resources from the cloud and adherence to the enterprise's governance, risk, and compliance requirements.

- Hybrid: Build infrastructure architecture that integrates with a legacy system based on business requirements for an intelligent and seamless utilization of public and private cloud.

- IT Service: Reform the enterprise's existing IT organization and optimize the IT service catalog to effectively meet business needs.

Conduct the Cloud Application Assessment

The enterprise needs to conduct a thorough assessment and plan to analyze all the existing legacy applications that need to be migrated to the cloud. The cloud application plan would include the target environment feature availability, application dependencies, and the enterprise's business availability and timeline. The cloud application assessment would confirm the migration type and effort and involve code-level assessment to determine the degree of fit for the target platform.

Applications are typically arranged in three migration types, each of which includes the varying level of effort and skills to migrate. The enterprise needs to segregate all the applications into these categories to assess and estimate the effort required for the migration.

1. Migration with Significant Remediation:
   - High level of complexity and effort required, with more than 15 integrations.
   - Applications that would require a major code change before they can be migrated to the cloud.
   - Validation would require a rigorous testing effort and thorough assessment.
   - There is a significant change in application platform, architecture, and engineering.
   - Deployment would require intensive automated and manual activities.

2. Migration with Minor Remediation:
   - Medium level of complexity and effort required, with 5 to 15 integrations.
   - Applications that would require a minor code change before they can be migrated to the cloud.

- Operating system changes, version upgrade, reference changes.
- Limited configuration changes.
- Automated and manual remediation; automated deployment.
- Requires fit-for-purpose migration testing.

3. Like-for-Like Migration:
   - Low level of complexity and effort required, with less than five integrations.
   - No code changes or remediation required.
   - Scripted/automated.
   - Minimal or no impact on business.
   - Minimal testing required.
   - Zero business downtime.

Conduct the Cloud Infrastructure Assessment

The enterprise needs to conduct the cloud infrastructure assessment and prepare the plan for the cloud platform and infrastructure deployment program. The assessment would include finding out which delivery and deployment model is the right fit for the organization – SaaS, PaaS, and IaaS including public, private, and hybrid cloud.

Use Case

Case Study: Large Postal Service Enterprise Implemented a Complete Cloud Strategy Program to Enable Their Digital Business Model of the Future

- Scenario
  - One of the world's leading postal services companies adopted the cloud as their enterprise strategy but struggled to progress because many individuals within the organization were not ready for this change due to fear of losing their jobs. The enterprise had a complex organizational structure – with culture, policy, process, and technology constraints, typical of any government organization, and was incurring significant costs related to traditional systems with limited capabilities, as well as a high degree of virtualization. Thus, the enterprise was unable to deliver a high-speed operating model that would enable a faster digital business execution.
  - Prior cloud strategies and initiatives were not executed due to organizational silos, lack of alignment, and an inability to gain traction from the stakeholders.
  - Some progress had been achieved in an unstructured adoption of SaaS, but PaaS or IaaS capabilities were only achieved via a shadow IT working around the internal IT organization.

- Approach
  - The CIO initiated the program to accelerate the development of an integrated, cohesive strategy to break down policy, cultural, process, financial, governance, operational, and other barriers to cloud adoption.
  - A complete cloud application and infrastructure assessment were done to identify current capabilities to design the target digitized organization.
  - The enterprise used industry-leading best practices and methodology to capture and validate findings and built a roadmap to cloud.
  - The enterprise built guiding principles to enable a digital business model of the future with secure access on any device with speed, quality, and low cost.
  - The enterprise defined the target state organization, processes, technology capabilities, and services.
  - The enterprise created an actionable and practical implementation roadmap that supported the design for the enterprise's cloud vision.
- Results
  - Managed to get all work streams and implementation teams on board with the vision, needs, transformation, and roadmap.
  - Captured the maximum possible savings in excess of $200 million over five years; networking capabilities enabled the high-speed digital business model and provided greater flexibility and adaptability for the enterprise.
  - Designed and implemented new security practices with the cloud solution.

Enterprise Migration Path to Cloud

The IT transformation journey to the cloud can be quite a rewarding experience for an enterprise, but it has to pass through the rigor and plan for the migration path. Listed below are some of the key activities that need to be considered when taking the transformation path to the cloud:

Evaluate Cloud Services

As the first step towards IT transformation using the cloud, the enterprise needs to evaluate the options delivered by the cloud service providers and how they will enable value within the enterprise business. The enterprise should conduct the following activities:

- Evaluate the cloud capabilities and options that are the right fit for the enterprise.
- Effort estimation and enterprise future roadmap assessment.
- Business value assessment for moving to the cloud.
- Security and risk assessment.
- Alignment of long-term cloud strategy with IT and business objectives.
- Enterprise change management readiness – people, process, business models.
- Enterprise IT organization readiness.

Select Cloud Vendors

Once the business case has been approved, the enterprise needs to select the right vendor to provide the services that meet the requirements of the enterprise. The enterprise should conduct the following activities:

- Develop the vendor selection criteria.
- Evaluate all major vendors.
- Select the top four to six candidates that fit the overall requirements.
- Solicit requests for proposals from all the selected vendors.
- Call the vendors to present their services.
- Assess the capabilities and services provided by each vendor.
- Negotiate the contract.
- Finalize the cloud service provider.

Conduct Cloud Migration Planning

Once the vendor has been selected, it's important to create the detailed migration plan for moving the applications to the cloud. The enterprise should conduct the following activities:

- Prioritize the applications that need to be migrated to the cloud.
- Consider the risk for business-critical applications.
- Develop the IT architecture and framework involving the cloud.
- Choose the cloud deployment model.
- Establish a governance and controls model to evaluate ongoing risks.
- Assess the integration with other enterprise-wide applications.
- Develop the detailed migration plan with minimum business downtime.

- Assess the gap in the skill set and evaluate training requirements for employees.
- Assign roles and responsibilities to manage the new IT infrastructure enabled by the cloud.

Manage Cloud Vendors and Applications

The enterprise needs to ensure that it has the vendor management policies in place so that the spending and performance of the SaaS applications can be tracked, optimized, and managed to achieve the KPIs and improve business outcomes. Some of the key activities would include:

- Define vendor management practices and strategies.
- Identify SaaS applications that are underutilized.
- Take action where SaaS vendors fail to deliver on signed contracts.
- Identify early any issues related to SaaS applications.
- Assess the strengths and weaknesses in the existing skill sets.
- Identify talent development programs for both local and global workforces to bridge the gap with the new cloud operations.
- Maintain the agility for continuous improvements in the application landscape to achieve new business capabilities and faster time to value for SaaS.

Use Case

Case Study: Enterprise Migration to the Cloud Using Amazon Web Services Cloud Computing Solution

- Scenario
    - One of the world's leading electricity and gas companies wanted to migrate to a global integrated operating model to better serve its customer's needs across all the geographies where the company operates.
- Approach
    - The enterprise assessed its ecosystem and infrastructure requirements and decided the journey to the cloud was the most cost-effective and efficient model.
    - The enterprise completed the migration to the cloud, leveraging Amazon Web Services to move more than 350 applications and 3,700 servers from an on-premise data center to AWS in just nine months.

- The enterprise opted for the cloud-managed services from the vendor including data center and network operations services for the migrated infrastructure on the cloud.
- Results
    - Utilizing AWS's cost model and agility was instrumental in the enterprise's move towards digital transformation and also resulted in significant global IT cost reduction over its previous on-premise model.
    - The global integrated operating model helped the enterprise to intelligently implement new services more easily and quickly and be even more responsive to its customers and stakeholders.

Key Cost Drivers

It is prudent that the enterprise evaluate the infrastructure and application total cost of ownership (TCO) savings on a five-year horizon to justify the business case for migration to the cloud. Some of the key drivers and a rough order of magnitude savings are described below, which can be used as a reference point and can vary from the enterprise's business and its industry:

Data Center and Security

20–35% range in data center savings or cost reduction:

- Sources of Savings
    - Electricity, UPS, air conditioning.
    - Land/building capital expenditure, if owned.
    - Leasing of floor space.
    - Infrastructure assets.
    - Security personnel.

Server

25–35% range in server savings or cost reduction:

- Sources of Savings
    - Provisioning of capacity based on average usage rather than peak usage.
    - Taking advantage of the elasticity of the cloud service provider.
    - Optimization of computational power based on high-traffic websites or seasonality.

Storage

25–35% range in storage savings or cost reduction:

- Sources of Savings
  - Intensive workload storage utilization in cloud.
  - Storage instances designed for high sequential read and write access to very large data sets.
  - Backup of archived data.

Network

20–30% range in network savings or cost reduction:

- Sources of Savings
  - Upgrade of network infrastructure.
  - Savings in bandwidth cost through internet peering. Peering is a relationship between two or more internet service providers (ISPs) where they share a direct peering network instead of routing traffic through the public internet. This direct connection increases speed, quality, and efficiency while bypassing the internet infrastructure and its associated bandwidth costs.
  - Using multiprotocol label switching (MPLS), which is a protocol-independent routing technique designed to speed up and route traffic across the enterprise-wide area and service provider networks.
  - Scalable pipe-to-cloud service provider to facilitate bursting.

Software

20–35% range in software savings or cost reduction:

- Sources of Savings
  - Upfront licensing fees.
  - Subscription fees.
  - Price increase at the completion of the term or contract.
  - Major upgrade-related costs.
  - Training costs each year.

Applications

15–25% range in application savings or cost reduction:

- Sources of Savings
  - Sunset of legacy systems.
  - Simplification of enterprise-wide IT architecture and landscape.

- Increased agility for business changes.
- Automating business processes.
- High cost of maintenance of legacy systems.

Enterprise Transformation to the Cloud

Enterprises can derive value by transforming their internal business operations to the cloud, thereby increasing operational performance. The cloud can be leveraged in the way of Software as a Service in various business functions such as sales and marketing, human resources, financial integration, or supply chain.

There are a plethora of cloud services that are available in the market as a result of the exponential growth in recent years. It is a daunting task for an enterprise to choose the right business model and cloud technology to meet their business requirements, enable innovation, provide superior customer service and drive their business process transformation journey. The enterprise needs to consider the following aspects and complexity of migrating or building new applications on the cloud.

Manage the Journey to the Cloud

The enterprise needs to acquire the skills and capabilities required to successfully manage the complexity of an end-to-end transformation while maintaining service to the business. Some of the key activities would include:

- Provide leadership, program management, governance, reporting, and control.
- Provide assurance to the stakeholders that all the components of the transformation are being executed in an appropriate way, to a level of quality which will deliver the desired business outcomes.
- Help manage risks and ensure compliance with regulations while the enterprise is transitioning to the cloud.
- Manage the initial and subsequent release management plan, including lines of business, to ensure that the dependencies between different initiatives are managed and the ability to continue to operate the legacy system is not impacted.
- Manage stakeholders and the transition of the technology organization to a new capability.

Manage DevOps

The enterprise needs to define, implement, and run DevOps to compete successfully in today's high-velocity business world, thus improving and accelerating delivery, resulting in a seamless path to production with dependable IT outcomes in application development and operations. Some of the key activities would include:

- Assess the maturity within the enterprise's development and operations teams and then create an implementation strategy and roadmap that sets the course for DevOps execution.
- Define an architecture supporting automated releasing, scalability, feature control, automated testing, instrumentation, and operability.
- Design and build a platform to support DevOps activities for development, testing, and production environments.
- Enforce organizational change management within the operating model and implement DevOps behavior.
- Translate the enterprise's business and IT strategies into a coordinated set of DevOps processes, roles, governance structures, performance metrics, and organization structures.
- Manage the resources for application design, development, and testing to enable the enterprise to achieve continuous delivery.

Develop the Cloud Architecture

The enterprise needs to define its cloud architecture so that they can integrate the Software as a Service solution into the existing IT landscape. The evaluation of SaaS vendors and solution providers would be an integral part of finalizing the services, which, in turn, would help the enterprise improve their business processes to support the digital transformation. Some of the key activities would include:

- Analyze the business benefits using the cloud.
- Define the target cloud architecture.
- Evaluate the proposal and select the correct SaaS vendor.
- Evaluate the new business capabilities using SaaS services.
- Assess the business, technology, and risk considerations for all business-critical applications before migrating to the cloud.
- Develop a robust strategy and methodology to integrate SaaS solutions into the existing environment.
- Analyze the integration impact on overall IT and cloud architecture.

Update Cloud Application

The enterprise needs to update the application portfolio so that it can maximize the value and benefits of the cloud. Some of the key activities would include:

- Analyze and evaluate scenarios to determine if the enterprise should consider updating to IaaS, PaaS, or SaaS as the future state solution.
- Consider the data migration from existing applications to the application on the cloud as part of the updates.
- Enable seamless integration between various applications, whether in the cloud or on-premise.
- Design applications to handle failures and have appropriate self-healing capabilities such as automatic shutdown, the ability to replay or restore state during start-up, and the ability to cover failing components seamlessly.
- Monitor applications based on anticipated volumes and trends and determine whether to add or shorten instances or recovery actions.
- Install advanced security features such as data loss prevention or advanced risk management to meet statutory and regulatory requirements.

Execute Custom Development on the Cloud

The enterprise needs to perform some custom development activities on the cloud to transform the existing applications by bringing over the functionalities that were customized in the legacy applications. Some of the key activities would include:

- Get the real-time data within the enterprise by modifying certain applications to work the way that the business operates.
- Reinvent the applications to keep pace with the current trends.
- Build intelligence within the applications to make smarter decisions.
- Build some interfaces to connect applications within and outside the enterprise.

Transform Cloud Infrastructure

The growing business demands and the drive to adopt the cloud highlight the need for enterprises to transform their existing infrastructures to be more cost-effective, scalable, and efficient. Enterprises need to design and build their cloud infrastructure requirements such as IaaS and PaaS to migrate workloads and operations platforms. Some of the key activities would include:

- Select Infrastructure as a Service (IaaS) or Platform as a Service (PaaS) as the cloud service delivery computing solution.
- Integrate all enterprise-wide applications to a common cloud management platform.
- Choose the right network to cost-effectively scale and transform the existing network environments to meet the growing connectivity demands of the digital business from cloud networking, wireless, Internet of Things, etc.
- Create a mobile workplace so that the enterprise can communicate and collaborate seamlessly and securely both internally and to the outside world across the digital supply chain.
- Develop a virtual office solution where applications and data are accessible to business users anywhere, anytime, and on any device.

Use Case

Case Study: Enterprise Transformation to the Cloud for Highly Complex Legacy Systems and Organizational Structure

- Scenario
  - One of the world's leading pharmaceutical conglomerates had a complex legacy environment with multiple operating systems in physical and virtual servers across 400 data centers globally.
  - Due to the highly complex structure of the enterprise, a wide variety of server and application management standards were created over time.
  - Manual server provisioning and deprovisioning through various IT management systems and groups for approvals could take up to six weeks, preventing the IT organization from quickly serving its business unit customers.
  - Application and server extension overtime had become a significant negative impact on the IT operation's bottom line.
- Approach
  - The enterprise deployed an industry leading design for a data center with network virtualization.
  - A data center environment fully automated by software was set up in North America, Europe, and the Asia Pacific regions.

- Application workload migration was at the rate of over 850 servers per month during the transformation period.
- Self-service catalog build time was reduced from 6 weeks to 90 minutes, which included compliance and regulatory requirements, performance monitoring, predictive analysis, virtualization infrastructure cost showback, and enhanced security through network segmentation and virtualization.
- DevOps and agile transformation strategy was implemented incrementally and iteratively over multiple sprints, leveraging kanban and scrum methods for tracking and predicting program outcomes in an optimized sequence.

- Results
  - The enterprise was able to achieve a savings of over $200 million in the IT operations from this transformation of infrastructure and services to the cloud.
  - 50–60% of workloads were migrated to on-premise private cloud.
  - 20–30% of workloads were migrated to a virtual public cloud solution.
  - The use of legacy infrastructure was reduced to < 20% of workloads, which itself resulted in more than $110 million in savings.
  - The new data center operating model resulted in 25% labor savings.

Enterprise Cloud Management and Optimization

Automated management tools and dashboards provide monitoring, cost control, governance, and accountability of the enterprise's cloud consumption. It's important that the enterprise's technology, skills, culture, and adoption continue to evolve in line with business needs.

Manage Cloud Operations

The enterprise needs to either manage the entire cloud operation in-house or outsource to a vendor who can provide services and support and manage cloud infrastructure. Some of the key activities would include:

- Support cloud infrastructure, mainly from a program management point of view while the technical aspect would be managed by the cloud service provider.
- Manage virtual servers/network and storage, maintaining configuration, recovery of infrastructure application servers, and cloud connectivity functions.

- Manage cross-functional areas to ensure all incidents, changes, capacity planning, service requests, delivery management reporting, etc., are serviced properly.

- The enterprise might open a shared service desk to provide first-level resolution to the tickets. A shared knowledge base and standardized processes help bring best practices faster to all the business units. Service desk people are the first voice of delivery to all the tickets that flow in from tools, phone, chat, e-mail, and other media.

- Manage cloud-based applications including support, ongoing maintenance, enhancements, and upgrades.

- The enterprise needs to constantly monitor for the visibility of the cloud infrastructure and application, which would help detect any system events or errors in advance for better management.

Manage Security Operations

The enterprise needs to either manage the entire cloud security in-house or outsource to a vendor who can provide flexible security operations services to secure environments and infrastructure in the cloud. Some of the key activities would include:

- Manage the security of the virtual machines in the cloud environment.

- Monitor the configuration and detect vulnerabilities existing in virtual machines in the cloud.

- Monitor the security events and incidents from the logs of various components of the virtual machines.

- Define controls as recommended by the compliance and regulations team.

Maintain Cloud Optimization

The enterprise needs to optimize the cloud services by monitoring the cloud spend through analytics, actionable recommendations, operational improvement and application remediation, and rearchitecture while balancing the business needs. Some of the key activities would include:

- Analyze businesses and their requirements and understand recurring infrastructure usage and the billing for all the services.

- Establish automated reports, alerts, and dashboards for better visibility, control, and analysis.

- Utilize industry expertise to produce optimization roadmaps tailored to the enterprise's business requirements.

- Implement recommendations through automated policies, rightsizing of resources, resource utilization, or contract mechanisms.
- Avail application remediation, architecture, or rewriting that is driven by ROI.
- Explore application support services to manage cloud-based applications.

Enhance Business Processes

The enterprise needs to enhance and automate the business processes using cloud technology so that they are reflected in the business results. Some of the key activities would include:

- Create process efficiencies and enable faster transitions by incorporating industry leading practices.
- Provide flexibility and scalability through a consumption-based model providing greater capacity elasticity to meet the needs of the enterprise's business.
- Reduce initial upfront and huge capital investments over the life cycle of the cloud-based model.
- Provide an innovative solution to the business so that it improves the speed to value while remaining scalable.

Implement Cloud Governance Framework

The enterprise should implement a cloud governance framework for the selection and consumption of SaaS services, address new business requirements, promote innovation while managing organizational risk, and achieve a future state operating model to maintain the right balance of autonomy and control. Some of the key activities would include:

- Define the governance process and framework.
- Define the shared accountability and responsibility of the enterprise and the SaaS service provider.
- Define the roles and responsibility of the business and IT within the enterprise.
- Frame the policy for the governance of data, processes, security, and service-level agreement with the vendors.
- Define sourcing and contracting strategies to ensure the best alignment of SaaS solutions to address business goals and capability requirements.
- Define the SaaS operating model, guiding principles, and criteria for success.

- Maintain the policies and procedures for contract negotiation and renewals.

Use Case

Case Study: Maximizing the Economies of Scale from a New Operating Environment on the Cloud

- Scenario
  - One of the world's leading metal and mining companies wanted to manage all its applications and infrastructure once it moved to the cloud.
- Approach
  - The enterprise created a cloud-based service model for its application development, maintenance, support, and infrastructure services.
  - The business received scalable support and development services to meet their demand at a much lower cost to the enterprise.
  - The enterprise's cloud-based infrastructure is managed through the cloud service provider, which delivers consumption-based billing.
  - The enterprise continuously monitors the utilization of resources with a rightsizing approach for cost-effectiveness.
- Results
  - The stakeholders of the enterprise made strategic decisions on how to improve the services and drive continuous innovation within the business units.
  - The enterprise experienced significant cost savings through the increased business agility and cost flexibility that are inherent in using cloud infrastructure and services.
  - The enterprise would additionally benefit from lower infrastructure prices in line with cloud economic trends.

Use Cases

Cloud use cases are certain scenarios where the goals and objectives of an enterprise are addressed. Some of the scenarios that could trigger an enterprise to take the transformation journey to the cloud include:

- The enterprise is expanding its line of business and wants to use the cloud for application development, deployment, and managed services, which could accelerate the time to market the product launch.

- The enterprise wants to update its ecosystem and architecture with new cloud-based applications.

- The enterprise is looking to grow and be competitive in the market by optimizing its IT resources.

- The maintenance of the existing legacy system might be expensive and cumbersome, with no path to digitization.

- The enterprise might acquire a company that has all its applications on the cloud. Thus, there is a compelling business case to integrate the acquired company's application and infrastructure with the existing IT by moving to the cloud and adopting the new operating model.

- The enterprise wants to consolidate its data centers located all around the globe to cloud platform.

- The enterprise wants to reduce its IT infrastructure and support cost and at the same time be agile.

Let's study some scenarios along with real-life case studies to see how the journey to cloud computing can be facilitated to result in an intelligent enterprise.

1. Case Study: Assessment of Infrastructure Architecture and Service Delivery Model to a Private Cloud for an Entertainment Company

   - Scenario
     - The enterprise had a complex infrastructure that was expensive to operate, slow to provision, and suffered from performance and availability issues.
     - The enterprise was interested in implementing a private cloud architecture and operating model to reduce cost, create provisioning agility, and improve the operating quality.

   - Approach
     - The enterprise assessed all components of its infrastructure and operating model and identified gaps in design, operating processes, and tools used.
     - Designed future state private cloud architecture and operating model.
     - The enterprise evaluated the cost structure of the cloud solution to validate cost savings and developed a framework for a new chargeback model.
     - Assessed private cloud vendors and obtained feedback from internal users of the private cloud to assess areas for improvement of customer experience.
     - Developed recommendations on changes in organizational design to improve accountability and operating outcomes.

- Results
  - Validated the business case for a private cloud and enabled CFO commitment to support the implementation project.
  - Enabled a metrics framework for tracking operational performance and continuous improvement.
  - Provided recommendations on changes in organizational structure to optimize service delivery.

2. Case Study: Creating Digital Connectivity Between Online and Offline Customer Experiences to Deliver Brand Promise for a Large Restaurant Chain
   - Scenario
     - The enterprise wanted to understand who buys their items in order to:
       - Build a direct relationship with their customers.
       - Build a cohesive vision and strategy for consumer engagement.
       - Know the customer's preferences and behavior.
       - Build the organizational capability, processes, and technology to track consumer activities and engagement with the brand.
   - Approach
     - Determine how a consumer used their products and identify ways to digitally enable these experiences utilizing the "social mobile cloud."
     - Build a consumer experience life-cycle model to illustrate the need to connect franchisees, restaurant, and corporate employees with consumers at every phase.
     - Review online customer feedback in order to highlight opportunities to improve consumer experience and impact.
   - Results
     - The potential of well over $250 million in annual incremental revenue with a created plan.
     - Built plan based on mobile order and payment, consumer knowledge, and encouraging adoption and development of full loyalty and feedback programs as adoption develops.
     - Built new capabilities and an experimentation-based culture.

3. Case Study: Moving Healthcare to a Cloud-based Solution
   - Scenario
     - A laboratory testing company in the healthcare solutions sector wanted to accelerate service delivery with 100% claims on a cloud-based solution. As a start-up, the company wanted to accelerate every aspect of laboratory care and service delivery.

- Approach
  - In the strategy phase, the enterprise decided to implement a cloud-based platform to avoid an extended timeline and the higher cost of building infrastructure in-house.
  - A portal for providers, patients, and health plans provided systematic access to data, claims, and prior authorization.
  - Detailed business rules and algorithms were developed that enabled processing in real time for submitted claims.
  - By fetching member and lab historical data in real time from the business partners, the service team was able to review claims for lab services providing the approval or rejection, all within the context of an insurer's end-to-end process of evaluating the full range of medical claims.
- Results
  - The new cloud-based service was implemented, demonstrating an ability to edit up to 150,000 claims per hour with 99% uptime and 99.5% accuracy, with a response time under a second.
  - The cloud-based solution was flexible with the ability to scale up easily.
  - The web-based platform was "future-proofed," meaning it can be easily updated by providing agility for payers to implement specific provider contracts or group benefits.
  - Advanced analytics was incorporated into the cloud model so that the growing volume of data can be harnessed for statistical analysis.

Conclusion

The pace at which businesses are getting disrupted along with the changing demands and expectations of the customers are forcing enterprises to challenge their existing business and operational models and leverage cloud-based solutions across various functions within the enterprises to streamline and scale operations and stimulate ideas for new products and services.

Cloud computing is now a matured platform for the enterprise to devise a strategy to move to the cloud and benefit from the explosion of cloud opportunities available, whether it is a single cloud application or a complete enterprise transformation.

The journey to the cloud by an enterprise involves setting the cloud strategy, identifying the right solution for their application portfolio, and restructuring the infrastructure by adjusting the applications within the ecosystem to take advantage of what the cloud can deliver.

CHAPTER 16

APIs

*T*his chapter provides an overview of the APIs that act as building blocks to allow enterprises to leverage the data and services in the digital ecosystem. It also discusses the architecture, business strategy, roadmap, and API development life cycle to help the enterprise integrate and become intelligent.

API Overview

An application programming interface (API) is a set of rules, procedures, and tools that allow applications to communicate and interact with each other. The convergence of mobile, data, cloud, and social media in today's economy has driven the universal need for APIs acting as new business channels and playing a major role in the integration of IT systems and architectures across industries. The explosive growth of mobile devices shifted the use from browser-based to device-based using apps and communicating through APIs.

In simple terms, an API is a messenger that takes requests from a mobile device app, as an example, and communicates with the back-end system for any particular action that needs to be performed and, then returns the response to the mobile app. Let's take a simple example. While booking a flight on any airline's website, a traveler fills out the requisite information, then the data is retrieved from the airline's database and provided to the portal. Similarly, when a traveler fills out the same information on an online booking site, the site fetches the information by interacting with each airline's API and the information is then retrieved from the database of each airline. This creates communication and connectivity between various applications, data, and devices.

Enterprises face a gap between systems of record comprising financials, inventory, HR, supply chain modules within the enterprise resource planning that exist, and systems of engagement, which are apps that deliver digital experiences to customers, partners, and employees. APIs fill that gap by providing integration to both these systems.

These systems of record require extreme stability and strict governance, and, by design, the changes are at a slower pace. On the other hand, many of the business apps, customer engagement, and partner engagement apps evolve faster, with changes occurring in weeks and days. They are usually consumed through mobile devices, and the volume is in billions of interactions compared to the smaller transaction and posting volumes in systems of record.

Types

APIs drive different levels of collaboration and innovation to accelerate business objectives for digital services. Listed below are the types of APIs that can be developed by the enterprise:

Private API

Private APIs are primarily used internally to facilitate the integration of various applications and systems used by the enterprise. They provides the following benefits:

- Reduction in cost
- Operational efficiency
- Streamlined infrastructure
- Improvement in flexibility

Partner API

Partner APIs are used to facilitate communication and integration of software between the enterprise and its business partners. They act as a collaboration tool between the enterprise and its partners. They provide the following benefits:

- Increase in revenues through cross-selling
- Value-added services to customers

Open APIs

Open APIs are used to provide information to the general public and services to third parties who may not have a business relationship with the enterprise. They open up the communication channel between the enterprise and the outside world. They provide the following benefits:

- Increase the exposure to the masses
- Lead innovation
- Open up the opportunity to create new business models
- Create new revenue streams
- Substantially increases traffic from the outside world

Benefits

Some of the key benefits of using APIs are listed below:

- Collaboration: Some of the most popular uses of APIs come from third-party developers working together and creating apps that define new markets and create new revenue streams for the enterprise.
- Customer Engagement: In the digital business, one of the most important aspects of the enterprise is to engage with its customers and provide exactly the data they need, and APIs facilitate this activity.
- Speed to Market: APIs can be provisioned quickly with minimal back-end refactoring.
- Security: The API gateways have been inspected for security and are compliant in most security areas.
- Product: An API is a product by itself and not just a means to access back-end services.

API Architecture

The API acts as an interface between the enterprise's data source and the application used by employees, partners, and consumers. A simple API architecture is illustrated in Figure 16.1.

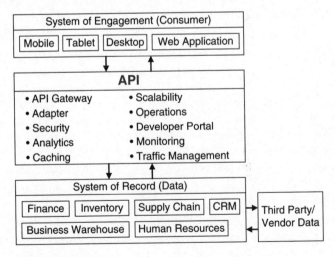

Figure 16.1   API architecture.

The API platform is capable of providing the following management services:

- Publishing APIs makes enterprises subject to the growing threat of cyberattacks. The security detection and protection service guards against API attacks and prevents data leakage.

- Unauthorized access is the biggest security and compliance exposure for APIs. The authentication and authorization service enforces and manages the trust relationship between API providers and consumers and provides the right level of access.

- Enterprises need to know the number of API calls made by consumers over a time interval. The traffic control service maintains counters that tally the number of requests received from individual apps, which enables enterprises to enforce limits on the number of API calls.

- Caching API calls and similar repeated data is the service that improves the performance.

- The transformation services help save costs, as changing the back-end applications cost a lot of time and money, while building an API to get the data is quite a feasible option.

- Routing service provides API request sequencing based on administrator-defined policies and logic. It routes requests based on their content or service availability and enables multiple back-end service calls to run simultaneously, which helps reduce overall latency.

- The analytics service provides visibility of data passing through the APIs with detailed metrics about how the API is utilized.

- The back-end integration service connects the API gateway to the back-end systems. This is done using the middleware data services.

- The developer portal service enables developers to register and request access to the APIs provided by the enterprise and provide reports on their usage and performance. It also provides the capability for the terms of service that need to be presented and accepted by developers as they request keys and enables developers to get support on issues regarding their use of the APIs.

- The API gateway service acts between API providers and app developers. It helps developers to learn about the APIs and help the apps to communicate with actual APIs.

- The app services enable developers to get their apps up and running quickly and are designed with a user-centric vision to enable users to talk to each other and connect to the cloud, to their data, and to APIs.

API Business Strategy

As enterprises adopt the digital business models, they need to ensure that everything and everyone is continuously interacting as one connected world. The business strategy is not just to enable mobile apps as part of the offerings or implement the Internet of Things, it is to have an API ecosystem that can drive the digital business of the enterprise.

API strategy should be framed by the enterprise with the following characteristics:

- A defined set of business objectives and tangible indicators to measure the value that will be achieved through the program
- An amazing set of services that will be integrated as part of the program to appeal and satisfy users
- A well-defined set of end users that are identified early in the program
- A structured governance and management model to be established for efficient operations

When an enterprise initiates an API program, it is critical to include business leaders and key stakeholders in defining the business strategy around the program. The business strategy should include the goals and objectives that the API program should accomplish. A number of themes driven by both business and IT can be used for API programs across the globe. The business strategies surrounding these programs comprise the following themes:

Accelerate Time to Market

The pace at which the mobile apps get built is quite different than for traditional enterprise systems. An API program enables the enterprise to accelerate the time to market for both internal and external solutions through enhanced service production and consumption operations, controls, and monitoring.

- The development cycles for the API products can be put on a fast track by creating an agile platform which can be reused and standardized across internal and external groups of developers.
- The platform cultivates an environment of cost-effective, fast, and efficient iteration of the design, build, test, and monitoring around business transformation and innovation that drives early adopters of API.
- Enterprises that are building apps for multiple platforms such as cloud, social, or mobile can construct common functionality through the use of internal APIs to standardize data and service access and minimize rework.

- APIs provide expedited onboarding and development capabilities that help enterprises accelerate the time to market and establish an effective API program.

New Business Opportunity

APIs play the role of business-level artifacts which provide the means to enable new business and revenue models. The digital business is closer than ever to the customers and provides an opportunity for the enterprise to act and reap the benefits; APIs provide the platform to facilitate the process.

- APIs aid in interaction with customers over connected devices, mobile, and social media channels that drive innovation through business partner and third-party apps and expose the services or data to customers or the public in general.
- APIs provide collaboration and new business partner relationships.
- They also help in monetizing the data and services for use by others, thus maximizing IT efficiency.

Provide Innovation

APIs provide an effective exposure of key functionality and data to enable a self-service model that provides access to internal groups, partner organizations, and independent developers to innovate and enhance the functionality on their own without being limited by the enterprise's IT department.

- A well-designed and creative API program extends the edge of the enterprise by creating an agile environment for innovation and growth.
- It provides an opportunity to leverage the capabilities of a developer community and independent developers as a part of the innovation strategy by harnessing the creativity and promoting a modern app development for the digital world.
- It also allows leveraging innovative resources that are even outside the realm of the enterprise to help grow the business.

Meet Customer Demands

API programs address the global demands of existing and new customers and enable business expansion, new outcomes, and brand building.

- API programs support digital business demands, drive global consumption models, and provide services to anyone, anytime, and anywhere.
- Extend the reach into new business channels, partners, customers, and market segments that may have not been considered or were previously deemed unreachable to realize new revenue streams.

- The successful and effective API programs make it simple, effective, and efficient to extend the brand, either through partner reuse or extended developer networks.

Evolution Through Analytics

Both the providers and consumers of the APIs benefit from the insights generated from analytics, which is still evolving with explicit designs.

- Analytics provides visibility into the APIs with the consumption patterns, relationships to apps, and internal consumers, which is extremely valuable in establishing a strategy-driven API program.
- Well-designed analytics allows enterprises to measure API effectiveness and compare it to goals and defined success criteria.
- An effective API analytics framework is composed of the back-end resources, the API façade, and the apps that leverage real-time analytics to feed the overall API program strategy and governance functions.

Governance Structure

Any API program needs to have a governance process whereby the enterprise defines the agile governance process for the API that can become part of the existing governance structure within the enterprise. Most of the API programs would present new demands on the existing governance processes, which should be addressed and added as part of the API journey.

- The enterprise needs to evaluate their existing complex, cumbersome, and time-consuming governance processes that have a negative impact to suppress benefits that can be achieved using the API program.
- As API programs are a little different than the traditional software implementations, their governance needs to be considered based on that context.
- Based on the new API products that are being developed by innovative business thinkers, enterprises need to create new roles to manage and support these products going forward.

API Life Cycle and Roadmap

APIs are the facilitators of the ever-growing digital business, where the enterprise should lay out the roadmap and approach the development of the API operating model with the end goal in mind. It's always beneficial for the enterprise to leverage the existing capabilities, functionality, and processes and then enhance or adjust some of the existing elements to support the development of APIs to align with the overall objectives and principles of the API program.

Some of the key components of the API life cycle and roadmap are listed below:

Strategy and Growth

The enterprise needs to develop an overall strategy and roadmap for the API program. This strategy will guide decisions around various elements of the program such as the capabilities that need to be built, the composition of the API portfolio, how it needs to be branded, the business model that needs to be implemented, target milestones around consumer channel exposure, delivery timelines, and the growth of the ecosystem. This strategy, too, must evolve over time and be supported by an organization and set of processes nimble enough to keep pace.

Architecture

The enterprise needs to define the API reference architecture for the program. It sets the direction on all common architecture elements that support the API portfolio and enables capability maturity across the model over time. The enterprise designs and implements the architecture framework with capabilities such as identity and authorization, service-level models, monitoring and reporting, performance management, and analytics that are set into action to execute the overall API strategy.

Design

The enterprise needs to establish the API design functionality to capture the core processes related to setting enterprise coding standards, pattern templates, and versioning standards, and creating a policy definition for development. Processes should be developed to support design and review sessions with API product owners to ensure collaborative discussions around architecture and how the API platform capabilities can enable better API products.

Development

The enterprise needs to develop and build the API within the defined framework, tools, and processes. Development should be integrated with an agile or continuous delivery model that provides automation wherever possible. Functions and processes within this area should mature over time with the introduction of more automation and development capacity where applicable.

Testing

The enterprise is responsible for defining the testing methodology for the development team by defining unit test cases even before the start of build activities. The test cases should cover all the detailed requirements, and the guidelines should be established to ensure that the processes for unit, integration, and user acceptance testing such as input and output artifact definitions, RACI definitions, coordination steps, and key activity descriptions are covered sufficiently based on API types. The requirements on regression testing, performance testing, and platform release testing also need to be established along with the governance on defect management.

Developer Experience

The way the enterprise interacts with the developers drives the developer experience. It incorporates onboarding and registration, the developer portal experience, development services, API catalog and documentation capabilities, identification of risks, and issues associated with the release. Creating a world-class developer platform to attract consumers to the APIs provides an unbeatable developer experience.

Governance

The enterprise needs to establish a governance function to maintain a standardized and consistent approach to the overall development of the program. The governance function must be accountable for elements of the program related to risk management, quality, success, the performance of the APIs, and the overall program.

Delivery

The delivery of APIs to the customers requires the design of the physical delivery model and the supporting processes required to support successful deployment. These processes include entry and exit criteria at each phase, release management, backlog prioritization, approval requirements, enterprise readiness, standard communication protocols, and deployment management.

Support

The enterprise needs to establish the support function for an effective API program and sustain it over time. It should be defined in a way that allows meaningful data to flow back to the API owners. It incorporates the processes for handling production API incidents, the approval process with API product owners, managing capacity against growth requirements, a robust set of reports to assess performance, traffic management thresholds and policies, and a continuous improvement philosophy.

Conclusion

In the digital economy, every enterprise needs to make IT a core competency to drive growth, sustainability, and successful business outcomes. The developer uses API to simplify the operations and provide functionality to enable and evaluate the business case for API in terms of providing efficiency, monetization, customer satisfaction, and innovation.

As a product, the API not only provides access to both data and services but also represents the brand. APIs should not be considered just an interface to the new technology; the enterprise needs to define the strategy around what to represent, when to display, and how to develop the APIs in the overall ecosystem.

PART V
Product Review

CHAPTER 17

SAP Leonardo

*T*his chapter provides an overview of the SAP Leonardo framework that connects the enterprise's business processes with emerging technologies, people, and things. It also discusses the architecture, application, and some of the typical use cases across business processes and industries where SAP Leonardo uses a combination of intelligent technologies, digital platforms, and an intelligent suite of applications to deliver an intelligent enterprise.

SAP S/4HANA ERP Overview

In this era of the digital world and global competition, enterprises are facing the challenge of gathering information from the environment and its ecosystem and analyzing the collected data to stay ahead of the competition. The enterprise needs to process both structured and unstructured data in a timely manner to make better decisions. SAP has been one of the leading Enterprise Resource Planning (ERP) providers for decades, and with its next-generation SAP HANA database with in-memory computing power, it has the capability to process huge amounts of data for analysis in a very short time. SAP S/4HANA represents the fourth-generation business suite and the latest evolution of SAP's core application platforms, designed and engineered to exploit the in-memory capabilities of the SAP HANA database.

SAP S/4HANA is a revolutionary innovation from SAP that adds transactional simplicity, advanced analytics, and enhancement of functionality compared to traditional SAP ERP. SAP S/4HANA leverages the new transactional and real-time analytical capabilities, delivered through a simplified and enhanced end-user interface based on SAP Fiori, available both in the cloud and as an on-premise solution. The SAP Fiori integrated user experience provides users with instant insight and works on any mobile device. It offers real-time operational analytics on the SAP ERP platform, reducing the data latency of SAP Business Warehouse reporting. SAP S/4HANA enables real-time collaboration with the SAP Ariba Network, Concur, etc., in the networked economy by providing integration with the Internet of Things.

Understanding SAP Leonardo

SAP Leonardo is the latest innovation from SAP comprising a portfolio of advanced products and solutions that connects the emerging world of intelligent devices with enterprise, people, and process to realize tangible business results. It combines several applications, big data, and connectivity in a bundled package to provide business solutions across functions and industries.

SAP Leonardo provides the IT function the platform to offer innovation to the lines of business while linking IT to the overall enterprise strategy.

It is a very powerful tool that provides an enterprise with an innovative solution portfolio to enable the digital transformation of the existing end-to-end business processes and provide an opportunity to create new business models to run digitally.

SAP Leonardo is the combination of an intelligent suite of applications, technologies, digital platform, and services to make the enterprise intelligent, as depicted in Figure 17.1. SAP Leonardo has been designed to enable businesses to leverage their data to detect patterns, provide insights, predict outcomes, and suggest actions. SAP Leonardo has been embedded directly into core the SAP S/4HANA ERP application to provide seamless integration for enterprises already using the core SAP infrastructure.

Creating Intelligent Enterprises

The intelligent enterprise is made up of three key components as listed below:

Intelligent Business Suite

The SAP intelligent suite enables businesses to automate their day-to-day business processes and operations and has better interaction with the

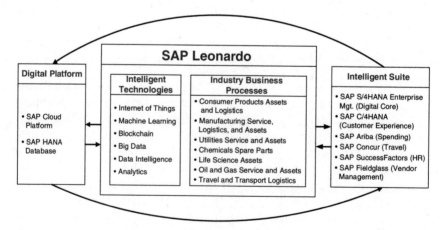

Figure 17.1 SAP Leonardo creating intelligent enterprises.

customers, suppliers, employees, and other business partners through applications that have intelligence embedded in them.

Digital Platform

The SAP Cloud Platform in combination with the columnar HANA database facilitates the collection and orchestration of data by maintaining the connectivity required to integrate and extend the processes within the intelligent suite.

Industry Business Processes

SAP provides industry innovation kits that combine business process best practices, intelligent technology, and pre-integrated software with services into industry solutions to solve critical industry problems in an accelerated way with reduced risk and cost.

Intelligent Technologies

SAP Leonardo plays a vital role in enabling the intelligent enterprise with intelligent technologies for every business process to create better outcomes. The intelligent enterprise can be considered as a virtual cycle where business actions executed by the intelligent suite layer generate data that is used to build intelligence that can be embedded in business processes.

The data from these business processes is combined with external data sources within the digital platform, where intelligent technologies are applied to generate better insights, which are then embedded back into the intelligent suite for process automation or making an informed decision.

Some of the key SAP Leonardo intelligent technologies have been elaborated below. Most of the time, two or more of these technologies work in conjunction with each other.

SAP Leonardo Internet of Things

The SAP Leonardo Internet of Things is SAP's holistic approach to intelligent applications, technologies, and services. In this digital era, a business is able to improve its outcomes by leveraging the intelligence generated from the IoT. Some of the key components that make up the SAP Leonardo IoT architecture are listed below:

SAP Leonardo IoT Architecture

The technology framework providing the end-to-end solution is built on the SAP Cloud Platform and includes the following architecture components, as illustrated in Figure 17.2.

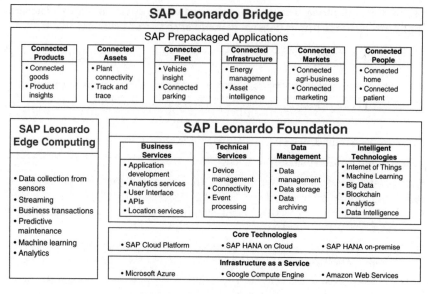

Figure 17.2   SAP Leonardo Internet of Things architecture.

- SAP Leonardo Bridge to transform the traditional supply chain components into live supply chain environments including connected products, assets, fleet, infrastructure, markets, and people.

- SAP Leonardo Edge Computing for real-time data collection, streaming, processing business transactions, and analytics.

- SAP Leonardo Foundation consisting of emerging technologies, business and technical services to enable devices, connectivity, and rapid application development with the intuitive user interface and APIs.

- SAP Cloud Platform acts as the strategic platform-as-a-service infrastructure that provides the SAP Leonardo framework for the Application Portfolio and SAP Leonardo foundation, which includes SAP Leonardo business services and SAP Leonardo technical services.

SAP Leonardo Edge Computing

The edge is simply a location close to the source of data where IoT devices such as sensors are placed to generate data. An edge location could be an offshore oil rig at sea, a moving vehicle, a retail store, or a manufacturing shop floor. The edge device which physically exists at these edge locations is referred to as the IoT gateway. These IoT gateways are computational devices that provide connectivity, data processing, analysis, and storage of data.

- The streaming service is one of the microservices offered by SAP Leonardo Edge Computing. It analyzes IoT data streams in real time based on rules and business logic and provides predictive insights.
- The policy service can be used to set up sophisticated rules and provides deployment and life cycle management of edge services.
- The persistence service locally stores the IoT data on IoT gateways that are synchronized with the SAP Cloud Platform, and it also enables execution of analytic models at the edge.
- The essential business functions service provides business data and processes at the edge so that they can be integrated with the IoT data to provide meaningful insights for the enterprise to take actions.
- The predictive analytics service helps the enterprise to create the models using SAP predictive analytics, open source, or any third-party tools; train the models in the cloud; and then deploy, execute, and update predictive models at the edge.

SAP Leonardo IoT Application Portfolio

The enterprise continuously collects valuable and huge data across the equipment, smart devices, and its own business processes. SAP Leonardo Bridge for IoT, for example, provides a cloud-based solution with real-time data from multiple sources to assess its impact on the business. It connects all data in one centralized operation command center, providing valuable insights and actual guidance in real time. It also allows integration of the business partner's data into the system by empowering collaboration and helping users run the business operations efficiently in the new connected environment.

Connected Products

In recent times, there has been a significant increase in the number of smart and connected products across industries in line with the demand for information and insight. The enterprises analyze the data from the embedded sensors, connected products, and other big data sources, to modify the product and satisfy the needs and requirements of the customers and tap the opportunity that leads to higher demand in the market.

- **Use Case.**   The pallets are embedded with sensors carrying the connected products that provide real-time tracking and visibility of in-transit deliveries. Based on rules and threshold, the sensors will send real-time data to SAP

Leonardo Bridge. With the sensors on the connected vehicle, the user can visually track the location and status of the delivery in real time. The user can also drill down into the business-relevant information on the vehicle such as the products that are being delivered, the customers receiving the deliveries, the estimated date of deliveries, etc.

The value proposition of the Leonardo Bridge lies where it correlates the sensor data from operations with the business process data to get the insights of the real problem that the enterprise might be facing. Real-time alerts and messaging can be propagated from the Bridge to the user to analyze the data and make smart decisions to resolve the problem. It provides end-to-end transparency and business visibility into the day-to-day operations to not only resolve an issue but proactively monitor it to prevent the issue from taking place.

Connected Assets

The manufacturing and maintenance business processes are connected to the fixed assets in the production systems to track, monitor, maintain, and analyze all fixed assets across the network with the objective to reduce operational and maintenance costs for the enterprise.

- **Use Case.**   Traditionally, fixed assets used to be maintained on a scheduled plan, but with connected assets, enterprises are able to conduct the real-time insights. SAP Leonardo Bridge provides an end-to-end solution for predictive maintenance of these fixed assets.

The customers, manufacturers, and service providers are all integrated through the asset network to collaborate and provide service on any issue, procure spare parts without human intervention, and schedule maintenance as suggested by the connected asset data. All the capabilities can be applied to enterprise-owned assets as well as those that are installed at the customer premises and covered by service contracts.

Connected Fleet

The enterprise that owns connected fleets of moving assets such as trucks, drones, robots, ships, planes, and forklifts collect real-time telematics and sensor data as generated by the devices. The data is then integrated with the business processes to improve driver behavior, tracking, security, and safety, and provide better services to the customers. It also enables enterprises to create new revenue and business models and reduce cost by utilizing the Internet of Things data.

- **Use Case.**   A connected fleet provides the capability to track and manage inventory in the supply chain logistics, which is one of the most critical elements in delivering the goods on time to the customers. It provides greater visibility of the inflow and outflow of goods in the enterprise's warehouse, which helps in the inventory planning.

The entire procurement process of ordering, delivery, and goods receipt is optimized and streamlined by integrating telematics, enterprise, and vendor information.

Connected Infrastructure

Connected infrastructure aids transformation by integrating sensors and control technologies embedded in the physical infrastructure assets with SAP S/4HANA enterprise business applications. The sensors are connected to SAP Leonardo Bridge, which generates real-time data and analytics, and its integration with the business processes helps forecast, plan, and take action in response to real-time conditions.

Integrating the real-time information with business data creates new infrastructure models, improves service and operational efficiency, mitigates risk, and maintains infrastructure compliance.

● **Use Case.**   Connected infrastructure provides a real-time dashboard with information on all the properties of the enterprise to maintain facilities, improve performance, and optimize energy consumption, thus reducing the utility expenditure.

Connected Markets

Connected markets provide transformation to local markets, cities, and urban and rural areas by optimizing the utilization and consumption of natural resources and assets, resulting in energy conservation, emission reduction, power usage, and environment protection.

● **Use Case.**   The agriculture industry has been in the limelight in terms of utilizing the digital solution to increase yield, reduce cost, adopt changes in the market, and meet the shortage of natural resources caused by the growth in population worldwide.

Sensors can be used by farmers in the farmland to monitor the crops, and with the development of big data and the Internet of Things, all the resources on the farm are connected to generate and analyze live data about the fields, crops, irrigation, etc.

SAP Leonardo Connected Agriculture also connects all machines and equipment used in agriculture to enable predictive maintenance, increase crop throughput, and optimize food supply chains. Farmers and growers residing in a remote rural area have the ability to connect with the global supply chain network using the IoT and mobile technology to sell their crops and get fair pricing.

SAP Leonardo can provide a revolutionary change in urban areas and city life by automating and letting people know about live traffic, parking availability, etc., and managing and optimizing the usage of open spaces, lights, and other infrastructure that creates an urban landscape.

Connected People

SAP Leonardo is a global platform that enables innovative applications and devices to connect individual users and consumer groups with various products, assets, and markets.

Enterprises now have the ability to offer connected people customized services in real time, catering to the individual's preferences, needs, lifestyle, and location. This not only creates new business opportunities for the business but helps improve the health and lives of people at the same time.

- **Use Case.**   A connected home with smart devices is an opportunity for homeowners to ensure safety and have the ability to manage the household systems from anywhere in the world using their mobile devices, such as opening the garage door remotely, managing the lights and air conditioners remotely, monitoring any intruders through the security cameras, etc.

Retailers have the opportunity to provide real-time personalized products to a consumer when he is passing through a particular aisle within the store based on past purchase records and behavior.

With SAP Leonardo Connected People, healthcare providers can access patient data through the wearables and provide a comprehensive and personalized health plan, which will improve the health and lives of people and lower the healthcare costs for the patients.

SAP Leonardo Machine Learning

Most of the large enterprises run on SAP systems, which cover 26 industries and 7 lines of businesses. This makes SAP the only system in the world to not only understand the business processes and their related data but also learn from the data and embed intelligence into the process in every industry and line of business.

As we know, machine learning algorithms have outperformed human beings in speech, image, and text recognition. SAP Leonardo Machine Learning helps in enabling the intelligent enterprise by leveraging SAP's core data assets and providing services in the following areas:

- **Process Automation.** SAP Leonardo machine learning provides the opportunity for the enterprise to fully automate their business processes in the areas related to human resources, cash applications, invoice processing, workflow approvals for purchase orders, and sales execution.

- **Dynamic Analytics.** SAP Leonardo machine learning provides the opportunity for the enterprise to proactively analyze new data types and discover unfamiliar patterns that can provide greater insights into the data.

- **User Experience.**   SAP Leonardo machine learning provides the opportunity for the enterprise to provide a next-generation user experience and increase business productivity by developing user experiences based on voice, vision, and messages that can replicate how people interact in real life.

SAP Leonardo Machine Learning Foundation

The SAP Leonardo Machine Learning Foundation provides users with superior application capabilities. It enables developers by providing reusable services and APIs that can be embedded into applications. It enables data scientists by providing core capabilities such as training as a service to build their own model, customize existing models with various data sets, or deploy their own model with data science results. It also allows the enterprise to embed new services into the enterprise business application with machine learning applications.

Some of the capabilities and services available in SAP Leonardo Machine Learning Foundation are depicted in Figure 17.3.

The SAP Leonardo Machine Learning Foundation consists of functional and core services integrated with core technologies and applications. Some of these services are described below:

Functional Services

The functional services include images, video, voice, and text data such as detecting objects in images, detecting keywords in text, or recognizing speech. Some of these services are elaborated below:

- **Image Services.**   The image classification service categorizes a digital image into generic categories such as vehicle types, food types, environment, animals, gadgets, or consumer goods. The customizable image classification service provides the ability to use a pretrained classifier to build a custom image classifier with the enterprise training data to recognize enterprise-specific object classes.

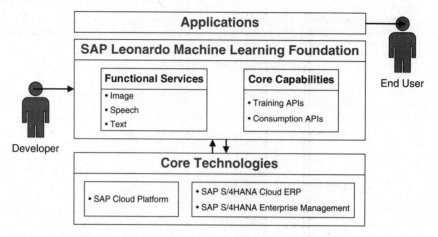

Figure 17.3   SAP Leonardo Machine Learning Foundation.

The optical character recognition service provides the ability to process document scans to extract structured text, while the scene text recognition service provides the ability to extract text from images. The human detection services allow detection of humans in images, while the face detection service allows detection of faces in images.

- **Speech Services.**   The speech processing capabilities provided by SAP Leonardo Machine Learning Foundation includes two services. The speech-to-text service converts the speech into text, and the text-to-speech service generates audio from the text.

- **Text Services.**   SAP Leonardo Machine Learning Foundation provides multiple text processing capabilities. The detection service extracts topics and keywords from documents and assigns the documents to the most relevant subject. The customizable text classification service uses custom text data to create an enterprise-specific text classification service. The text feature extraction service is used to retrieve similar documents in the future. The language detection service detects the language of a given text. The translation service translates texts from the source language to a different target language to cater to any localization requirement.

Core Capabilities

The core capabilities of the SAP Leonardo Machine Learning Foundation include the ability to customize machine learning services with enterprise-owned data using training APIs or deploying custom models. The SAP Leonardo Machine Learning Foundation allows the ability for consumers to quickly and easily enrich their apps with machine learning.

Core Technologies

The core enterprise system, consisting of either SAP S/4HANA Cloud ERP or SAP S/4HANA Enterprise Management, connects and integrates with the Machine Learning Foundation using the Cloud Platform Connector.

Applications

The applications at the top are infused with intelligent machine learning services using SAP Leonardo Machine Learning Foundation for the end user benefits.

SAP Leonardo Machine Learning Architecture

SAP Leonardo Machine Learning Foundation architecture, as illustrated in Figure 17.4, provides an overall understanding of how the foundation is organized within the SAP Leonardo framework.

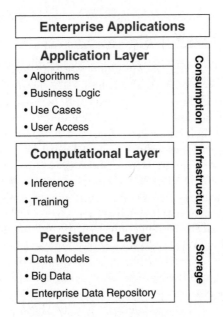

Figure 17.4   SAP Leonardo Machine Learning Foundation architecture.

The SAP Leonardo Machine Learning Foundation architecture comprises three tiers:

Persistence Layer

The bottom tier of this architecture is the persistence layer, where data and models are stored.

Computational Layer

The middle tier consists of the computational layer, which hosts the infrastructure that is required for inference and training the models to make them intelligent. Various services are consumed in this layer by the developers and data scientists.

Application Layer

The application layer at the top provides the ability to consume the services made available by SAP Leonardo from the inference and training APIs. This tier also holds the components required for hosting the algorithms and business logic for different applications and the requisite components for providing access to various users.

SAP Leonardo Blockchain

In the coming decade, the world, economies, and businesses will rapidly change and move towards the path of the intelligent enterprise. IT systems are getting more intelligent, integrated, and increasingly self-optimized. Innovation in technology has enabled computers to handle repetitive end-to-end tasks while humans can focus on solving strategic problems and look for new opportunities. Business ecosystems will change and have a seamless connection to the network of business partners that would enable more flexible value chains. This will create new trust layers for sharing data, processes, and algorithms across value and supply chains, which will be developed based on technologies such as blockchain.

The enterprise needs to be certain that the information coming out of sources that they don't own or control is true, unaltered, and can be trusted, or else it cannot be utilized in the business process and no decisions can be made based on that information. Thus, trust, security, transparency, and protection of intellectual assets are the foundation of any shared ecosystem where enterprises and their competitors conduct business within the same network. Sharing data in a trusted environment using blockchain allows execution of processes more efficiently and sustainably, which leads to network-based, multiparty business model innovation.

SAP Leonardo Blockchain is an innovative way for enterprises to test and deploy distributed ledgers and blockchain technologies in a protocol-agnostic way. As part of SAP Cloud Platform, blockchain comes either as Hyperledger Fabric or as MultiChain to underline SAP's technology-agnostic approach.

SAP HANA Blockchain service provides an adaptor to integrate blockchain data into the core HANA database. This allows integration into the database and business transactions, and thus blockchain appears just like a typical database transaction to end users. The next step for the enterprise is to integrate blockchain data with advanced analytic engines such as a graph, geospatial, text analysis, and machine learning.

SAP Leonardo Big Data

Enterprises receive, collect, and store massive amounts of data coming from IoT sensors in the data lakes and cheap storage on various cloud environments. Various technologies and cheap data storage and computational power have solved the data volume issue; the challenge remains in the formats and the structure of the data.

Once the unstructured data from various streams such as IoT, social media, blogs, search engines, pictures, and videos are all ingested into the system landscape, it needs to be prepared and structured before meaningful insight and analytics can be generated. Once the data is ready, the data can be processed using machine learning services, predictive algorithms, and analytics, and then integrated into the systems to enrich the existing transaction and master data.

SAP Leonardo Big Data leverages different technologies, different data storage options, and different possibilities within the landscape to achieve centralized control without storing, owning, or creating another massive data warehouse solution.

This solution overcomes the challenge of persisting the data at one central location by building a logical hub in the landscape to combine the data and the processes within the landscape.

SAP Leonardo Big Data provides all of the functionalities that are needed to establish the end-to-end processing of data within the landscape such as collecting, consuming, connectivity of, streaming, and storing the data. It helps in processing the data where it's stored at the centralized location instead of moving it around into a different target or environment using the transformation tool. This is accomplished through the product called Data Hub, which can be deployed on-premise or within the cloud. Data Hub provides the infrastructure to process the data, integrate, and get results out of it. It has the ability to use the machine learning algorithms for execution and brings together different pieces and technologies within the SAP Leonardo portfolio.

SAP Leonardo Data Intelligence

SAP Leonardo Data Intelligence aids in delivering the intelligent enterprise by fueling the power of connected data and extracting maximum value out of it. The key business outcomes of data-driven innovation are listed below:

- Serve the customers better by going beyond their expectations at the right time and context.

- Achieve operational excellence by using connected data to reimagine the entire business process, understand the behavior of the enterprise, and take appropriate actions.

- Use data to generate new revenue streams or new business models for extraordinary growth.

In order to get the most value out of data, it needs to be refined, processed, and put into a ready-to-consume format that can automatically be fed back into the business process and close the loop between front-office and back-end processes, and extend the insights to connected ecosystems and customers. SAP Cloud Platform has the capability to turn the enterprise data into live customer data. Though the platform is essential for the making of the intelligent enterprise, right data expedites the process.

Live Customer Cloud is a turnkey solution for data intelligence that is run on the cloud to provide speed and focus on business outcomes, relieving the enterprise from any bottlenecks with technology. It comes pre-integrated with connectors and ready-to-use data services across various industries, thus helping the enterprise to achieve the business outcomes of serving its customers better, developing new business models, and reimagining new business processes with data.

SAP Leonardo Analytics

SAP Leonardo applies the correct technology to the right part of the business process for each industry that makes every process smarter. The integrated solution provides context for the data that needs to be presented to a user with proper insights so that strategic decisions can be made. This is where analytics becomes a critical component of the intelligence enterprise.

SAP Analytics Cloud in combination with Digital Boardroom provides the business intelligence, planning, and predictive analytics solution as a service through the public cloud to meet the needs of an intelligent enterprise for today and in the near future.

SAP Analytics Cloud uses predictive modeling, simulation, and machine learning to understand enterprise data and business processes and bring intelligent insights to the users to make informed decisions. All SAP business applications are embedded in SAP Analytics Cloud to provide visualizations and machine learning capabilities to users in the context of the business processes, essentially making them part of that intelligent enterprise.

SAP Leonardo Enterprise Engagement

Enterprises that are looking forward to innovating and creating digital businesses would engage in implementing SAP Leonardo using a design thinking approach to solve some of the challenges faced by the business. Though there are various technologies that can be enabled using the SAP Leonardo digital platform, the enterprise needs to adopt one that delivers real-time insights, forecasts customer preferences in advance, and, most importantly, provides business value.

Listed below are the key phases during an SAP Leonardo engagement for an enterprise where the design gates are built at the end of each phase to perform an audit and ensure that the design and quality standards are maintained:

Explore Phase

In the Explore phase, the enterprise needs to identify the use cases as applicable to its business process that can be explored for digital transformation and can be investigated further during the SAP Leonardo implementation process.

Once the use case is identified, the project needs to identify the duration to deliver the proof of concept, the effort required during the engagement, the solution to solve a specific business problem, and the cost involved from the initial idea to a working prototype.

At the end of this phase, the enterprise should have the following outcomes:

- Identified use cases
- Prioritized business scenarios
- Implementation approach using design thinking
- Potential design
- Key stakeholders
- Approved funding
- Technology to be used
- Project plan

Discover Phase

In the Discover phase, the enterprise needs to deploy subject matter experts to conduct requirements-gathering workshops and research. During the workshops, the end user requirements are identified based on the current business process within the enterprise.

The "to-be" business process is defined based on the future state-of-the-technology that needs to be deployed using SAP Leonardo. The initial prototype is developed by the team to validate the solution.

At the end of this phase, the enterprise should have the following outcomes:

- Document the "as-is" business process.
- Identify pain points and areas of improvement across business processes.
- Define the "to-be" process with feedback from end users and customers.
- The initial round of prototyping.
- Simulated build for initial user verification and validation.

Build Phase

In the Build phase, the enterprise needs to demonstrate the functionality using the initial prototype and conduct playback sessions with the users during the advisory session. The project team needs to prepare, monitor, and track all the detailed activities that need to be executed among various teams. Finally, the initial prototype is converted into concrete digital solutions in this phase.

At the end of this phase, the enterprise should have the following outcomes:

- Prototype verified and validated by the business user.
- Digital solution ready for testing.

Test Phase

In the Test phase, the enterprise needs to integrate the digital innovation and solution within its ecosystem by thoroughly testing the solution and resolving all the defects before moving to the next phase.

At the end of this phase, the enterprise should have the following outcomes:

- Executed and successfully passed test cases.
- Integrated test scenarios.

Deliver Phase

In the Deliver phase, the enterprise needs to validate the prototype with the development architect and the proof of concept with the end users and business stakeholders so that the solution meets the design and business requirements. Finally, the feasibility of the project is checked along with the scalability of the solution so that it can be implemented enterprise-wide.

SAP Leonardo allows a flexible design where an enterprise can implement just the portions needed with a seamless and easy connection to the SAP S/4HANA core system and multiple legacy systems, technologies, and data.

At the end of this phase, the enterprise should have the following outcomes:

- Implemented proof of concept validated by business users.
- Reference architecture validated by the development team.
- Technology blueprint for the landscape.
- Value realization assessment.

Conclusion

All enterprises that are working on SAP ERP systems are looking to apply digital innovation within their organizations. The need to apply design thinking methodologies, the way SAP executes business processes, optimize customer experience, and deploy emerging new technologies led to the innovation of SAP Leonardo. This is an innovative system that has been designed to help the enterprise in its digital transformation journey with minimal disruption to its existing business and infrastructure.

Innovation within an enterprise cannot just happen with a single intelligent technology in a silo. It, rather, happens in combination with multiple innovative technologies such as blockchain, which builds trust and transparency within the network, and the Internet of Things, which connects to the real world, which would then generate big data that would need analytics, machine learning, and artificial intelligence on top of it to make sense of it and interpret it for the business.

Various areas within each industry are being identified where a prototype can be built with SAP Leonardo to make it even better, with a robust application portfolio, in the future.

ABOUT THE AUTHOR

Anup Maheshwari is a proficient SAP S/4HANA Finance, Business, and Digital Transformation thought leader with 21 years of IT and business consulting experience in presales, managing, and delivering complex projects globally. Anup is a native Finance professional and has now accomplished himself in the emerging technology space with a goal to build intelligent enterprises.

As a trusted business advisor, Anup has successfully led and managed more than 13 full life-cycle, global rollout SAP core business and digital transformation projects across North America, Europe, and the Asia Pacific region. Anup also led the initiative of building and integrating the SAP S/4HANA Finance solution with IoT, robotics process automation, and machine learning.

His core values include continuous learning, innovation, building relationships on trust, teamwork, and helping enterprises in their transformation journey. Anup has expertise in defining the roadmap and strategy using design thinking, driving design validation workshops, delivering industry-leading practices, providing business value, and collaborating with enterprises to create competitive advantage and improve digital outcomes.

Anup is also the author of *Implementing SAP S/4HANA Finance* (1st and 2nd editions). He has spoken at forums like Sapphire and also written a white paper titled "Fusion of SAP S/4HANA Finance with Artificial Intelligence."

Anup has an MBA and an MS in Project Management from The George Washington University. He is a Stanford Certified Project Manager and a PMI Certified Project Management Professional (PMP). Anup also has an Enterprise Architect Certificate from Carnegie Mellon University. He is a Chartered Financial Analyst and has Global Certification in SAP S/4HANA Finance.

Anup resides with his family in McKinney, Texas, and can be reached at anupmah@gmail.com.

INDEX